TUDOR TEXTILES

TUDOR TEXTILES

ELERI LYNN

Yale University Press   New Haven and London

For round about, the walls yclothed were

With goodly arras of great majesty,

Woven with gold and silke so close and nere,

That the rich metal lurked privily,

As faining to be hid from envious eye;

Yet here, and there, and every where unawares

It shewed it selfe, and shone unwillingly;

Like a discolourd Snake, whose hidden snares

Through the greene gras his long bright burnisht backe declares.

Edmund Spenser (1552–1599), *The Faerie Queene* (1590),
Book 3, Canto XI, stanza xxviii

In memory of Florence

First published by Yale University Press 2020

302 Temple Street, P. O. Box 209040, New Haven CT 06520-9040

47 Bedford Square, London WC1B 3DP

yalebooks.com | yalebooks.co.uk

ISBN 978-0-300-24412-0 HB

Library of Congress Control Number: 2019949027

10 9 8 7 6 5 4 3 2 1

2024 2023 2022 2021 2020

Copyedited by Rosemary Roberts

Designed by gradedesign.com

Printed in China

Front cover: Curtain, early 17th century, linen embroidered in silk (see fig. 70).
Back cover: Spinning and weaving wool. Isaac Claesz van Swanenburg, *Het
spinnen het schere van de ketting, en het weven*, 1594–6 (see fig. 87).
Frontispiece: Detail from the Bacton Altar Cloth, *c.*1600, silk and silver camlet
embroidered with silk and metal thread (see fig. 18).
p.V: Detail from a watercolour drawing by Jacques Le Moyne de Morgues, 1585
(see fig. 128).
p. XIII: Tapestry, *c.*1585, wool and silk (see fig. 15).
p. XV: Cushion cover, late 16th century, needlework slips on velvet (see fig. 47).

Contents

VIII Acknowledgements

X Preface

XII Abbreviations

XIV Notes for the Reader

1 INTRODUCTION

6 1 THE GLOBAL STORY
Tudor Textiles in Context

28 2 POWER AND LIGHT
Textiles and Meaning at the Tudor Court

74 3 PRIVATE SPACES
The Textiles of the Privy Chambers

104 4 THE GREAT WARDROBE
The Administration of Royal Textiles

116 5 TUDOR TEXTILES
Materials and Techniques

160 6 EPILOGUE

164 Glossary

169 Notes

177 Bibliography

186 Index

192 Picture Credits

Acknowledgements

Many people have helped to bring *Tudor Textiles* to print. I am so grateful to my colleagues at Historic Royal Palaces (HRP), primarily, Joint Chief Curator Tracy Borman for her advice and encouragement, and to Lucy Worsley, John Barnes and Adrian Phillips for their support. I am indebted to Susan Mennell and Clare Murphy, and to HRP's Research Advisory Board – namely, Maria Hayward, Maurice Howard and Thomas Betteridge, without whom this idea would never have become a reality. Thanks also to Anthony Musson, Alden Gregory, Charles Farris, Matthew Storey, Rebecca Wallace and Libby Thompson, and also the wider Conservation and Collections Care team at Hampton Court Palace.

I express my grateful thanks to the team at Yale University Press, including Mark Eastment, Anjali Bulley and Julie Hrischeva, for their expertise and advice, to Rosemary Roberts, to Peter Dawson and Alice Kennedy-Owen at Grade Design, and to Elizabeth Scott-Baumann, Samin Saeed, Virginia Novarra, Cynthia Jackson and Constantina Vlachou for their advice on the text. I am deeply indebted to Lisa Monnas, for her generosity in sharing her time and advice; I (and this book) have benefited enormously from her knowledge, encouragement, and expert eye. My thanks also to Jan Graffius at Stonyhurst College, to Vicky Perry at Hatfield House, and to Kent Rawlinson for introducing me to Wolsey's George Cavendish. My thanks, too, to the staff of the Victoria and Albert Museum's Clothworkers' Centre, the British Library, the British Museum, Amgueddfa Wlân Cymru (National Wool Museum, Wales), the National Trust at the Guildhall of Corpus Christi in Lavenham, and the Weald and Downland Museum in West Sussex. I am indebted to a number of other curators and specialists who have spent many hours with me studying the Bacton Altar Cloth, including Clare Browne, Susan Kay-Williams, Karen Hearn, Helen Hackett, Hester Lees-Jeffries and Veronica Horwell, and to Stephanie Selmayr and Louise Baldock at Past Pleasures. I am grateful for the help of Ruth E. Richardson, the PCC and church of St Faith, Bacton, and Charles and Susan Hunter.

I should also like to take this opportunity to acknowledge the intellectual debt I owe to the scholars whose work has informed my own. I am indebted to the curators of the Furniture, Textiles and Fashion Department at the Victoria and Albert Museum, which I joined as an assistant curator in 2003. The privileged access I had to the collection over a ten-year period and the expertise of curators and former curators is the inspiration for much of the work presented in *Tudor Textiles*. I owe a great deal to the work of Maria Hayward on the wardrobe, textiles and inventories of Henry VIII's reign.[1] The transcription by David Starkey and Philip Ward of the 1547 Inventory of Henry VIII's possessions, published in 1998, has been invaluable, as has the analysis of it by Thomas Campbell, Maria Hayward, Donald King, Santina Levey, David Mitchell and Lisa Monnas, published by Hayward and Ward in 2012.[2] The research presented in other monographs by many of these same authors has also contributed significantly to the story told in the following chapters. Lisa Monnas's work, in particular, is the destination for those wishing to understand more about the technical construction of Renaissance textiles, though that subject is not covered here as the remit of this book is to explore the role of

Tudor textiles at court rather than to present an in-depth analysis of materials and techniques.[3] I would be remiss if I failed to mention the influence of the late Janet Arnold through her transcription and inspiring scholarly analysis of the inventories of the wardrobe of Elizabeth I.[4] Works by Stephen Alford, Jerry Brotton, Nandini Das and Lisa Jardine on the cross-cultural exchanges and expanding global horizons of the Tudor monarchs, their courtiers and merchants, have given me a framework within which to contextualise the story of sixteenth-century elite textiles and to show their role not just as décor or dress but as an influential and important global commodity.[5]

Finally, my thanks to Kate Harris for her unfailing support and her contributions to this book. And warmest thanks to my family, to Dom and Daisy for helping me to juggle everything, and particularly to Luke, Awen and Tal.

Preface

The writing of *Tudor Textiles* has been inspired by a number of factors. As a curator at Historic Royal Palaces, I care for around ten thousand items, which include royal, court and ceremonial dress dating back to the sixteenth century, and a number of textiles. Historic Royal Palaces is the independent charity that looks after the Tower of London, Hampton Court Palace, the Banqueting House at Whitehall, Kensington Palace, Kew Palace, and Hillsborough Castle in Northern Ireland. The Tower and Hampton Court, in particular, were the setting for many major Tudor events. We welcome millions of visitors to our sites every year and endeavour to tell the stories of the palaces and their people in a way that inspires our visitors and transports them to the past. With this in mind, the last few years have seen various projects under way to interpret the wider Tudor story. Part of my job is to advise on the role of textiles within the Tudor palaces, and my aim is to communicate the primacy of textiles within the decorative context of the court, and within the courtier's understanding of royalty and magnificence. For the visitors and groups with whom I speak, the fact that tapestries were prized more highly than paintings is a surprise, and the sums of money spent on decorative textiles, such as cloth of gold, an absolute revelation.

Hampton Court Palace is the home of a number of significant Tudor textiles, including Henry VIII's 'Abraham' tapestries, woven with precious metals, which have hung in the palace for centuries (fig. 1). In recent years, textiles have come to the fore in a number of projects undertaken by Historic Royal Palaces, notably research into Tudor tents and temporary lodgings by my colleague Alden Gregory, and the re-presentation and

FIG. 1 The Great Hall of Hampton Court Palace, hung with Henry VIII's tapestries of the biblical story of Abraham.

planned refurbishment of a number of Tudor apartments at Hampton Court. In late 2019, over a thousand hours of painstaking conservation work on the Bacton Altar Cloth was completed and the cloth went on public display, contextualised for the first time as an item of *c.*1600 elite court dress, alongside contemporary portraiture, herbals, embroidery pattern books and embroidery slips. Research undertaken as part of that conservation process uncovered new evidence about the cloth and is presented in the following chapters. Last but not least, the publication of *Tudor Textiles* coincides with the 500th anniversary of the Field of Cloth of Gold, the meeting of Henry VIII with his French counterpart, Francis I, in the Pale of Calais in 1520. The meeting is to be celebrated by a series of spectacular re-enactments and events at Hampton Court, and a major exhibition featuring objects from HRP's own collection, alongside significant international loans, reuniting Tudor objects for the first time in centuries within the apartments of the historic palace.

The aim of *Tudor Textiles* is to situate textiles as an important part of visual and material culture, for those interested in the Tudor monarchs, their courts and sixteenth-century art and design. As a curator, I am used to telling stories through objects, and the illustrations have been researched and carefully selected to communicate this focus on material culture. The book is presented in a narrative style, with the aim of conveying the role and importance of textiles in an accessible way for a broad audience, and I therefore assume that the reader is a non-specialist. I have, however, endeavoured to credit the sources of arguments and findings by means of rigorous referencing, so that scholars wishing to trace the origins of the work outlined here will be able to do so.

The importance of textiles to the display of Tudor magnificence, and the complexity of their construction, dissemination and usage are the very reasons why the subject has so often been covered in separate categories, such as tapestry, embroidery or velvets, or contextualised within the reign of one monarch rather than across the

entire Tudor period. This book attempts a survey of the subject as a whole, but its breadth means that it can serve as no more than an introduction, albeit one that attempts to present a holistic interpretative narrative of the period and a comparative study of changing textile fashions at the royal court. Within its pages I present new research and make new connections; I also draw on the work of a number of academics, conservators and curators, alongside original sources and documents, experimental and living history, contemporary literature, portraiture and, of course, the textiles themselves, which are this book's primary source and inspiration.

Abbreviations

1547
Inventory Inventory of the movable goods of Henry VIII, begun after his death in January 1547, Society of Antiquaries, MS 129, and BL, Harley MS 1419. The inventory is fully transcribed by Philip Ward, edited by David Starkey and indexed by Alasdair Hawkyard as *The Inventory of King Henry VIII: Society of Antiquaries MS 129 and British Library MS Harley 1419*, vol. I: *The Transcript* (London: Harvey Miller Publishers for the Society of Antiquaries of London, 1998).

BL British Library, London

BM British Museum, London

BNF Bibliothèque Nationale de France, Paris

HRP Historic Royal Palaces

LP *Letters and Papers, Foreign and Domestic, of the Reign of Henry VIII*

NPG National Portrait Gallery, London

ODNB *Oxford Dictionary of National Biography*, online edition

RCIN Royal Collection Inventory Number

TNA The National Archives, Kew

V&A Victoria and Albert Museum, London

Notes for the Reader

SPECIALIST TERMS

Textile terms are defined in the Glossary (pp. 164–8); more obscure terminology is also glossed at the first occurrence in the text.

CURRENCY AND VALUES

Monetary values are expressed in pounds, shillings and pence. The values are indicated by the abbreviations £ *s. d.*, except in quotations, where *l.* stands for *livre* ('pound'). In that currency:

> £1 (or 1*l.*) = 20*s.*
> 1*s.* = 12*d.*
> 1 guinea = £1 1*s.*

The English crown (struck in gold or silver), first minted in Henry VIII's reign, had a currency value of 5*s.* The florin, originally a Florentine coin, played a significant part in European trade, as it was adopted by many countries, though not by England (except for a short period in the fourteenth century); because of its widespread use, values in florins appear in Tudor records. The ducat, introduced in Venice in the thirteenth century and modelled on the florin, was also widely used in European commerce.

I provide approximate twenty-first-century values, where appropriate, in the text and notes, using 'The National Archives Currency Converter', 1270–2017; this deploys data from historical records, such as those of the royal household and exchequer, to give a general guide to historical values and purchasing power.

WEIGHTS AND MEASURES

In the Tudor period, units of weight and measure were those we now refer to as 'imperial'. Lengths of cloth might be measured in yards, feet and inches as follows (metric values are here rounded to two decimal places):

> 1 yard = 36 inches = 91 cm
> 1 foot = 12 inches = 30.48 cm
> 1 inch = 2.54 cm

Other expressions of length were the ell and the nail. The ell was originally the length of a man's arm from the elbow to the tip of the middle finger (about 18 inches). By Tudor times the length of an ell was fixed, but differed from one country to another; in England it measured 1¼ yards, in the Low Countries ¾ yard, in France 1½ yards. The nail as a unit of measurement was 1/16 of a yard.

> 1 English ell = 45 inches (114.3 cm)
> 1 nail = 2¼ inches (5.72 cm)

Weight was expressed in stones, pounds and ounces:

> 1 stone = 14 pounds = 6.35 kg
> 1 pound = 16 ounces = 0.45 kg
> 1 ounce = 28.35 grammes

TITLES OF PUBLISHED WORKS

For works published up to 1800, titles are given as cited in the English Short Title Catalogue.

INTRODUCTION

In June 1520, King Henry VIII (1491–1547) met his French counterpart, King Francis I (1494–1547), in the (then) English province of Calais.[1] The two kings were young, educated, athletic and – especially with each other – competitive. For more than two weeks, the kings held a festival of chivalry, which included jousting tournaments and other sports, feasting and an unsurpassed display of wealth and magnificence. The meeting was designed to cement the peace established by the Anglo-French Treaty of 1514 and the 1518 Treaty of London, which allied them as Christian kings. Each king brought an entourage of six thousand. Key courtiers and officials were dressed in the finest cloth of gold.[2] The encampments and tents were constructed of 'material woven from gold' or 'were everywhere cloaked with golden hangings'.[3] It was the most lavish and costly spectacle of either king's reign. The profusion of rich textiles gave the event its name – the Field of Cloth of Gold (fig. 2).

FIG. 2 British School, *The Field of Cloth of Gold* (detail), *c.*1545, oil on canvas. The English delegation arrives at the meeting, with the king in the midst of the procession, resplendent in cloth of gold, and Cardinal Wolsey mounted on a donkey to his left. Royal Collection, Hampton Court Palace.

The Field of Cloth of Gold shows, perhaps more clearly than any other occasion of the Tudor period, the status of textiles at the European courts of the sixteenth century, and their use as the ultimate projection of wealth and taste. However, the numerous accounts of court décor, pageants and ceremonial processions invariably contain awestruck descriptions of the comparably rich textiles on display. The cost of these textiles demonstrated wealth beyond the reach of the average person, and indeed even beyond the reach of most of the nobility. For example, in August 1509, the young Henry VIII paid the mercer Charles de Florence £117, equivalent to ten years' pay for a skilled tradesman, for just 18 yards of cloth of gold.[4] The staggering quantity of rich textiles on view at the Field of Cloth of Gold was a tangible display of the vast and almost unimaginable power held by monarchs. It was also a manifestation of the primacy of textiles above all other decorative art forms: the court artist Hans Holbein was paid £30 per annum, while a set of tapestry cost fifty times as much, at £1,500.[5]

Years later, textiles took their usual starring role in the 1559 coronation of Henry's daughter Queen Elizabeth I (1533–1603). As one observer noted, she processed through the City of London under a rich canopy of cloth of gold, and the streets were decorated with

> riche hangings, as well [. . .] tapistrie, arras, clothes of golde, silver, velvet, damaske, sattin, and other silks, plentifullye hanged all the way as the Quenes Highnes passed from the Towre through the Citie. Out at the windowes [. . .] of every house did hang a number of ryche and costlye banners.[6]

In addition to their intrinsic value, textiles conveyed figurative meanings too. Arms, emblems or narratives might contain messages of loyalty, piety, courtly love or martial power, among other things, to both the court and the wider public. Another reason for the ubiquity of textiles in Tudor décor and ceremony lies in their portability. The royal court moved on a regular basis, and the ability to reconstruct magnificent surroundings quickly in different locations was paramount.

This book tells the story of the textiles used at the royal court during the long Tudor century, from the accession of Henry Tudor to the throne as King Henry VII in 1485, to the death of his granddaughter Queen Elizabeth I in 1603. It follows the publication of my *Tudor Fashion* (2017),[7] which concentrated on dress at the royal court. In *Tudor Textiles*, I endeavour to avoid the ground covered by *Tudor Fashion*, and consequently the study of textiles as dress is limited in what follows. Instead, the book explores the use of textiles for purposes other than dress – specifically for interiors, including woven fabrics for hangings, carpets, tapestries, upholstery and cushions, bedding, cloths of estate and so on. It also includes textiles for tents, pageants, revels, and some aspects of ceremonial use (which was not covered by *Tudor Fashion*, since ceremonial dress was not, and is not – given that much of it remains unchanged to this day – subject to the vagaries of court fashions per se). It considers the manufacture, trade, sourcing and procurement of textiles that entered the court as cloth destined for the Wardrobes and its storage for various uses. And it focuses upon the administration and management of those stores of textiles and the court's relationship with merchants.

The opening chapter introduces the wider international story of Tudor textiles, demonstrating how important the textile industry was to the fortunes of both country and crown, and how textiles were the foundation of the English economy and the monarch's wealth. Rather than sitting aside from the great constitutional and political issues of the day, textiles were at the very heart of matters, shaping domestic and foreign policy. Throughout the Tudor period, the political and religious changes wrought by the Reformation, by the religious and dynastic struggles across Europe and by the voyages of discovery across the Atlantic shaped the textiles that were available and fashionable at the royal court. The story begins with English wool, guilds, and trade with the Low Countries, and ends with silks, dyes from Mexico and the first whispers of empire.

The second chapter examines perceptions of textiles at court, chronologically across the Tudor period. Its title, 'Power and Light', illustrates two important functions of textiles within the Tudor paradigm. Firstly, because of their intrinsic value and their capacity for symbolic story-telling (in figurative tapestries and embroideries, for example), textiles were highly prized conveyors of social power and prestige. This chapter discusses the ways in which Tudor monarchs used textiles to convey their own messages and meaning, and how the textiles in question moved in and out of fashion according to the political context and vagaries of each reign. For example, ostentatious commissions of allegorical tapestries and extravagant militaristic tents typified the visual style of Henry VIII's reign, reflecting Henry's own perception of himself as a classical hero and chivalric knight. By contrast, the reign of his daughter Elizabeth found tangible expression in a visual culture of intimate and coded emblems in the form of portrait miniatures and symbolic embroidery. Secondly, light is a key factor in understanding Tudor ways of seeing textiles, and should be considered an important factor in their study. Alum was a vital mineral compound in the production of the best dyes, and was given the name *dare la lume* ('to give light'), or simply *lume* ('light').[8] This terminology provides an insight into the purpose of textiles within the court context. In most accounts of court spaces, textiles are displayed alongside cupboards containing metal plate, usually gold- or silverware (fig. 3).[9] Naturally, plate held significant value of its own, but, interestingly, accounts often prioritise its use as a reflector of light, working in combination with the metal or silk highlights of elite textiles. Cloth of gold transcended even the value of its material worth when combined with light, and took on an added quality. In dim or dark candle- or torch-lit spaces, light was necessarily useful but – more than that – to the Tudor eye it might seem ethereal, maybe divine. A French account of the English encampment at the Field of Cloth of Gold in 1520 noted that 'tapestries with golden figures shine radiantly [. . . and] the elevated vault [. . .] glows with gold, everywhere glittering'.[10] Such an effect could only have been within the gift of royalty or princes of the church. It would have been a rare sight. As the Elizabethan poet Edmund Spenser wrote over half a century later:

[. . .] round about, the walls yclothed were
With goodly arras of great majesty,
Woven with gold and silke so close and nere,
That the rich metal lurked privily, [. . .]
Yet here, and there, and every where unawares
It shewed it selfe, and shone[.][11]

The third chapter continues to explore the meaning of textiles, but now as applied to the private spaces inhabited by the Tudor kings and queens. The discussion of Tudor monarchs' privacy is problematic, however, because they

FIG. 3 The frontispiece of the Duke of Montmorency's translation of Cicero's 'Four Orations', 1531–3, tempera and gold on parchment. The French baron and members of his household are assembled in a richly decorated chamber: a cupboard displays gold and silver plate, and millefleurs tapestries, lining the walls, are hung on hooks for ease of removal. J. Paul Getty Museum, MS Ludwig I 15, Getty Epistles.

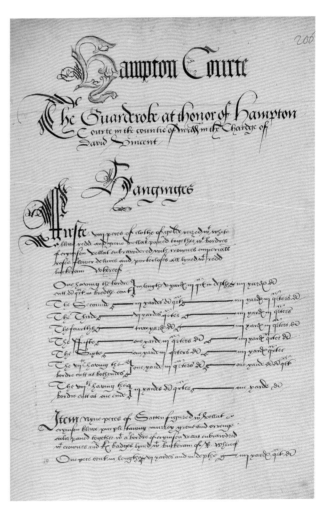

FIG. 4 A page from the inventory of Henry VIII's assets taken after his death, known as the 1547 Inventory. It shows the beginning of the list of hangings in the Wardrobe at Hampton Court. BL, Harley MS 1419 A, fol. 206.

had none, and certainly not as we would recognise it today. They and their nobility were attended at all times, even when they slept or went to the toilet; assembled courtiers often watched the monarch dining. The notion of intimacy was nevertheless of paramount importance to the court. The concept of closeness to the monarch was a key factor in the construct of the court's hierarchy. At Hampton Court Palace, the Great Hall was just the first space along a route that led to the Great Watching Chamber, and thence along corridors to the council chambers and then the privy chambers. Progression from one space to the next depended on rank and favour. The bedchamber represented the ultimate proximity to the king or queen, and consequently the royal bed was imbued with symbolism and meaning. It was a place of intimacy and private counsel, and, as such, was also of huge political significance.[12] The textiles of the privy chamber, and especially the bedchamber, were among the richest at the

royal court. Moreover, the descriptions in the inventories make it possible to discern differences between the textiles on display in the more public and the more private apartments. These small but tantalising differences allow us to inquire into the idea of the monarch's own private taste, in addition to offering glimpses of the personal interests and idiosyncrasies of the Tudors.

An important moment for the Tudor dynasty, and, indeed, for English history, is captured in an unassuming textile receipt for March 1522.[13] Richard Gibson, an official of the royal household, wrote that he bought 24 yards of fine yellow satin from mercer William Botry, at 8s. a yard.[14] The satin was for 'making [. . .] 8 ladies' garments' for the costumed pageants, known as 'revels', so enjoyed by Henry VIII. The ladies were afterwards permitted to keep the garments as a gift from the king. The *Château Vert* pageant took place at Whitehall Palace on Shrove Tuesday in the same month; this was a chivalric allegory in

FIG. 5 British School, *The Family of Henry VIII*, *c.*1545, oil on canvas. Henry is seated under an elaborately embroidered cloth of estate, his feet resting on a large embroidered foot cushion with an imported Eastern carpet beneath. He is shown with his son and heir, Edward, and his third wife, Jane Seymour (depicted posthumously); his daughters, Mary and Elizabeth, stand to the sides. Royal Collection, Hampton Court Palace.

which the ladies (representing the Virtues) were freed from a castle by the king and his companions. Among the ladies were the king's younger sister, the Countess of Devonshire, and one Mistress Anne Boleyn. This is the first record of Anne Boleyn's presence at Henry's court. This account testifies to the role of textiles in the story of the Tudors. Textiles were esteemed for their intrinsic worth, and were itemised and recorded to the nearest nail (fig. 4).

Accounts such as Richard Gibson's – aside from incidentally recording historic moments such as Anne Boleyn's debut – were fastidiously accurate, showing the value placed upon textiles, and indicating the complexity of the administrative apparatus charged with their care. The fourth chapter takes a step away from the royal chambers, and looks instead to the offices and storerooms of the Great Wardrobe – the vast bureaucratic and logistical machine responsible for the procurement,

maintenance, storage, transport and implemented use of textiles at the Tudor court.

The final chapter is a thematic overview of the raw materials and basic techniques of Tudor textiles, from 1485 to 1603. It summarises how fifteenth- and sixteenth-century industries took fleece, flax, silkworms and precious metals, and produced woollen cloth, fine linen, silk and metal thread. It also looks at the raw materials and processes required for dyeing yarn and cloth. And it sets out the broad technical categories of luxury Tudor textiles: weaving – of cloth, carpets, tapestry, napery and lace – and embroidery. In summary, this book tells the story of Tudor textiles as a key element of sixteenth-century material and visual culture. It is the story of the royal court, of wool and silk, of merchants and expanding global trade, of spies and hidden codes, of Renaissance and Reformation, and ultimately of the competitive magnificence of the Tudor monarchs at the heart of it all (fig. 5).

e	Nichome		iz	a	
f	dis		i	b	Geruasii
g				c	
a			9	d	
b	Bonifacij			e	
c			17	f	·Vigᵃ
d	Luciane		6	g	Marcholus
e				a	Eligne c'
f			14	b	Iohanis
g	Landoldis		3	c	
a	Barnabe·			d	Vigᵃ
b	apli;		11	e	Petri & p̃
c				f	Comeoreo
d	Basilij e		23	;	pauli;

1 THE GLOBAL STORY

Tudor Textiles in Context

The story of Tudor textiles is the story of Tudor England itself. It is intricately interwoven with the wider political, social and religious changes of the late fifteenth and sixteenth centuries. The fashion for certain types of fabric, or for particular tapestries or embroideries, directly relates to these changes, and to the expanding global horizons that accompanied them.

The Tudors came to power in August 1485, when Henry Tudor (1457–1509) defeated King Richard III (1452–1485) at the Battle of Bosworth, and assumed the throne as King Henry VII. The England of Henry's early reign was dramatically different from the one his granddaughter Elizabeth I would inhabit, and Europe, too, changed radically in the seventy years that separated their accessions.

FIG. 6 Sheep shearing in late spring, *c*.1540, manuscript painting from a book of hours known as the 'Golf Book'. After the sheep were washed and sheared, the wool buyers would offer prices based on the colour, texture and length of the fleeces. BL, Add. MS 24098.

WOOL AND ENGLAND'S WEALTH

During the late Middle Ages, the production and sale of wool accounted for over half England's wealth; in 1420 it contributed three-quarters of the government's export revenue.[1] Wool was known as 'the jewel of the realm' and was the foremost fabric of England and of the royal court.[2] Indeed, from the fourteenth century onwards, a bale of wool covered in red cloth, known as the 'Woolsack', was the seat of the Lord Chancellor of England (now of the Lord Speaker) within the House of Lords, as a tangible reminder that wool was the foundation of England's economy.[3]

The flocks owned by monasteries and by manorial lords formed the basis of wool production. The quality of their fleeces was well regarded and commanded good prices (figs 6 and 7). These landlords built fulling mills and tenter yards (for the manufacture of woollen cloth) on their lands, and their estates became power-houses of production and industry.[4]

Trade was closely regulated by guilds. These were associations that oversaw the trade practices of their members in their respective areas, guarded trade secrets, ensured the quality of the product and lobbied against

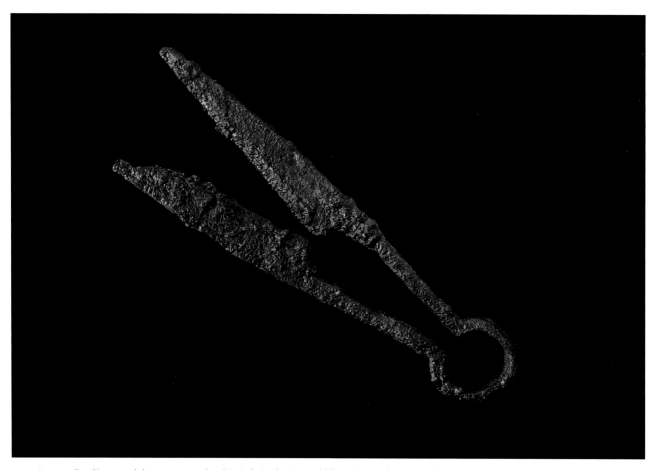

FIG. 7 Late medieval iron wool shears, excavated at Criccieth Castle, Gwynedd (length 9.5 cm). Amgueddfa Genedlaethol Cymru / National Museum Wales, 41.299/ 1.

unregulated competition. One had to be a member of a guild to legally conduct the business of the craft or trade in question. Guilds included the Drapers (wool and cloth), Tailors (known as Merchant Taylors from 1503), Haberdashers (clothiers), Dyers, Weavers, Broderers (embroiderers), Woolmen, Fullers and Shearmen.[5]

English wool was in high demand, and the Staplers – dealing in bales of raw wool – were the wealthiest of all the wool merchants and the dominant presence in England's export economy.[6] Through duties paid on their goods and through their own amassed wealth, merchants became major financiers of the crown, and were granted concessions on duties and taxes in compensation for personal loans to the king.[7]

Around the end of the fourteenth-century, however, the market for raw wool exports began a steady decline. Under the Yorkist king Edward IV (1442–1483), membership of the Staplers' Company exceeded 300, but by 1525 that number had halved.[8] Instead, demand shifted

towards manufactured woollen cloth during the fifteenth century, and English kersey and broadcloth were successful exports. Weavers in the Netherlands attempted to imitate the lighter, cheaper fabric of the English kersey that was so popular across Europe, and particularly for warmer climes such as Italy.[9]

A pamphlet written during the reign of Edward IV, entitled *England's Commercial Policy*, captured the importance of wool to the economy and the mindset of the country. It stated that merchants from 'divers lands far beyond the sea' desired 'to have this merchandise into their country', and that, by means of English wool, England 'might rule and govern all Christian Kings'.[10] In reality, the England that Henry Tudor seized at Bosworth was a relative backwater, and was neither inclined nor powerful enough to think in imperial terms about ruling 'all Christian Kings'. That would change during the reign of his granddaughter Elizabeth, but, in the late fifteenth century, English trade was relatively limited. It was

FIG. 8 Maarten van Heemskerck (1498–1574), portraits of a merchant (8a) and his wife (8b), 1529, oil on panel. The sitters were possibly Pieter Gerritsz Bicker and Anna Codde and these are among the earliest portraits of Dutch citizens. The man is engaged with his accounts, the woman with her spinning wheel and distaff. Rijksmuseum, Amsterdam.

dominated by the export of wool and woollen cloth to the Low Countries and, from there, the import into England of goods from the East and the Mediterranean, such as spices, almonds, fruit, wine, oil and – importantly for our story – luxury textiles.[11]

The area known as the Low Countries was the lowland region of north-western Europe, loosely consisting of modern-day Belgium, the Netherlands, Luxembourg and part of north-eastern France. The area consisted of regions and fiefs ruled by the dukes of Burgundy, including Flanders, Brabant, Hainault, Holland and Zeeland. The region's cities of Bruges, Brussels and Ghent were among the most important trading cities of the late Middle Ages (fig. 8). Bruges had been the dominant trading centre, but in 1478 the powerful Medici family abandoned the city as the result of heavy losses from the Bruges branch of their business: debts were owing from Charles the Bold, Duke of Burgundy (1433–1477), and an

attempt to assume control of the Western European supply of alum (a compound essential to dyeing textiles) had failed.[12] Trade shifted towards Antwerp, and around the time that Henry Tudor was establishing his dynasty in the late fifteenth century the city was establishing itself as the main port of the Low Countries. Geographically, Antwerp held a secure inland position, but it was located on the river Scheldt, whose deep waters provided a good harbour and easy access to the sea. By around 1490 it was Europe's major trading hub, surpassing even Venice, and was the termination of trade routes from as far afield as India and Africa.[13] The merchants of the German Hanse, the Baltic states, the Italian city-states, Spain and Portugal traded here, and English merchants had little need to look for other markets while the mighty port of Antwerp lay open, just a stone's throw away across the North Sea (fig. 9).

England's foreign and economic policy focused on keeping wool and cloth flowing to the Low Countries.

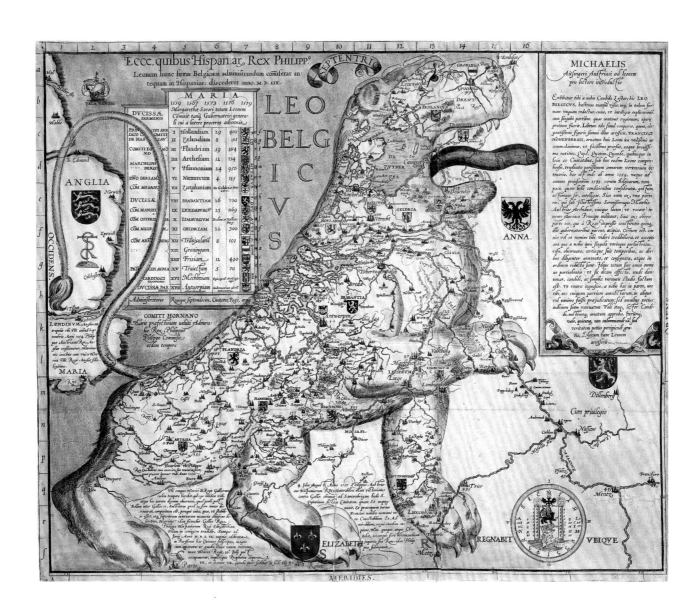

The trade was threatened by the support of Margaret of York (1446–1503), third wife of Charles the Bold and protector of the Duchy of Burgundy after his death, for rival claimants to the Tudor throne. Margaret was the sister of two Yorkist kings, Edward IV and Richard III, and she actively supported a challenge to Henry VII in the shape of Perkin Warbeck (c.1474–1499), who claimed to be her nephew, Richard, Duke of York (b. 1473), one of the lost 'princes in the Tower'. In response to this threat, Henry issued a trade embargo, forcing English merchants to relocate from Antwerp to Calais. When the embargo began to bite on the economies of England and the Low Countries, the Intercursus Magnus treaty was signed in February 1496.[14] The treaty re-established favourable trading arrangements, on condition that Margaret accepted the Tudor succession.[15]

COMPETITION IN EUROPEAN TRADE

While England focused on Antwerp and on eradicating threats to the Tudor claim, Portuguese and Spanish explorers were beginning to exploit the vast riches of the New World. In 1503 the Casa de la Contratación de las Indias ('House of Commerce of the Indes') was established as an agency of the Spanish crown to collect duties on the vast cargoes of gold and silver, gems, pearls and costly spices being brought back from overseas. This new wealth swelled the royal coffers and enhanced Spain's reach and power (fig. 10).[16]

The merchant bankers of the different states we now know as Italy also had significant reach – and ambition, too. Cities such as Genoa and Venice were major trading players in the Mediterranean, dominating the flow of luxury commodities and textiles from the East.[17] Their commercial and financial power equated to considerable

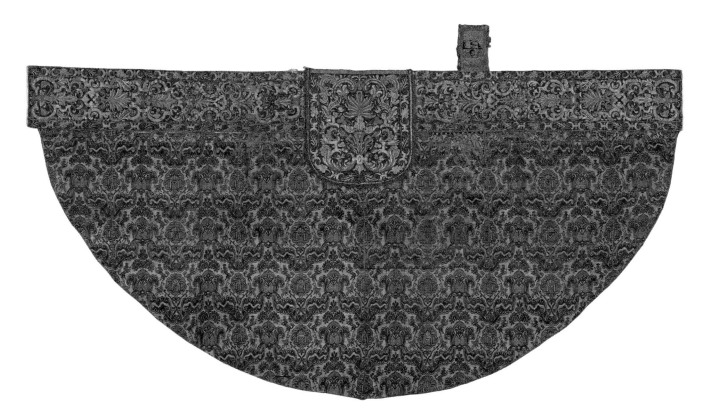

FIG. 9 (OPPOSITE) Michael Eytzinger (c.1530–1598) and Frans Hogenberg (1535–1590), the Low Countries depicted as a lion, 1583. The map shows the different states of the Low Countries, and also the proximity of the main ports to the east coast of England ('Anglia', left). Private collection.

FIG. 10 (ABOVE) Cope, 16th century, Spain, silk, dyed with cochineal from Mexico, with embroidery of silk and metal threads. Metropolitan Museum of Art, New York, 51.129.7.

political power and leverage. Edward IV had borrowed significant sums from the Florentine Medici and their agents to fight the dynastic war of succession now known as the Wars of the Roses, from which Henry Tudor emerged the victor. Lorenzo and Giuliano Medici and the merchant banker 'Thomas Portunary' (Tommaso Portinari) had lent Edward an eye-watering £5,000, which roughly equates to £3.5 million today.[18] For this outlay, the Medici and Portinari were able to gain favourable terms on customs due, and benefited from a relationship with the king. Portinari was pivotal to the fortunes of Henry VII, too, as a negotiator of the Intercursus Magnus, and the Portinari were still merchants to the royal court during the reign of Edward's grandson Henry VIII, enjoying safe conduct and the king's protection.[19]

As early as the mid-twelfth century, the poet Thomas of Britain described how his protagonist Caerdin entered London disguised as a mercer, sailing 'upriver with his merchandise [. . .] straight up to London beneath the bridge, and there displays his wares, unfolds and spreads his silks'.[20] That silks were being transported to London from afar is also demonstrated in trading regulations dating to around 1130 and 1150, concerning the 'emperor's men' – that is, men from the Holy Roman Empire.[21] The regulations dictated that, once past London Bridge, the ships had to wait in the harbour to show their wares to the king's chamberlain, who had the right of first choice so that the king might have the finest of the goods.

Medieval mercers had to agree that their wares were subject to valuation by London's own merchants.[22] These silks may have been coming from as far afield as China, Syria, Persia or Constantinople, or from al-Andalus, the Muslim-ruled region of southern Spain, where *tiraz* workshops (producing silk, woven or embroidered with inscriptions) were established as early as the eighth century.[23] Italian merchants had trading posts in the Syrian city of Aleppo, at the western edge of the silk roads (the network of trade routes connecting East and West), where silk and spices were traded.[24] Silk was also imported from Spain, Sicily and the Middle and Far East – areas where silkworms could be cultivated locally.[25] Venice, the main exporter of Eastern silk to Western Europe, began to weave its own silk cloth in the twelfth century, as did Florence, Lucca and Genoa.[26] The Italian weavers wove the fibre with especial expertise, and their silks became a prized luxury textile (fig. 11).

The Italian merchants – along with others groups, such as the German merchants of the Hanse, resident in London from the late thirteenth century[27] – had branches in major ports across Europe. Collectively known as 'Lombards' by Londoners, after the Italian province of Lombardy, they had houses and warehouses in the City of London, where their former presence is still recorded in the name Lombard Street.[28]

Italian silks have been found in the archaeological record in London dating from the fourteenth century.[29] However, these fragments represent what was still a rare commodity. Although we know that Edward IV spent lavishly on silks, including damasks and velvets when he could, the small number of accounts that survive from his reign show that his wardrobe included a high proportion of fine woollen cloth, and only a small amount of imported fabric.[30] This may suggest that Edward was leading by example in support of his powerful domestic industry or, more likely, that imported luxury cloth was not as abundant or as easily procured as it would be for his Tudor successors. Indeed, in the 1547 inventory of Henry VIII's goods recorded over 1,000 metres of cloth of tissue, while just a hundred years earlier, in 1443, less than 2 metres of this luxurious textile were purchased for use by Henry VI.[31]

An important moment of change seems to have occurred around the turn of the sixteenth century, when imported silks decisively replaced domestic woollen broadcloth as the textile of choice at the English royal court. English merchants naturally objected to this threat, and the guilds lobbied the authorities and government, but to little avail.[32] One reason for this change might be that the Italians were able to produce greater quantities of silks following the discovery of alum at Tolfa, in the Papal States, in the 1460s. Alum was a vital mordant used in the dyeing process; before this point it had been found only in Ottoman-controlled territories, and in small quantities in Spain. The Medici took on the management of the alum mines, which subsequently strengthened and enriched the silk industry of the Italian city-states.[33] The invasion of Italy in 1494 by Charles VIII of France (1470–1498) may also have been pivotal in this change, as the French nobility were exposed to Italian fashions that drove the demand for fine silks westward to Paris and on to London, where the elite were always eager to follow French style.[34]

It was during Henry VII's reign, too, that the fashion for imported Eastern carpets took root in England. The trend had spread through Europe from Italy, where Islamic prayer rugs can be seen adorning window ledges and tables in Italian paintings of the fifteenth century.[35] They can be seen, too, in Netherlandish paintings, almost exclusively those produced in Bruges and later Antwerp – the main commercial hubs of the Low Countries and at the termination of trade routes from Asia via Italy.[36] The Genoese notary (and friend of Christopher Columbus) Antonio Gallo bought fifty Turkish carpets in the early 1490s, and sent forty of those to London in exchange for English woollen cloths; this transaction was evidently profitable, as the venture was repeated a number of times.[37] As with all fashions, the ability to display such carpets demonstrated sophistication and taste to a contemporary audience, and appealed to the desire for status as conferred by rare and exotic imported commodities. They may also have indicated – from the fifteenth- and sixteenth-century viewpoint – the ideological triumph of Christianity over the Ottoman Turk, particularly when they were depicted under the feet of the Virgin in paintings and frescos (fig. 12).

FIG. 11 The signboard of the Guild of Silk Weavers in Venice, 16th century, oil on panel. Museo Correr, Venice.

THE POWER OF THE MERCHANTS

When Henry VII died in 1509, his 17-year old son became King Henry VIII. It was the first peaceful transition of power in almost ninety years. Henry VII, who had won his throne in battle, had spent much of his reign eradicating threats and securing the Tudor succession. One of the ways in which he did this was to emulate, or continue, the styles of his Yorkist predecessors. The young Henry, on the other hand, was the model Renaissance prince. He was young, exceptionally well educated and ambitious, and, thanks to his father's care over the treasury, he was also very rich. Henry was eager to compete with his fellow princes on a European stage and to play an increasing role in continental affairs. Along with his principal minister for domestic matters, Cardinal Thomas Wolsey (1473–1530), Henry absorbed European artistic and chivalric models and aesthetics, particularly from Italy and Burgundy. Merchants played a vital role in creating the conditions for these models to reach the royal court.[38]

Wool, and the production of woollen cloth, remained profitable for the English economy and for the crown. The castle built by the Heydons of Baconsthorpe in Norfolk from the late fifteenth century to the mid-sixteenth century testifies to this. The family had prospered during the Wars of the Roses (often switching sides), but under Tudor rule they had little need to fortify their estates, and instead turned the castle at Baconsthorpe into a wool 'factory' for an estimated flock of 30,000 sheep, transforming the east range of the castle into an area for the production of woollen cloth, with large windows providing light for the spinners and weavers.[39] There was demand for their output, for just as the merchants brought silks, alum, dyes and wines to London so they exported profitable English woollen cloth (and kerseys in particular) back to the continent – usually via Antwerp.[40]

So important was the contribution of the merchants to the national economy and to the crown that they were often targeted in the course of political wargames. In September 1511, Thomas, Baron Dacre (1467–1525), Lord

Warden of the Marches, made complaints to the wardens of Scotland for the 'robbing and spoiling of English merchants' goods' and the taking of the ship 'Mary of Roken with 150 fardels [bundles] of linen cloth worth 1,400*l*. [. . .] from Maurice Dee and Davy Welshman'.[41] King James IV of Scotland dismissed these complaints, claiming that the raids were beyond his control, being the work of pirates in the pay of the French, and so the looting continued.[42] Thomas Spinelly, Henry VIII's representative in the Low Countries, wrote directly to the king from Brussels in July 1512 that the Scots were still 'entering the ports of Zealand [. . . and] pillaging English merchants'.[43] Lord Dacre also reported that James IV met with a representative of the French king on board his great ship, where he was presented with gifts of arms, wine and '8 stick [presumably ell-sticks] of cloth of gold [. . .] The Scots will assuredly help the French'.[44] All this occurred during a time of nominal peace, but the raids on merchant ships were antagonistic and can now be seen as a prelude to the war with France and Scotland in 1513, and the Battle of Flodden of that year, in which James IV himself was killed.

Italian families such as the Cavalcanti, the Frescobaldi and the Bonvisi were active in Tudor London, and vital to the crown. The Florentine company of Giovanni Cavalcanti (1480–1544) and Pierfrancesco de' Bardi (d. 1534) was based at Austin Friars in the City of London, where in due course Thomas Cromwell would make his home. They were often exempted from paying customs, and the king was often in their debt – facts that were not unrelated. Their property comprised accommodation, a parlour, gardens, a counting-house and a large warehouse for storing cloth. At a time when even members of the nobility struggled to afford counterfeit arras, the rooms of the Cavalcanti and Bardi property served as a showcase, decorated with eleven cloths of arras, and rich lampas cloth of gold.[45] The King's Book of Payments shows that the Cavalcanti and Bardi company provided most of the textiles for the Field of Cloth of Gold.[46]

Meanwhile, English merchants were trading on the continent. The Gresham family were prominent merchants to the royal court. Brothers Sir Richard (*c*.1485–1549) and Sir John (*c*.1495–1556) Gresham exported English wool and woollen cloth, and imported tapestries, carpets, silk, linen, fustian and grain.[47] Sir Richard Gresham was an important figure in the history of court décor: he was

FIG. 12 Jan Van Eyck (*c*.1390–1441), *The Madonna with Canon van der Paele*, 1434–6, oil on panel. The Virgin and Child are shown enthroned under a cloth of estate on a dais laid with an Eastern carpet. St Donatian (*left*) is dressed in a cope of blue and cloth of gold in a typical Renaissance pattern; behind the canon stands St George. Groeningemuseum, Bruges.

charged by Cardinal Wolsey to buy tapestries for Hampton Court, not by subject matter but rather by the yardage required to fill the vast empty walls of his new palace.[48] Gresham served Wolsey and the king, and his family rose in prominence. His son Sir Thomas Gresham (c.1518–1579; fig. 13) founded London's Royal Exchange in 1568, based on Antwerp's *bourse*, and endowed Gresham College (which came into being after his widow's death).[49]

Thomas Gresham was an agent of the state, and Queen Elizabeth's merchant. He conducted much of his business in Antwerp, a converging point for merchants and manufacturers from across Europe. As such, in letters to William Cecil, Lord Burghley (1520/21–1598), Elizabeth's secretary of state, Gresham was able to relay news from the Low Countries, but also intelligence from Italy, Turkey and Spain. Hundreds of letters from Gresham attest to his importance in shaping England's foreign policy through his 'advertisements'.[50] Gresham paid his own network of servants to send 'daily advertisements . . . if it were but to know who cometh and passeth from thence'.[51] Indeed, English merchants were so powerful that the crown was reliant upon *them* for finance and subsidy. Henry VIII's principal agent in Antwerp was the London merchant Stephen Vaughan. He arranged and then managed the repayment of loans to Henry to finance his war with the French.[52] On 17 June 1544, Vaughan wrote to Secretary Thomas Wriothesley (1505–1550) that he was negotiating the 'bills of credence for 100,000 crowns' with merchants in Antwerp, such as Bartolomeo Compagni (fig. 14).[53] Lenders had to forgo the usual interest payments,[54] but merchants financing the king might hope for favourable trading concessions instead. In the early years of Edward VI's reign, 'Bartholomew Compagny, Florentine, [. . . was] appointed the king's merchant for provisions of silks, clothe of gold and sylver [. . .] tapissery, lynnen cloth [. . .] and velvettes, dammaskes, sattyns, taffeta and sarcenettes, all maner of works of Venyce golde and sylver, Dammaske gold and sylver', which he was allowed to import at a favourable rate, paying the same duties as 'natural born subjects'.[55]

FIG. 14 Pier Francesci de Jacopo Foschi (1502–1567), portrait of Bartolomeo Compagni (1503–1561), Florentine merchant to Henry VIII and Edward VI, 1549, oil on panel. Cummer Museum of Art and Gardens, Jacksonville, Florida.

A GROWING CRISIS

A crisis was brewing. The English economy was largely dependent upon a single commodity – woollen cloth – traded in a single market – Antwerp; but growing religious persecution and unrest in the 1540s and 1550s made Antwerp much less stable and accessible than it had been. The population of the Low Countries was largely Protestant, but the region was ruled by Roman Catholic Spain through a series of marriages and for lack of direct male heirs. When Charles the Bold, Duke of Burgundy, died without a male heir, rule of the region passed to the Habsburg dynasty by the marriage of Charles's daughter, Mary of Burgundy (1457–1482), to Archduke Maximilian I (1459–1519).[56] Their son, Philip of Habsburg (1478–1506), known as 'the Fair', became Philip IV, titular Duke of Burgundy in 1482, and then in 1506 was proclaimed King of Castile through his wife, Joanna (1479–1555). Through this dynastic confluence, Philip and Joanna's son, Charles (1500–1558), inherited the Low Countries as Duke Charles II, the Holy Roman Empire as Charles V, and Spain as King

FIG. 13 Antonis Mor (d. 1576?), portrait of Sir Thomas Gresham (c.1518–1579), merchant to the royal court, c.1560–65, oil on panel. Rijksmuseum, Amsterdam.

Charles I.[57] Mary I (1516–1558), the only surviving child of Henry VIII and Katherine of Aragon, married Charles's son, who, in 1554, became King Philip II of Spain (1527–1598). She did not interfere with Habsburg policies in the Low Countries, though she did initially – on the advice of her council – refrain from supporting Philip's war with France, as it would be detrimental to trade.[58]

The persecution of Protestants in the Low Countries was fierce, and from 1567 to 1571 an estimated 18,000 people were killed for their religion.[59] Many of the Flemish and Dutch Protestants fleeing persecution settled in Elizabeth's Protestant England. The impact of this was dramatic. Skilled immigrant weavers brought new techniques to England, simultaneously revitalising the English economy under Elizabeth and slowing that of the Low Countries.[60] Between 1583 and 1589, the population of Antwerp, Ghent and Bruges halved.[61] This had ramifications for the specialized textile industries of both the Low Countries and England, with repercussions for the availability and fashions of court textiles.

In September 1591, an agent acting for the Earl of Essex was trying to procure tapestries in the Low Countries. There was some choice in Antwerp, but nothing in Brussels.[62] Elizabeth Talbot (née Cavendish), Countess of Shrewsbury (1527?–1608), who is better known as Bess of Hardwick, was also tapestry shopping in the 1590s. She bought a set of tapestries depicting the story of Gideon, which bears witness to the faded glory of Flemish tapestries. She purchased them from the heir of Queen Elizabeth's favourite, Sir Christopher Hatton (1540–1591), who had commissioned the thirteen large panels in 1578 in an attempt to attract the queen to visit his house at Holdenby, Northamptonshire. The set was expensive and Hatton had incurred huge debts. Even so, the panels are made of low-quality materials and dyestuffs, and though they are vast in scale, much of the detailing is completed in a dark or black paint. Recent conservation by the National Trust has revealed that this set was made in Oudenaarde, a less prestigious weaving centre than either Brussels or Antwerp.[63]

It is not by chance that the decline in the traditional tapestry-weaving centres of the Low Countries coincided with the development of an English tapestry industry, particularly after the 1560s, when Flemish immigrants brought their weaving skills to bear on hangings, table carpets, coverlets and cushion covers produced in England.[64]

In the late 1560s, William Sheldon set up a new tapestry-weaving business in Warwickshire, continued from 1570 by his son, Ralph (1537–1613). He employed one Richard Hyckes (or Hicks; c.1524–1621), an émigré Flemish weaver,[65] who was appointed by Queen Elizabeth as her 'arras-maker' in 1569 (see p. 31),[66] responsible for the repair and upkeep of the some 2,500 tapestries in her collection. Sheldon called Hyckes 'the onely auter and beginner of this arte within the

realm'.[67] When the town clerk of Warwick asked for help from Robert Dudley, Earl of Leicester (1532/3–1588), to alleviate the town's poverty, his response was to

> marvaile you do not devise someways amongs you to have some special trade to kepe your poore on work as such as Sheldon of Beolye devised which [to] my thinking should not only be very profitable but also a

FIG. 15 Tapestry, c.1585, wool and silk. This luxurious piece is attributed to the Sheldon tapestry workshop in Warwickshire. Victoria and Albert Museum, London, T.320-1977.

meanes to kepe your poore from idelnes or the making of clothe [...] or some such like.[68]

A surviving tapestry featuring the arms of the Dudley family was probably made for the Earl of Leicester's London residence, Leicester House (fig. 15). It has been traditionally attributed to the Sheldon workshop, though it is of higher quality than most of their output. The artistry of the weaving suggests skilled Netherlandish involvement, so perhaps the importance of the commission caused skilled weavers to be employed specially to fulfil the order.[69] The composition certainly demonstrates sophisticated Renaissance aesthetics. A central coat of arms is surrounded by depictions of formal classical gardens, fountains, foliage and birds that come straight from the engravings of pattern books, including a turkey from the Americas, partridges, quail, a heron, and a hawk or egret.[70]

The crisis in the Low Countries had an impact on textile manufacture in other ways, too. Just as émigré skills contributed to the Dudley tapestry, so also did they affect the core historic woollen industry. Norwich had long been a centre of production of traditional English worsteds, but by the 1550s the area's woollen industry was in decline, despite the efforts of the guildsmen. Some of the city's merchants and officials recognised that only a radical departure from traditional products would allow Norwich to compete with the continental woollen industry.[71] During the 1560s, Norwich welcomed Protestant Dutch, Walloon and Flemish asylum seekers, who were admitted partly so that the city might share in their textile-weaving skills and knowledge. The house in which these refugees lodged and worked became known as Strangers' Hall.[72] Much of the prosperity of Norwich and Norfolk from this period onwards can be traced to the influx of refugees and the growing manufacture of the 'new draperies' – half-worsteds, which were lighter, finer and cheaper than old English broadcloth.[73]

While urban centres were booming as a result of the immigrants from Flanders, old wool towns like Lavenham, just 50 miles to the south of Norwich, were in decline. Although it is no more than a village to modern eyes, in the 1520s Lavenham was the fourteenth richest town in Britain, paying more tax than the cities of York and Lincoln. It was one of the great centres of medieval wool production, famous for its blue cloth, dyed with woad. Like many of the old wool towns, it was unable to compete with urbanised trade and the new draperies.[74]

The cloth trade in the Low Countries continued to be England's single largest export market for the rest of the sixteenth century, but exports of English cloth to Antwerp fell from 130,000 standard lengths of cloth (as set by the customs authorities) in 1550 to around 80,000 per annum in the 1570s.[75] Elizabeth's own position further endangered trade with the Low Countries. Her reinstatement of the Oath of Supremacy, first established by her father, which positioned her as Supreme Governor of the Church, pitted her against the Catholic powers of Europe. The hostility of her brother-in-law, Philip II of Spain, Lord of the Netherlands, could easily disrupt or halt English trade with Antwerp and the Low Countries.[76] Concern over the risks of trading with Antwerp caused William Cecil to draw up a series of questions for consideration and discussion (dated 23 January 1563). He asks:

> 1. In what Countrie are these Commodities of England most used and consumed, viz. Cloth, Woll [wool], Leade, Tynne, and such like. 2. Whether may not those Commodities of Woll, Cloth, Leade and Tynne be transported [...] and solde in other Countreys, as well as in the Low Countreys; and what Countreys those be [...] 5. What wares be they that com through the Low Countrey from other Countreys; or growe not, or be not wrought in the Lowe Countreys. 6. Which of the same are most necessary for England, and which may be spared. 7. How many and which of them may be brought out of other Countreys.[77]

English merchants got used to a war footing, and became pawns in diplomatic disputes.[78] Their ships were seized, and in April 1576 Cecil directed the Lord High Admiral to 'equip and send five of Her Majesty's ships, to wit the Dreadnought, the Swiftsure, the Foresight, the Achates, and the Handmayden' to protect merchant ships in the channel and North Sea.[79] For the first time in a long time, English merchants – and the English crown – had cause to look elsewhere for new markets.[80]

FIG. 16 Emblem celebrating Sir Francis Drake's circumnavigation of the world in 1580, coloured woodcut from Geoffrey Whitney, *A choice of emblemes* (1586); Whitney's book represented key virtues and ideas by symbols and other devices, a concept that became highly fashionable at the Elizabethan court.

GLOBALISATION

English merchants, however, were at a disadvantage. Part of their problem was that no English mariners could navigate the new global routes, and English merchants had no experience of the kind of major Asian, transatlantic or even trans-European trade that other countries had, such as Italy, Spain and Portugal.[81] Spain, which had conquered Mexico in the early 1520s, was, by the middle of the sixteenth-century, plundering its natural resources and precious metals. Shiploads of Mexican cochineal red dye were transported across the Atlantic and traded from Spanish ports to the Netherlands, Venice and the Ottoman Empire, and the product became Spain's second largest source of income after Mexican silver.[82]

The establishment of the first English joint-stock trading company began to redress the problem. Established originally under the governance of the Italian explorer Sebastian Cabot (*c*.1474–*c*.1557), who had arrived in Bristol, probably in 1548,[83] the company was granted its first royal charter by Queen Mary I in 1555, and was called the Merchants Adventurers of England for the Discovery of Lands, Territories, Isles and Seigniories Unknown.[84] (Even though Mary was married to Philip II of Spain, England did not profit from the Spanish voyages to the New World, and Mary would not countenance privateering or piracy by Merchant Adventurers against her husband's Habsburg fleet.)[85] The venture relied on collective investment, and it was hoped that expeditions undertaken by members of the company would yield sizable profits. A significant number of noblemen and courtiers invested in the company's voyages, including:

> William, marquis of Winchester, lord high treasurer, Henry, earl of Arundel, lord steward of the Household, John, earl of Bedford, lord keeper of the privy seal, William, earl of Pembroke, William, lord Howard of Effyngham, lord high admiral [. . .] Sir John Gage, knight of the order, lord chamberlain of the Household, Sir Robert Rochestre, knight, controller of the Household, Sir Henry Jerningham, knight, vice-chamberlain [. . .] Sir Edward Walgrave, knight, master of the wardrobe of robes [etc.][86]

'Sir William Cicille' also supported the venture. The company's charter was reconfirmed by Elizabeth in 1566, under the name Fellowship of English Merchants for Discovery of New Trades.[87] It was known informally as the Muscovy Company. Other companies followed,

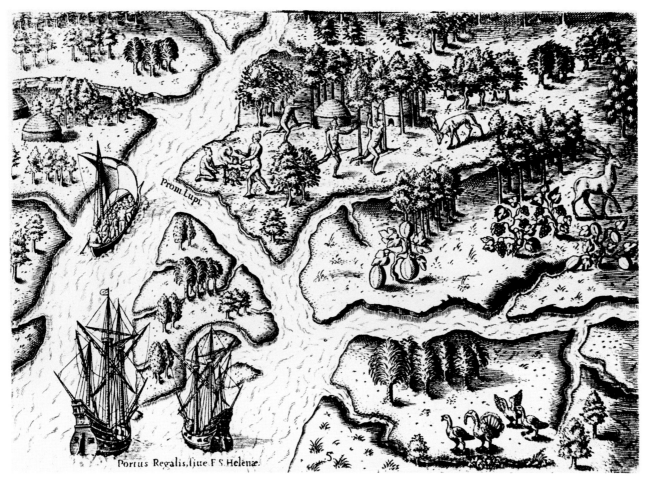

FIG. 17 Theodor de Bry (1528–1598), the arrival of the French at Port Royale in 1564, engraving after a drawing by Jacques Le Moyne de Morgues, published in volume II (1591) of de Bry's *Great and Small Voyages*. Part map, part illustration, the drawing shows indigenous flora and fauna and the activities of the local people. Library of Congress, Washington, DC, G159.B7, [plate] 5.

including the Levant Company in 1581, and the East India Company, granted its royal charter by Elizabeth in 1600 (see fig. 16).[88]

The eagerness with which English merchants began to broaden their horizons can be discerned in *The principall navigations, voiages and discoveries of the English nation, made by sea or over land, to the most remote and farthest distant quarters of the earth* by Richard Hakluyt (1552?–1616), first published in 1589. The first edition was dedicated to his patron Sir Francis Walsingham (*c*.1532–1590), Elizabeth's principal secretary. The second edition was dedicated to Robert Cecil (1563–1612), then a rising star at Elizabeth's court. An elder cousin of his, another Richard Hakluyt (*c*.1530–1591), was a lawyer in London, and though he never travelled he compiled a huge array of information and advice from merchants and mariners who did. These accounts, along with the younger

Hakluyt's own additions, were published in *Principall navigations*, and were intended for merchants travelling abroad, particularly those involved in the cloth trade.

In 1579 the elder Hakluyt wrote notes for one Morgan Hubblethorne, dyer, who was travelling to Persia under the auspices of the Privy Council.[89] Hakluyt wrote that Hubblethorne should look at how Persian carpets – 'the best of the world' – were dyed, and ascertain how that might be used for English wool. The aim was to investigate

the dyeing of foreign countries [. . .] for the satisfying of the lords, and of the expectation of the merchants and of your company, it behoves you to have care to returne home with more knowledge then you carried out [. . . for] the price of a cloth [. . .] riseth by the colour and the dyeing.

He was instructed to learn the different ingredients the Persian makers used in dyeing, and to acquaint himself with any dyers from Russia, China 'or of the East part of the world' to be found there and to learn what he could from them. The ultimate aim was to increase England's competitiveness, provide work for the poor, and extend the business of the merchant companies, for 'thereof will follow honour to the Realme'.[90] The Hakluyts' aim seems always to have been the advancement of English trade for the prosperity and profit of England.[91] Consequently, *Principall navigations* has been seen as an early seed of British Empire.[92]

Connections to this proto-globalisation can be found in the details of surviving textiles of the period – for example, in the floral motifs of Jacques Le Moyne de Morgues's embroidery patterns. Le Moyne (*c.*1533–1588) was a French artist and a Huguenot (a French Protestant). He was a member of the French expedition of 1564 across the Atlantic to the colony at Port Royale, in modern-day Florida, tasked with drawing maps of the coast and towns, and recording details of the native people and aspects of their culture. The expedition was a disaster, bedevilled by mutiny, starvation and a massacre of the French by the Spanish. But Le Moyne escaped and returned to France,[93] and Hakluyt used his drawings in *A notable historie* (1587), his translation of an account of the voyage by René Laudonnière;[94] Hakluyt calls Le Moyne 'an eye-witness of the goodness and fertilitie of those regions'.[95] By this point, Le Moyne was living in London, having left France in 1580 to avoid religious persecution. He settled in Blackfriars, and found important patrons such as Sir Walter Raleigh (1554–1618) and Mary Herbert (née Sidney), Countess of Pembroke (1561–1621).

Engravings by Theodor de Bry (1528–1598), a Protestant Fleming who fled Spanish persecution, are reputedly based on Le Moyne's drawings and paintings from the expedition.[96] They were published in de Bry's *Great and Small Voyages* collection (1590–1634), which chronicled early expeditions to the Americas. One engraving shows galleons arriving, alongside Native Americans hunting in a forest (fig. 17). Shown too, are turkeys, plants, berries and fruit that are distinctly recognisable as the stylised motifs of Le Moyne's *La clef des champs* ('The key of the fields'; 1586), which was used by noble ladies of the court as an embroidery pattern book

(see p. 63). Their appearance, out of scale and in fantastical motif format, is curious: maybe the use of Le Moyne's designs added interest or points of recognition for a European audience, showing the commodities and fruitfulness of the country.[97] Arguably, when de Bry or Hakluyt used engravings such as these – which Hakluyt did only sparingly – the goal was to encourage English expeditions by advertising the riches on offer, which would necessitate clear recognition by the viewer.[98] These same motifs, inspired by or copied from Le Moyne, can be seen on surviving textiles such as the Bacton Altar Cloth, where they feature alongside little embroidered sailors and mysterious sea creatures (fig. 18), which loomed large in the Tudor consciousness as a result of these voyages.

MANUFACTURING INNOVATION

While expeditions and voyages were expanding England's horizons, changes were also taking place to the traditional order of manufacture. For centuries, guilds had monopolised their trades. The guilds ensured the uniformity of the product, but at the same time guild regulations hampered innovation and competition.[99] The art of the dyers, for example, had remained unchanged for over a thousand years, and master dyers were not permitted to move from town to town.[100] In order to maintain their trade secrets, they were even known to keep people away from their workshops by spreading scare stories of ghosts and demons.[101] Some dye recipes had been published in *Tbouch va[n] wondres* printed in Brussels in 1513, but it was not a technical manual, nor was it directed to the dyer, but rather to a domestic audience. Some of the recipes would later be translated by Leonard Mascall (d. 1589) in *A profitable boke declaring dyvers approved remedies, to take out spottes and staines* [. . . *and*] *how to die velvets and silkes, linnen and Woollen, fustian and threade* [. . .] *englished by L.M.*, first published in London in 1583.[102]

The first technical book on the art of dyeing fabrics was published in Venice in 1548 as *Plictho de larte de tentori* (fig. 19).[103] In this work, the author, Giovanventura Rosetti, who was superintendent of the armoury in Venice, gathered together the dyeing secrets of Venice, Genoa, Florence, other Italian cities and areas of the Near East. It was a controversial move on his part, as the book exposed guild secrets; Rosetti's justification for doing so has echoes of Protestant Reformation in its language:

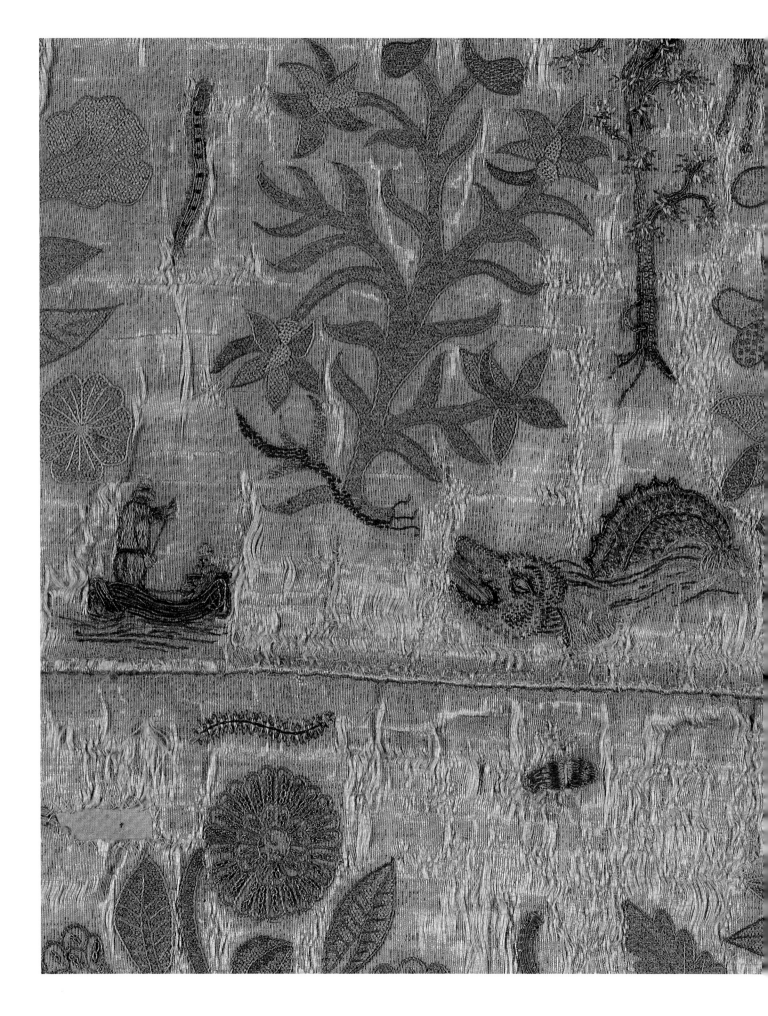

FIG. 18 Detail from the Bacton Altar Cloth, c.1600, silk and silver camlet embroidered with silk and metal thread. Among the motifs are boats and a large sea creature, conjuring up the Tudor fascination with voyages to distant lands in the age of exploration.

You must know that this is a work of Charity that I bequeath for the public benefit, and which has been imprisoned for a great number of years in the tyrannical hands of those who kept it hidden and thus subject to Evangelic indignation [. . .] Wherein sweetest Readers, I cajole you not to be subject to apostatic censure by dulling the virtue that the glorious GOD has wanted that men be endowed with [. . .] These works of mine have been published for the benefit of the people of this illustrious City of Venice.[104]

In 1549, during the reign of Edward VI, the first *Book of Common Prayer* was published in English, with the aim of delivering the word of God directly to the congregation in a language they could understand, rather than in the traditional Latin. The *Plictho* may be read as an application of the same doctrine to the mysteries of trade and manufacture. It was hugely popular, and numerous editions and translations followed for decades.[105]

The *Plictho* also provides evidence of the importance of international trade to the quality of cloth and dyestuffs. Rosetti writes about 'grain' – that is, kermes, the species of insect that was ground to make red dye – from Corinth (Greece), Valencia, Provence and Barbary (north Africa), and outlines the qualities of the product from these different places: 'Here will I tell the nature of grain and the region that produces the highest value [. . .] And actually the grain of Armenia is numbered among the good, and second is from Asia [. . .] The third is Spanish.'[106] Rosetti also mentions some of the dyes available through the new trade of the sixteenth century – namely, brazil from the Americas and indigo from India.[107] Brazilwood yielded a plentiful but slightly ineffective red dye, which only really worked in combination with other ingredients, but may have been valued for its New World origins. Rosetti did not mention Mexican or American cochineal. This was still viewed with suspicion and prohibited by Italian guilds, though shortly after the publication of the *Plictho* guild dyers conducted experiments and found it acceptable.[108] Recent conservation work has uncovered evidence of Mexican cochineal dye along with (probably) Indian indigo in the coloured silk thread embroidery of the Bacton Altar Cloth (see further pp. 64–7), providing direct evidence for the dissemination of dyes at the English court.[109] Global trade was evolving.

* * *

By the late sixteenth century, the textile trade had changed in marked ways from the early Tudor years of the 1480s. An account published by William Stafford in 1581 of the 'ordinary complaints' of Englishmen – *A compendious or briefe examination of certayne ordinary complaints [. . .] of our country men in these our dayes* – noted that even as recently as the 1540s imported goods were rare. He writes:

there is no man can be contented now with any other gloves than is made in France or Spain; nor kersey, but it must be of Flanders dye; nor cloth, but French or Friseadowe;[110] nor [. . .] brooch, or agglet, but of Venice making, or Milan [. . .] I have heard within these forty years, when there was not of these haberdashers that sells French or Milan caps [. . .] not a dozen in all London: and now from the town to Westminster along, every street is full of them, and their shops glitters and shines.[111]

FIG. 19 The dyeing of silk yarn, engraving from Giovanventura Rosetti, *Plictho de larte de tentori* (1548). Getty Research Institute, Los Angeles, TP897.R81 1560, [plate] 2.

LIBRO CHE INSEGNA A TENGERE SEDE DI
ogni colore persettamente, secondo Firenza & Genoua.

Notandissimi secreti per tengere sede in diuersi colori boni: & persetti
magistrali. Prima bisogna che se tu uogli fare colore che sia bono che tu
facci che la seda sia bianca:& a uolerla cocere bisogna che facci come inten
derai leggendo. Et in che modo si debbe stuffare & cocere & solsarare,ten
gere & retengere la seda particularmente colore per colore,& generalmen
te di quelli che uanno lauadi secondo il consueto de li maestri Fiorentini,
& consueto de tutti li maestri di Italia, e perche intendi la caggione & l'or
dine, perche se debba stuffar la seda. Tu sai che come la seda è filada & per
uolere tengerla torta,sala stusare come intenderai.

F

2 POWER AND LIGHT

Textiles and Meaning at the Tudor Court

Textiles were valuable, and the ability to acquire rich and intricate hangings or tapestries demonstrated significant financial clout. Textiles were also practical and portable, affording comfort and luxury for courts on the move. But there were a number of other factors at play in the choice of the textiles displayed at court: the influence of continental royal fashion, political competition and religious reformation; the development of humanism and a focus on classical narratives and scholarship; and the emergence of the printing press as a force for the dissemination of imagery and subject matter. Added to these were the personal stories and tastes of the Tudor monarchs themselves, which can be read in the style and content of their textiles.

FIG. 20 'The Arrival of Queen Penthesilea at Troy', 1475–90, tapestry, wool and silk, woven at Tournai. Several sets of the Troy tapestries were provided to the courts of Europe, including those of Charles the Bold of Burgundy in 1472 and Henry VII in 1488. This tapestry was one of the set made for Charles VIII of France and was listed in his inventory in 1494. Victoria and Albert Museum, London, 6-1887.

HENRY VII: HERALDRY AND ARMS

The dynastic wars that we now call the Wars of the Roses came to a decisive conclusion at the Battle of Bosworth in August 1485. The exiled Lancastrian heir, Henry Tudor, faced a superior Yorkist force and a battle-tested king, Richard III. Henry had a weaker force and a tenuous claim. He was the outside chance. His fortunes swung on the decision by his stepfather, Thomas Stanley, 1st Earl of Derby (c.1433–1504), to switch sides at the last minute, and on the failure of Richard's doomed final charge at Henry himself. Richard was surrounded and killed. Henry emerged from the battle as the victor, and took the crown as King Henry VII. Throughout his reign, he would fear usurpers and challenges to his throne, and was dependent upon the support, or at least the compliance, of the nobility. Much of his reign would be spent demonstrating his legitimacy to rule and securing the Tudor succession. It was an obsession of the new regime to get things right.[1]

Henry had spent a considerable part of his adult life in exile in Brittany and France, and was not accustomed to the conventions and practices of the English royal court. In the winter of 1496, a Venetian visitor to England wrote that Henry did 'not change any of the ancient usages of

England at his court'.[2] It seems he established power by demonstrating continuity with his Plantagenet predecessors' rule and style.

Henry gained a reputation as a miser, for frugality – as one contemporary observer noted – even 'to excess'.[3] However, he also knew when to spend, and did so lavishly in the display of majesty and ceremony that was a key expectation of royalty in the fifteenth century.[4] This manifested in the purchase of textiles, as both the archives and rare extant textiles demonstrate. In 1501, for the marriage of his heir, Prince Arthur (1486–1502), to Katherine of Aragon (1485–1536), the king's lodging at Baynard's Castle was lavishly decorated. At the far end of his chamber was 'a sete regall covered over with a cloth of estate precious and riche costly, where under his magestie was sitting upon cusshions of cloth of golde [. . .] his dere and wilbeloved sons, the Lord Prince on the right hand and the Duke of York on his left hand'.[5] His spending on the trappings of kingship, such as rich tapestries and furnishings, resulted in the punning nickname 'Rich Mount' for his palace of Richmond.[6]

An exceptional commission of Henry's survives in the form of ecclesiastical items now known as the 'Stonyhurst vestments'. The cope, a much altered chasuble and a (probably composite) chalice veil were part of a set of twenty-nine copes and matching vestments commissioned by Henry in 1500 and later bequeathed in 1509 to Westminster Abbey.[7] They were woven to shape, with the Tudor and Beaufort heraldic designs – the arms respectively of Henry's father and mother. They are richly brocaded, feature gold loops and are woven with silver and gold wound around silk cores. Antonio Corsi of Florence was paid £287 6s. 8d. for part of the set in 1500.[8] The commission was too big to be handled by Corsi alone, however, and the Bonvisi family of merchants were also involved.[9] It was a demonstration of piety, arguably even of thanksgiving for God's blessing upon the house of Tudor, whose rose and portcullis badges were woven into the fabric alongside the religious imagery of the embroidered orphreys and the hoods of the copes. The vestments were certainly meaningful objects to Henry, who listed them in his will, stating that 'of late at our proper costs and charges' they were 'made, brought and provided at Florence in Ittalie'.[10] They are among only a very few items whose origins were named in the will, and

clearly they held significant prestige in the demonstration of both the wealth and the cultural reach of the new dynasty.[11] This set of twenty-nine pieces remained unsurpassed. Indeed, Henry VIII would borrow them from Westminster Abbey to take with him to the Field of Cloth of Gold in 1520. The items that survive do so because the Jesuit order secretly shipped them out of the country, apparently in the early seventeenth century, to the College of Saint-Omer in Artois, which was then part of the Catholic Netherlands.[12] Most of the remaining vestments of the set – along with other valuable Tudor textiles – were bought by a London goldsmith, one John Bolton, as part of the Commonwealth Sale of royal goods after the Civil War. They were probably burned in order to recover the gold and silver bullion content.[13]

The vestments were part of a court aesthetic that communicated Tudor heraldry through magnificent commissions in cloth of gold. In 1499, the same Antonio Corsi supplied a cloth of estate to Henry for an incredible £11 per yard, equivalent to a full year's wages for a skilled craftsman.[14] It is possible that a cloth of estate recorded in the 1547 Inventory of Henry VIII's possessions described this very item. The inventory detailed a cloth of estate that was 'raised with crimson vellat pirled and portecloses of tissue crowned having iiii borders of S and Rooses of Tissue withowte armes Borders or other Badges embraudered'.[15] The similarity of these motifs to Corsi's Stonyhurst vestments might suggest they were contemporaneous and, if so, were plausibly the output of the same workshop.

The Corsi orders were magnificent new commissions, but many of the textiles in Henry VII's possession were inherited from his predecessors, including a large number of tapestries. This collection numbered several hundred, including some pieces dating from the reign of Edward III (1312–1377) and his grandson, Richard II (1367–1400), showing religious scenes that tally with descriptions of panels given to Richard by Philip the Bold, Duke of Burgundy (1342–1404).[16] Others may have been spoils of the Hundred Years War with France, such as the six panels at Windsor depicting a tourney (jousting tournament), and a ten-piece set of heraldic devices taken from the French royal collection by John of Lancaster, Duke of Bedford (1389–1435), in the 1420s.[17] This period was marked by English emulation of continental chivalric and artistic ideals.

French and Burgundian courts were in pursuit of the ideal of 'magnificence', the concept of which was intended to emphasise the divine authority and earthly glory of the sovereign.[18] The treatise *Toison d'Or* ('Golden Fleece') by the churchman and humanist Guillaume Fillastre (*c.*1400–1473), written for Charles the Bold, Duke of Burgundy, at some time between 1468 and 1473, pronounced that 'magnificence' was a quantifiable virtue, and one upon which other noble virtues, such as justice and mercy, established their foundation.[19] Magnificence, to the fifteenth-century mind, was a vital component of strong and good governance. It was virtue made tangible and it manifested legitimacy to rule.

As a result of this ethos of magnificence, the Burgundian and French courts spent extraordinary amounts of money on textiles and tapestries.[20] Their production cost much in terms of skills, materials and time, and the end product could be both beautiful and symbolic – perfect for the display of wealth and taste. Tapestry production in the Low Countries developed apace in response to this demand, particularly in the city of Arras, where some of the very finest tapestries were made, and which, consequently, gave its name to tapestries woven with gold and silver. Edward IV collected a number of tapestries from the Low Countries, in emulation of the Burgundian court.[21] He entrusted the procurement of tapestry to the officers of the Great Wardrobe, but Henry VII created a new court position of 'royal arras-maker'.[22] The royal arras-maker probably undertook repairs and minor weaving, such as adding badges of the house of Tudor to existing panels, but the role was perhaps indicative of a new emphasis on tapestries. A second appointment was made to this role in the person of Pasquier Grenier (1447–1493) of Tournai, merchant-weaver to the court of Burgundy, who had provided sets to Edward IV and, as royal arras-maker working out of the Low Countries, would go on to provide many of Henry's tapestries.[23]

Henry began to commission his own sets of tapestries from Grenier. He ordered a set depicting scenes of the Trojan War (fig. 20). This eleven-piece set had a cumulative length of about 100 yards. It was delivered by Pasquier's son, Jean (d. 1520), in the spring of 1488. Tapestry designs were often duplicated as, once the original cartoon was drawn, multiple weavings of the same design were possible. Sets of the 'Troy' tapestries were also woven for Charles the Bold of Burgundy, and Federico da Montefeltro, Duke of Urbino (1422–1482). Henry may have seen a set from the first weaving of the 1460s, done for a French nobleman, which hung at the French court during his exile there in the 1480s.[24] On 13 March 1488, Henry wrote to Richard Fox (*c.*1448–1528), Bishop of Exeter and Keeper of the Privy Seal, regarding his recent purchase from 'John' (Jean) Grenier of the eleven 'clothes of Arras' of the history of Troy, instructing Fox to direct the port of Sandwich, 'where the said clothes were discharged', that no customs or duties should be demanded from Grenier.[25] Henry evidently thought that the Troy tapestries reflected well upon him, as pieces from the set were hung at the church of Saint-Pierre in Calais on 9 June 1500 for a meeting between Henry and Duke Philip the Fair of Burgundy, and again in 1501 in the Great Hall at Richmond during the festivities to celebrate the wedding of his heir, Prince Arthur, to Katherine of Aragon.[26]

We know that some of these panels survived into the early nineteenth century, as five of them appear in a collection of sketches of the Painted Chamber at Westminster Palace, dating from around the turn of the century (figs 21 and 22). The artist, John Carter (1748–1817), made the drawings for the *Gentleman's Magazine*, by way of a protest at the proposed removal of the tapestries and the rebuilding of the palace. Despite the protest, they were sold, and nothing was heard of them after their sale to one Mr Teschemacher for 60 guineas in the 1820s.[27] In addition to the Troy tapestries, Henry owned a number of other sets of Grenier tapestries, including 'The Siege of Jerusalem', 'The History of Alexander', 'The Passion', and (probably) 'The Siege of Mount Alba'.[28]

The battlefield images of the Troy tapestries and others may have had a special resonance for Henry, whose victory at the Battle of Bosworth had won him the crown. Indeed, he was evidently proud of the battle as proof of divine favour, as he commissioned an expensive arras depicting his victory. The order reads: 'item, one pece of Arras of the comyng into Englonde of king henrye the vijth taking with the one hand the crowne from king Richard the thurde usurper of the same, & with thither hand holding a rose crowned'.[29] The set of which the battle scene was part also contained a piece that showed a wedding – possibly his marriage to Elizabeth of York (1466–1503) – reflecting

52

Stone

yellowish
boards —

some very dirty stone

pieces of wood which supported the Tapestry
by being nailed a hays.

dirty stone color

Tapestry

crimson

Tapestry

yellow curtain

Tapestry

Tapestry

bench

bench
&

Green
baize
door

matting

Matting

Matting

bench

Matting

Matting

Matting

Matting town
shewing stone behind.

floor covered with matting

V. A. M.

Henry's attempt to mythologise the Tudor story not as usurpation but as a Burgundian heroic epic and chivalric romance.[30] It is probable that this 'Tudor cycle' was among the first commissions given by Henry to the Brussels workshop of Pieter van Aelst of Enghien (*fl.* 1450–1530) in late 1500, for a payment of nearly £800.[31]

Henry also purchased a set of custom-designed armorial tapestries, showing the royal arms with millefleurs backgrounds, one of which survives at Haddon Hall in Derbyshire (fig. 23). Other dynastic textiles were recorded in the stores of the Tower of London. They included vast hangings of woven textiles, with borders of the king's arms. One was as wide as sixty-seven loom widths; some were made of crimson and purple fabrics paned together, others in the Tudor colours of green and white.[32] The fashion for tapestries featuring heraldic devices was particularly an early Tudor phenomenon. Henry VIII inherited about twenty tapestries featuring arms, dating to the reign of his father.[33] During the course

of the 1490s, Brussels weavers developed techniques that reproduced the light, shadow and detail achieved by oil painting, and, perhaps as a result, in the sixteenth century figurative narratives became more fashionable than the rather medieval heraldic tapestries.[34]

Contemporary records demonstrate how Henry VII formalised the hanging of tapestries and textiles for court events in strictly hierarchical order throughout the court, defining the status of the space by the value of the textiles adorning it.[35] The wealth of the textiles on display and their integral role in proceedings is clear. For the christening of a prince or princess, it was written that:

> the church or chappell dore must bee hanged with cloth of gould, roofe and all, and carpets under the foote [...] and the font to bee hanged with a riche siller [celure or canopy], and laid about with carpettes [...] and the font hanged round about with cloth of gould, and within laid in plates many fold of linen-cloth, and the church all to bee richlie hanged; the highe altar likewise to be arrayed in the richest manner with carpets.[36]

By these accounts, it would seem fair to say that rich textiles were the one key ingredient required to transform a space from the commonplace to one worthy of royalty.

Of course, not everyone was invited to experience royal spaces or to progress through the court, but for those who were, the environment became more rarefied with each step, reflecting the privilege of moving ever closer to the monarch. During the reign of Henry VII, the outer chambers were hung with woollen tapestries, inner chambers were hung with tapestries of wool with highlights of silk, and the still more important ones were hung with arras. The innermost chamber was hung entirely with gold-brocaded silk damask or velvet, embroidered in gold and silver with the Tudor royal arms.[37] In this, Henry was again following precedent. The European Habsburg, Valois and Portugese Aviz dynasties were all using tapestries and heraldic banners and textiles to project dynastic and imperial strength or legitimacy – to the extent that the aesthetics and symbolism of

tapestries from this period are intimately defined by their purpose as tools of royal myth- or image-making.[38]

One of the primary forces in the construction of Henry's image was his mother, Margaret Beaufort (1443–1509), Countess of Richmond and (following Henry's victory at Bosworth) of Derby (fig. 24). Although she was still married to Lord Stanley, after Henry's victory Margaret was granted the right to hold her wealth and property independently from her husband, and she did much to promote her own credentials as the matriarch of the house of Tudor. She invested in a ten-piece, custom-made set of tapestries featuring the Lancastrian red rose, the Yorkist white rose and her own emblem – the Beaufort portcullis. They were 'peces of verdures with rosys white and rede and porteculis of yellow every pece containing in length viij yerdes iij quarters [8¾ yards]'.[39]

The Lady Margaret's lodgings in the Tower of London were located next to her son's bedchamber and the council chamber, from where she maintained a discreet but pervasive control over court life and protocol;[40] in 1498, the Spanish ambassador noted that 'the king is much influenced by his mother'.[41] From 1499 she took a vow of chastity in the presence of the Bishop of London, allowing her unprecedented independence from her husband.[42] Despite her deeply pious countenance, the themes of her own tapestries and hangings were battles, campaigns, and the heroism of Hercules, Alexander and Hannibal. Others featured the biblical kings Saul and Nebuchadnezzar and the powerful Samson.[43] These themes were fashionable at the court of Burgundy, and consequently at her son's court too. That said, the adversities and dangers that Margaret and Henry had faced together – through exile, plots and battlefield, to threats to the throne of England itself – created a strong bond that may have revealed itself in their taste for epic narratives woven into tapestries.

Maintaining her pious reputation, and demonstrating the vast wealth accumulated by her as the king's mother, Margaret Beaufort bequeathed a significant number of her household textiles to Christ's College in the University of Cambridge, which passed to the college after her death in 1509. The list contains dozens of copes, altar cloths and other religious vestments, all of richly coloured damasks and velvets, often with embroidery and imagery. She gave:

FIG. 23 Tapestry of millefleurs ('thousand flowers') with the English royal arms, c.1485–1509, wool and silk, woven in the southern Netherlands. Haddon Hall, Derbyshire.

a cope of rede clothe of gold tissue ofreide with blewe velvett with Jhesus & portcullis full garnished [. . .] ij copes of blew satyn of Bruges embroidride with Rede rosis & white… orfreide with rede Satyn of Bruges enbrodered with portcullis [. . .] and] a paire of alter clothes of rede cloth of gold of Tyssue pained with blew velvet enbrodrid with Jhesu and portcullis & my ladys arms having a Coronall with a Crucyfyx in the myddys.[44]

Her commission of these pieces, depicting her portcullis badge alongside the embroidered figure of Jesus, is typical of an approach that was nothing short of a coherent and deliberate public relations campaign, mounted to validate Henry's lineage and exalt the new dynasty.[45]

Henry VII died in April 1509. His mother, Margaret, was executor of his will and arranged the coronation that celebrated the peaceful succession of her grandson Henry VIII. She died five days later, on 29 June 1509. The day before she died, Henry had turned 18. A second Tudor king sat on the throne and her work was done.

HENRY VIII: COMPETITION AND CLOTH OF GOLD

The young Henry's coronation established a precedent for his reign. He was crowned jointly with his queen, Katherine of Aragon, on 24 June 1509. Writing a few decades later, the chronicler Edward Hall (1497–1547), Henry's near contemporary, wrote of Henry's princely bearing and of his many virtues, which were so great and indefinable that the only way to represent them was through a description of his apparel, and that of his horse: 'I cannot express the giftes of grace and of nature, that God hath endowed hym with all: yet partly, to describe his apparel, it is to bee noted, his grace wore [. . .] a robe of Crimosyn Velvet [. . .] his jacket or cote of raised gold [. . .] Diamondes, Rubies, Emerauldes, great Pearles [. . .] The trapper of his Horse, Damaske golde.'[46]

Hall also wrote of the most lavish of coronations, unlike any that had gone before, and again exemplified by its textiles. 'This I dare well saie,' he wrote, 'there was no lack or scarcitie of cloth of Tissue, clothe of Golde, clothe of Silver, Broderie or of Gold smithes worke: but *in more plenty and abundaunce than hath been seen or redde of at any tyme before*' (my italics).[47] This is certainly supported by the King's Book of Payments for that year, which shows large outlays to Italian merchants. June, the month of Henry's accession saw the biggest outlay: to 'Lewis de la Fava, 58*l*. 10*s*.; and Guydo Portunary, 53*l*. 20*d*. for cloth of gold [. . .] Charles de Florence silks and cloth of gold, 281*l*. 6*s*. 2*d*. Benedict Morvello, same, 4 parcels, 198*l*. 2*s*. 8*d*.'[48]

So lengthy would the list of precious fabrics be, wrote Hall, that the best he could do to express the magnitude of the spectacle was to write of the almost indescribable workmanship on show:

> If I should declare what pain, labour, and diligence, the Taylers, Embrouderours and Golde Smithes tooke, bothe to make and devise garments for Lordes, Ladies, Knightes and Esquires, and also for deckyng, trappyng, and adornyng of Coursers, Jenetes, and Palffreis, it wer too long to rehersse, but for a suretie, more riche, nor more straunge nor more curious works, hath not been seen, then wer prepared against this coronacion.[49]

The streets were also richly adorned and dressed: 'His grace with the Quene, departed from the Tower, through the citie of London, against whose comyng, the streates where his grace should passe, were hanged with Tapistrie, and clothe of Arras. And the greate parte [. . .] with clothe of gold.'[50] Of course, all these descriptions may be compromised by the passage of time, flattery and exaggeration, and yet, to all intents and purposes, that matters not. The crucial factor here is the role of textiles and their use as recognised devices in conveying status, occasion, wealth, taste and a sense of the magnificent. The truth of this statement is irrefutable when considered alongside the reams of other contemporary records that prioritise the descriptions of textiles as the primary mode of conveying social prestige, and particularly accounts of the events of June 1520 – the Field of Cloth of Gold.

In October 1518, Cardinal Wolsey announced the Treaty of London, a multilateral agreement among Christian kings to unite against the Ottomans. This served

FIG. 24 Rowland Lockey (c.1565–1616), after Meynnart Wewyck (*fl.* c.1502–1525), Lady Margaret Beaufort (1443–1509) at prayer, 1598, oil on panel. Lady Margaret kneels beneath a cloth of estate of gold pomegranate design, featuring the Tudor rose and Beaufort arms; the same cloth is shown on her prie-dieu. An embroidered hanging behind her features the Beaufort portcullis. St John's College, Cambridge.

FIG. 25 Tent design, probably for the Field of Cloth of Gold, 16th century, watercolour on paper. The tents are dressed in red cloth decorated with Tudor mottoes, and the tent poles terminate in the king's heraldic beasts. British Library, London, Cotton MS Augustus III, fol. 18.

as the precursor for the 1520 meeting near Calais, a celebratory event that was to mark a peace between the kings of England and France, with each perceiving himself a victor.[51] In preparation for the meeting, Wolsey entertained the French ambassadors at Hampton Court Palace, where he gave the command 'neither to spare for any cost or Expence, nor Pains to make them such a triumphant Banquet, as they might not only wonder at it here, but also make a glorious Report, to the great honour of our King and this Realm'. The great waiting-chamber and presence chambers were 'richly hang'd with cloath of arras' and set with great lights, and a fire of wood and coal; cupboards were laden with white plate (silverware) and four great plates 'to give the more light'.[52] The use of plate as a reflector of light explains the positioning of cupboards

arrayed with gold- and silverware in prominent positions within the rooms. This device must have been of significance in otherwise dimly lit rooms. And the gold in the cloths of arras must also have reflected light, pinpointed and accentuated by the touch of daylight or torchlight.

Preparations for the great 'conference' of 1520 began as early as 1515, when the idea was first raised. The idea prompted immediate and extravagant investment. The Venetian ambassador, Sebastiano Giustiniani (1460–1543), who had heard it from the Florentine merchant Leonardo Frescobaldi (1485–1529), wrote to the Doge of Venice that Henry had 'despatched a messenger post haste to Florence for a great quantity of cloths of gold, and of silks so as to meet this most Christian King [Francis] with honour' (fig. 25).[53] By 1520, Henry had also gone a long way towards

the tent panels of canvas and their fine covering fabrics were packed up and transported to the meadow near Ardres, where the French king's camp would be set up. Among them – as one account recorded – was the king's

> great pavilion [...] as high as the highest tower, and three of a middle size, as high as the walls of a town, of wonderful breadth, covered with cloth of gold outside, and inside cloth of gold frieze. The great one was covered at the top with cloth of gold frieze, and below with velvet *cramoisy* [crimson] violet, powdered with gold fleurs de lis.[59]

Another account of the French pavilion said that it was 'raised the height of the sky' with four tents, spherical 'in the manner of the pyramids [...] on the outside they are all of gold, remarkable for its varied designs [...] within it was of pure gold, the most precious that could be [...] Gold is the material, and material woven from gold [... but] the rich workmanship surpassed the material.'[60] Rather devastatingly for the French, high winds blew the pavilions down and they were unusable for the entire fortnight. Francis and his retinue stayed in Ardres itself.[61]

Edward Hall's description of the English encampment once again reads as an itemised list of rich textiles, emphasising the cost of the new arras and carpets. He describes

> a royall rich tent, all of clothe of gold, and riche embroidery of the kyng of Englandes [...] within hanged of the richest Arras, *newly contriued and made, that euer before was seen* [...] with two chayers and rich cusshyns therein: the ground was spred with Carpettes, of newe Turkey making, all full of bueautie.[62]

The pièce de résistance of the English encampment at Guynes was a temporary palace, built of timber and canvas. A French account described the interior as 'everywhere cloaked with golden hangings, or else with every variety of embroidery'.[63]

On Sunday 10 June, each king left his own camp – at Guynes and Ardres – to dine with the other's queen. Henry, dining at Ardres, wore a double mantle of cloth of gold embroidered with jewels. The French queen and her ladies were dressed all in cloth of gold. The king's

accumulating the largest collection of tapestries and hangings ever owned by a European monarch.[54] Tapestries were both magnificent and portable – perfect for transportation between palaces or to a temporary encampment. One of the sets paid for in 1520, and taken to the Field of Cloth of Gold, depicted King David, a biblical model of kingship.[55] The set was probably the same as the one on display at Greenwich Palace when Henry staged a lavish tournament in May 1527, when it was called 'the most costly tapestry in England'.[56]

Preparations on the French side were no less intense. French tailors prepared 72,544 fleurs-de-lis made of gold thread and 327 pounds of silk fringe to adorn the pavilions.[57] Material for the 300–400 tents of the French encampment was made in Tours (an important cloth town), where some 170 men and 120 women were put to work in the palace of the Archbishop of Tours, sewing and constructing them in consecutive shifts, working day and night.[58] Once ready, mother was also in attendance and wore a robe of cloth of gold embellished with diamonds, dressed – as contemporary observers noted – 'so richly as it would be impossible to express'. On 11 June, the kings met each other. The French arrived to the sound of artillery, in a procession of archers, trumpeters, stewards, officers, the marshals of France, the Grand Seneschal with some two hundred gentlemen, and the king's gentlemen and chamberlains, most of whom were dressed in cloth of gold, though some wore crimson or coloured velvets; the French king rode a horse caparisoned in gold embroidery and wearing a mantle of cloth of gold. And 'thus accompanied, the king arrived at [. . .] the pavilion in which they were to confer, very rich and covered with cloth of gold'.[64]

As may be seen very clearly in these descriptions of the Field of Cloth of Gold, tents and cloth-covered temporary structures were an important part of Henry VIII's construction of kingship. They were integral to his beloved revels and jousting tournaments. The tents and galleries erected for the tournament to celebrate the birth in 1511 of the short-lived Prince Henry, Henry's son by Katherine of Aragon, demonstrated their importance (fig. 26). They were swathed in textiles that were a triumphant celebration of dynasty – Tudor green and white, the Beaufort portcullis, the Tudor rose, elaborate horse trappings and a canopy carried over Henry as he rode onto the field, as a sort of mobile cloth of estate. During peacetime, tents possessed chivalric and martial connotations that supported Henry's view of himself as a

FIG. 26 Detail from the Great Tournament Roll of Westminster, 1511, watercolour and gilding on vellum. The illumination shows Henry jousting, while the queen looks on, recuperating under a cloth of estate after giving birth to their son, Prince Henry. The horse trappers and the decorative textiles of the spectators' stand are richly coloured and patterned. College of Arms, London.

warrior, and it is interesting to note that the reigns of his children would not feature tents to the same extent.[65]

Even in war, Henry was conscious of maintaining his regal status. The encampment of tents reflected the court structure, with ewery, larder, laundry, scullery, wardrobe and kitchen, and a progression of spaces mirroring the arrangement of the king's privy lodgings in one of the royal palaces.[66] When Maximilian I (1459–1519), Holy Roman Emperor, rode into the English encampment in Picardy in 1513 during the War of the League of Cambrai, he found an arrangement of tents that 'looked like a castle or little town' (fig. 27). The exterior of the king's tent was overlaid with cloth of gold from top to bottom, which must have prompted discussion, as it is noted that the emperor's tailor estimated it was worth 33 florins an ell.

The interior of the tent was covered with rich cloth of gold of pure drawn-gold thread from floor to ceiling, furnished with a sideboard of gold plate and cups. The interior of the tent that served as the council house was hung with golden tapestry and 'therein stood the king's bed, hung round with a curtain of very precious cloth of gold'.[67]

Temporary structures allowed impressive and novel demonstrations of magnificence at a relatively lower cost than permanent architectural construction. In June 1518, the Venetian ambassador was received at a banquet aboard a galley on the river at Hampton Court, 'which had really been prepared royally, with a spacious platform decorated with every sort of tapestry'.[68] In 1527, a temporary banqueting house was built at Greenwich to

FIG. 27 Flemish School, *The Meeting of Henry VIII and the Emperor Maximilian I*, *c.*1513, oil on panel, probably painted for Henry. The king (*right*) and the emperor (*left*) are shown on horseback in the centre, their coats of arms displayed prominently on their tents. In the distance, the Battle of the Spurs is taking place, with the towns of Thérouanne and Tournai under siege. Royal Collection, Hampton Court Palace.

host the French ambassadors. It was 100 feet in length, and covered outside with purple cloth decorated with roses and pomegranates. Inside, it was 'richly hanged' and full of gold and silver plate to reflect the light. Cloths painted by none other than Hans Holbein (1497/8–1543, later to be painter to Henry VIII), depicted the cosmos, the earth and the sea 'like a very mappe', and also the siege of Thérouanne of 1513, a rather overt way of reminding Henry's court and his French guests of his military victories in France.[69]

In the 1547 Inventory, spectacular hangings of embroidered silk are listed. Many feature bold colours

paned together, richly embroidered with the royal arms. These include 'a hanging of purple and crimson tissue Churche worke paned togethers enbrawdered together with the bourders of the kings Armes and badges and lined with bockeram contenying lxvij panes euerye pane being in depthe iiij yards quarter and one nayle'.[70]

The 1535 inventory of Katherine of Aragon's goods lists a similar wall hanging, made of seven pieces of red and green velvet paned together, lined with buckram and 'everye of them [. . .] enbrowdered with the arms of Englande and Spayne, crowned with a crowne Imperialle, having boordres likewise enbrowedered with rooses,

flouredelucis [fleur-de-lis], and pomegarnettis'.[71] A similar set is recorded in the 1547 Inventory as being at the Tower, described as thirteen 'peces of Crymsen and blewe damaske paned together [. . .] enbrawdered aswell with tharmes of England and Spayne joyntely asallso with lettres H and K knyette togethers'.[72] Yet another set, brought from Westminster to the Tower Wardrobe, shows that the style was not restricted to Henry's early reign, as the item describes a 'hanging of red and grene vellat paned togethers embrawdered with borders of cloth of golde, upon the vellat the king and Quene Janes armes' – a reference to Jane Seymour, Henry's third consort, whom he married in 1536.[73] The length of these paned pieces suggests that they were used to cover significant areas, to line temporary structures like tents or the galleries constructed to watch jousting. The contrasting nature of

the colours and badges certainly echoes the bold heraldic patterns on the 1511 Westminster Tournament Roll (see fig. 26). Indeed, some of the pieces moved to the Tower from Westminster were inventoried in 1542 and the records confirm that they were used for tents.[74]

As important as tents were to Henry's communication of magnificence, it was tapestry that provided the most significant source of figurative subject matter at the Tudor court.[75] Upon his death in 1547, the inventory of his possessions detailed almost 2,500 tapestries and wall hangings. Hampton Court Palace was the most sumptuously furnished of all Henry's residences, containing 430 tapestries, 120 of which were cloths of arras, woven with gold or silver.[76] A significant number of these tapestries were inherited directly from Cardinal Wolsey, who began building Hampton Court Palace for himself in 1515, but gave it to the king in 1528 in an attempt to placate him for Wolsey's failure to secure Henry's divorce from Katherine of Aragon.

Wolsey's collection was second only to the king's, and was indicative of the ambition for which he was criticised so frequently by courtiers jealous of his position.[77] It seems that Wolsey was less concerned with the narratives depicted in the tapestries than with ordering sufficient quantities to furnish Hampton Court. He commissioned the merchant Sir Richard Gresham to take the measure of eighteen chambers at Hampton Court, and then to sail to the Low Countries to buy tapestries to fit the said chambers.[78] Surviving pieces from Wolsey's collection at Hampton Court suggest they were of good but not outstanding quality – they were counterfeit arras (silk not gold) and tapestry (wool), lined with buckram.[79] A 1530 inventory of Wolsey's possessions sheds more light on his collection.[80] Most of the tapestries he purchased depicted biblical scenes, though some showed classical themes beloved of humanist scholars in the Renaissance, including – as the 1530 inventory reads – 'Parys and Atchilles, Jupiter, Pluto and Ceres, Hanyballe, Virtue, and hunting'.[81] Fifty-seven of his tapestries were verdures, featuring flowers and beasts. He purchased an allegorical series of 'The Triumphs of Petrarch' (based on *I trionfi*, a series of poems by

FIG. 28 'The Triumph of Death over Chastity', from the series 'The Triumphs of Petrarch', 1503–23, Flanders, tapestry, wool and silk. Atropos (representing Death) sits enthroned in a triumphal car, drawn by oxen, with Chastity supine at her feet; the car is accompanied by boys riding unicorns, as described by the poet John Skelton. Royal Collection, Hampton Court Palace, RCIN 1270.

Francesco Petrarch (1304–1374), showing the triumph of Death over Chastity, Fame over Death, and Time over Fame) from the executors of the Bishop of Durham in 1523 (fig. 28); another set of the same theme is recorded, which may have been a gift from the king himself.[82] Surviving panels (from one set or a mixture of the two) have been on display at Hampton Court since 1842.[83] The imagery of these particular tapestries seems to have been uppermost in the mind of the poet John Skelton (c.1460–1529) in his work satirising the power of avaricious churchmen, more concerned with building palaces than churches. He describes how they built their royal mansions with hangings of 'clothes of golde' and 'arras of ryche aray', depicting the rather immodest forms of 'dame Dyana naked' and 'lusty Venus' riding in chariots 'conveyed by olyphants [...] and by unycornes'.[84] Wolsey's palace was certainly 'richly arrayed' in this manner. In October 1519, even before the delivery of Gresham's tapestries in the early 1520s, the Venetian ambassador, Sebastiano Giustiniani, wrote that Hampton Court was 'a very fine palace, where one traverses eight rooms before reaching his audience chamber and they are all hung with tapestry, which is changed once a week [...] in his own chamber there is always a cupboard with vessels to the amount of 30,000 ducats, this being customary with the English nobility'.[85] Wolsey's chambers were furnished with chairs of cloth of gold tissue, some with embroidered cardinals' hats and Wolsey's coat of arms wrought in crimson satin and venice gold, and also cushions of cloth of gold and different coloured velvets.[86]

Wolsey was stripped of his government offices in 1529. His gentleman usher described how Wolsey called his officers before him, to take account of all his possessions. He wrote that set upon tables were 'silks of all colours, velvets, sattins, musks [damasks], taffaties, grogarams, scarlets, and [...] a thousand pices of fine hollands [linen], and the Hangings of the Gallery with Cloth of gold, and Cloth of Silver, and rich cloth of [...] divers colours [...] to be delivered to the King'.[87]

While Wolsey thus provided a significant number of textiles to the king's Wardrobe, the sets of arras tapestries commissioned by Henry for himself offer a more interesting insight into the man. It is clear that the story of King David resonated with Henry. In addition to the set he ordered in the late 1510s and paid for in 1520, which he

took to the Field of Cloth of Gold, he ordered another on the same subject around 1526. The merchant Sir Richard Gresham delivered the gold-woven set of ten panels in October 1528.[88] The subject matter may have held a particular significance at this point in Henry's reign. The biblical story of David tells of God's favour for his chosen king. In all things, David enacts God's will, apart from an affair with Bathsheba, the wife of one of his soldiers, Uriah the Hittite, who is murdered at David's behest. As a result of this sin, David's first-born son by Bathsheba dies. At around the time this tapestry set was commissioned, Henry had begun to question whether his marriage to Katherine would produce a male heir. By the time the tapestries were delivered, believing that he would never have a healthy son by her, he was seeking an annulment of his marriage on the grounds that he had contravened God's law (as written in Leviticus 20:21) by marrying his late brother's widow.[89] We know that Renaissance kings modelled themselves on the biblical King David, but Henry arguably felt the parallel keenly (see fig. 79, which depicts Henry as David, in the pages of his own private psalter). Indeed, while Francis I of France seems to have spent vast amounts of money on tapestries designed by Raphael and other Italian artists, apparently in appreciation of their aesthetic and artistic value, Henry seems to have been primarily concerned with finding narratives that he related to, or that defined his position at the time.[90]

Another set of tapestries commissioned by Henry in the early 1530s – by which time he was moving towards separation from both his queen and the Roman Catholic Church in order to marry Anne Boleyn – depicts the story of the Trojan hero Aeneas (fig. 29).[91] Aeneas is bound to marry the Carthaginian queen, Dido, but the gods persuade him that he must leave her in order to fulfil his destiny. The idea of Henry as the hero who must cast aside his wife as the result of divine intervention must have been a powerful narrative for the Tudor king, and a powerful piece of propaganda to a court well versed in

FIG. 29 Aeneas encountering his mother Venus, from a series illustrating the story of Dido and Aeneas, early 1530s, tapestry, wool and silk with gilt-metal- and silver-wrapped thread, woven in Brussels. The goddess, with Mercury delivering a message from Jupiter, tells the Trojan companions that Aeneas must leave Dido. Royal Collection, RCIN 1255.1.

CVI·MATER
MEDIA·SESE
TVLIT·OBVIA
SILVO·

CVI·MATER
MEDIA·SESE
TVLIT·OBVIA
SILVO·

FIG. 30 'The Departure of Abraham', from a series illustrating the story of Abraham, 1540–43, tapestry, wool and silk with gilt-metal-wrapped thread, designed by Pieter Coecke van Aelst (1502–1550), woven in the workshop of Willem de Pannemaker (c.1510–1581) in Brussels. At the behest of God (who appears in the sky), Abraham and his household leave Ur of the Chaldees for Canaan. Royal Collection, Hampton Court Palace, RCIN 1046.6.

heroic and classical allusions.[92] The set is of woven wool with silk and gold and silver threads; five of the panels still hang at Hampton Court Palace. The relatively smaller dimensions of the panels suggest they may have been intended for the more private rooms of the palace – for Henry and his senior courtiers rather than the larger assembled court.

Two important sets of arras were commissioned by Henry and delivered in 1543 and 1544. They portrayed respectively the stories of Caesar and Abraham, and were made by the Brussels workshop of Willem de Pannemaker to designs by Pieter Coecke van Aelst (1502–1550; not to be confused with Pieter van Aelst, the tapestry weaver and seller). The Caesar set disappeared some time in the early nineteenth century, but the Abraham set survives today and still hangs in the Great Hall at Hampton Court Palace. The panels contain a breathtaking amount of gold, which has now oxidised so as to appear grey (figs 30 and 31). They depict the lives of Abraham and Isaac, showing God appearing to Abraham and the passing of God's covenant

from the father to his son – a clear parallel for the royal succession and Henry's joy at the birth of his son and heir, Edward, in 1537. At the time of the Commonwealth Sale in 1649 the set was valued at over £8,000, far in excess of any other work of art in the royal collection and far more than the next most valued works, the Caesar set, valued at £5,022.[93] Two other high-quality weavings of the Abraham tapestries are recorded, one in the Spanish royal collection in Madrid and the other in the Habsburg collection in Vienna, but neither of these features the gold and silver gilt thread of the Hampton Court set.[94] Henry's ability to spend such extortionate amounts at this point is not unconnected to the wealth that was coming his way as a result of the dissolution of the monasteries (1536–41).

Decades later, Elizabeth Talbot, Countess of Shrewsbury, known as Bess of Hardwick – the second richest woman in England after Henry's daughter Queen Elizabeth – spent a significant amount of money furnishing Hardwick Hall with tapestries and hangings. In the early 1590s, she bought four tapestries depicting the

FIG. 31 'The Oath and Departure of Eliezer', detail (31a), from the tapestry series illustrating the story of Abraham, wool and silk with gilt-metal-wrapped thread. In 2009 the HRP Conservation Team digitally re-created the original colours, using the unfaded threads at the back the tapestries (31b) as a guide. Royal Collection, Hampton Court Palace, RCIN1046.8.

story of Abraham;[95] Bess's Abraham panels were simplified, smaller versions of the ones ordered by Henry for Hampton Court, and of the four, only one was enhanced with gold thread. No other tapestries at Hardwick, which in 1553 had numbered some forty-eight panels, contained gold. Tapestry was a sign of wealth, but none could match Henry's expenditure or ambition. The pinnacle that Bess could hope to reach was a very humble version of the tapestries ordered by Henry some fifty years earlier. Such was their quality that Henry's Abraham tapestries remained important signifiers of power and prestige into the following centuries. They were hung in Westminster Abbey for the coronation of Henry's daughter Elizabeth in 1559. The Stuart monarchs used them for the same purpose during the seventeenth century.[96]

EDWARD AND MARY: LEGACY AND RELIGION
Following Henry VIII's death in January 1547, his 9-year-old son inherited the throne as King Edward VI (1537–1553).

Most of Henry's possessions passed to his son, but provision was made for the princesses Mary and Elizabeth. Over a hundred tapestries, for example, were delivered to Mary after Henry's death. It would be interesting to know if Mary was able to choose them personally, or if they were a random selection based on quality or size or some other factor, for some of them featured apocalyptic scenes of fire and judgment that seem retrospectively meaningful, given the nature of her reign.[97] Was the subject matter somehow indicative of the personality of the recipient? A significant number of the tapestries delivered to Elizabeth were classical in nature, or featured hawking and hunting scenes.[98]

Other portions of the vast stocks of textiles accumulated and stored by the officers of the Wardrobe during his father's reign were put to use for Edward's coronation. The ancient wooden coronation chair – known as 'St Edward's chair' – at Westminster Abbey was covered with 17 metres of the finest white baudekin woven with flowers of gold. More cloth was issued to the members of the court as livery, the quality of the cloth defining hierarchy – silk velvets for the senior officials, wool for the lower orders.[99] Edward's coronation procession is recorded in an eighteenth-century watercolour made from a mural painted for Anthony Browne (1500–1548), master of the horse, at Cowdray House, Sussex (fig. 32).[100] The mural is now lost, but the watercolour depicts streets festooned with fine textiles of tapestry, hangings and banners, not just to decorate the streets but also to honour the new king. Because he was not of age, Edward ruled under the protectorate of his maternal uncle, Edward Seymour, Duke of Somerset (c.1500–1552). Lady Somerset (c.1510–1587), Seymour's wife, was seen removing silks from the Wardrobe store, 'trussed up in a sheet', with the help of her half-brother, Sir Michael Stanhope (c.1508–1552).[101]

Edward's reign was defined by his youth, and by the men who ruled the country in his name, the Duke of Somerset and then John Dudley, Duke of Northumberland (1504–1553). Edward was an intelligent and accomplished

child, but we cannot assume that he had much agency in the decisions regarding the presentation of his court. The young king was paraded through London whenever rumours circulated about his poor health, and portraits showed him as a robust young king – a mini-Henry in physique, stance and dress – surrounded by the accoutrements of magnificence, such as cloth of gold and Turkish carpets (fig. 33). Demonstrating continuity may have been politically astute, but may also have been dictated by the less than full coffers left by Henry.[102]

Indeed, the Revels Accounts for 1552 contain a complaint that the garments of the gentlemen were not worthy, and they would not stand 'apon their reputacion' to be seen in London thus.[103]

Edward died in 1553 at the age of 15. He left behind him a succession crisis in which his half-sister Mary was pitted against the 'nine-day Queen', Lady Jane Grey (c.1537–1554), the daughter-in-law of the powerful Duke of Northumberland. Mary emerged the victor and was crowned at Westminster Abbey in October 1553. The

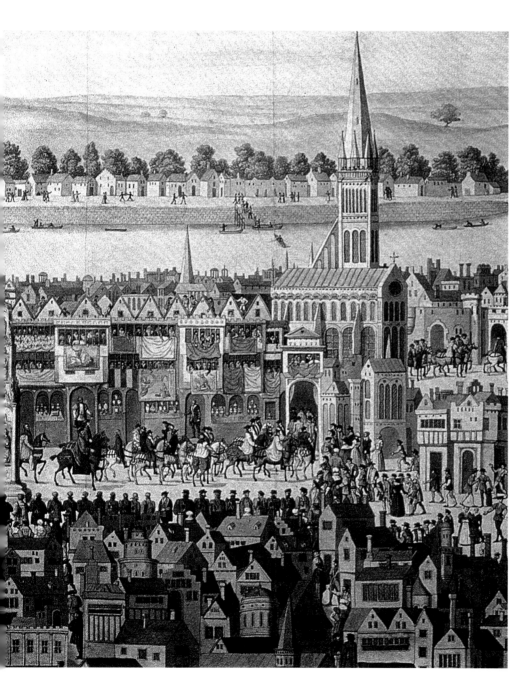

FIG. 32 The coronation procession of Edward VI (detail), 18th century, hand-coloured engraving after a watercolour of a lost mural at Cowdray House, Midhurst, Sussex. Rich tapestries and hangings are suspended from the upper windows and galleries of the houses, to beautify the city and to declare its wealth and sophistication. Society of Antiquaries, London.

FIG. 33 Workshop associated with 'Master John', portrait of Edward VI, c.1547, oil on panel. The young king is shown standing beneath a cloth of estate, bordered with pearls, on a richly coloured Eastern carpet; behind him is a chair with lions' feet, with a fringe of silk and tasselled cushions. National Portrait Gallery, London.

FIG. 34 Hans Eworth (d. 1574), double portrait of Philip II of Spain and Mary I, 1558, oil on panel. Philip stands beside an embroidered chair of estate, while Mary is seated on an identical chair, on a large cushion; over each of them hangs a cloth of estate of cloth of gold. A bulky cushion fills the window sill. Woburn Abbey, Bedfordshire.

FIG. 35 Replica (mid-18th century, wool and silk) of a panel from the series 'The Conquest of Tunis', original 1546, tapestry, wool and silk with metal thread, designed by the Flemish painter Jan Cornelisz Vermeyen (c.1504–1559) and woven in the workshop of Willem de Pannemaker (c.1510–1581) in Brussels. The original set was commissioned by Charles V to commemorate his sack of Tunis in 1535, and was sent as a gift to Mary I. Alcazar Palace, Seville.

following July, she was married to Philip II of Spain at Winchester Cathedral (fig. 34). An eighteenth-century publication, said to be an official account recorded by the heralds, describes the cathedral church as richly 'hanged with arras and cloth of gold'.[104] Marc Antonio Damula, the Venetian ambassador to the court of Philip's father, Emperor Charles V, noted that Charles had sent 'beautiful tapestries representing the Tunis expedition, and a quantity of jewels, as a present to the Queen of England' (fig. 35).[105] The tapestries were commissioned by Charles in 1546 to commemorate his military conquest in Tunis over Khayr ad-Din Barbarossa (c.1478–1546), pasha and Ottoman admiral of the fleet, in July 1535. The panels were based on sketches and drawings made by the Flemish painter Jan Cornelisz Vermeyen (c.1504–1559), who had been ordered to accompany Charles's expedition to record it for posterity. The cartoons for the tapestries, depicting

military victories and the slaughter and enslavement of civilians, survive in the Kunsthistorisches Museum, Vienna. The pieces were considered as glorious celebrations of Charles's victories, and above all of the victory of the Catholic faith over infidel Turkish and Moorish forces. A contemporary account describes 'xii pieces of arras worke, so richlie wroughte with golde, silver and silke, as none in the worlde maye excel them. In which peces be so excellentlye wroughte and sette out all the emperoures majesties proceedings and victories againste the Turkes'.[106] They represented the single most important tapestry set commissioned by the sixteenth-century Habsburg court.[107] The weaver, Willem de Pannemaker, was bound by a strict contract wherein the amount of silk and gold thread was distinctly specified – not to save money but to make sure that enough should be used. The finest materials were ordered, along with the richest dyes.[108]

Charles V was already aware of Mary's admiration of his expedition to Tunis. In the autumn following his victory, she had written to Nicolas Perrenot de Granvelle (1486–1550), adviser to Charles, calling the enterprise 'triumphant and holy', and 'most necessary'.[109] At the time Mary wrote, in October 1535, her mother, Katherine of Aragon, had been banished from court, her twenty-three-year marriage to Henry having been declared illegal by Archbishop Thomas Cranmer in May 1533. Henry and Anne Boleyn had already married in secret in November 1532. In July 1535, while Charles was besieging Tunis, Sir Thomas More was executed for refusing to acknowledge Henry as Supreme Head of the Church of England and recognise his divorce from Katherine. By the winter of 1535, it was clear to all that Katherine's life was drawing to a close. She had not been permitted to see her daughter. Mary's letter was an appeal to Charles V, her cousin, for aid, as 'he cannot appreciate the weight, importance, and danger of affairs here, and the whole truth cannot be conveyed in letters'. She besought him,

> on the part of her mother and herself, for the honor of God, and for other respects as well, to attend to their condition and make provision for them. In so doing he will perform a service most agreeable to almighty God, nor will he acquire less fame and glory to himself than in the conquest of Tunis or the whole of Africa.[110]

Mary saw the conquest of Tunis as a necessary holy war. She evidently sought to convince her cousin that the situation in England and within her own family warranted no less, and would bring him as much glory. Charles's gift of the tapestries may have held the symbolic message that with Mary's marriage to his son and heir, God's will had indeed been realised.

Mary's reign was relatively brief, and she died in 1558 at the age of 42. She had experienced the personal tragedy and political disgrace of two false pregnancies, and had, in the end, reluctantly named her Protestant half-sister, Elizabeth, as her legal heir.[111]

ELIZABETH: SECRETS AND SMALL THINGS
Henry VIII had spent lavishly on his palaces and textiles. His coffers were full, as the result of his father's financial acumen and the dissolution of the monasteries in his own

time. However, his extravagant spending and his military campaigns meant that his own children inherited a greatly depleted treasury. As a result, Elizabeth did not undertake major textiles commissions as her father had done.[112]

It is possible that some tapestry was commissioned during Elizabeth's reign. For example, the Royal Collection features a four-piece set of 'The Planets', dating to the last quarter of the sixteenth century. They find a parallel with a set purchased by Bess of Hardwick in 1591–2, bearing the same weaver's mark of a shield flanked by two Bs (indicating that the set was woven in Brussels).[113] The Royal Collection set is not woven with gold and the Collection's first record of them is from 1860, when Prince Albert had them moved from Windsor to Holyroodhouse.[114] In practical terms, however, there was hardly a need to commission new works, as Elizabeth inherited the largest collection of tapestries of any European monarch. It is equally true that Elizabeth had not the purchasing power of her father, and that the tapestry industry of the Low Countries was not as it had been in the first half of the century.[115]

The political stability of the later Elizabethan period may also have played a part in the absence of major tapestry commissions during those years. Textiles had been considered movable décor in the reigns of her father and grandfather but, by the late sixteenth century, the nobility were investing fortunes in substantial grand country houses, hoping to entice the queen and her court to stay with them on her summer progresses.[116] This investment in permanent luxury may have reduced the queen's need to move her own furnishings. Certainly, it seems that the textiles at Hampton Court remained largely in situ during the Elizabethan era. A contemporary account noted that, though the Queen had 'recently progressed [...] to Nonsuch with some three hundred carts of bag and baggage as is her custom', tapestries and gold, silver and pure silk hangings still hung in the apartments at Hampton Court, of which 'the like is nowhere to be found in such quantity in one place'.[117] This continuity may also have helped to reinforce her dynastic legitimacy, and records suggest that a number of her palaces were well-maintained relics or showpieces of her father's reign.[118] Tourists allowed to take tours of Hampton Court described its treasures: rooms filled with fine royal beds, canopies and chairs, bed hangings worked by the

'queen's mother and her ladies', and chambers 'hung with ancient tapestries', including the Caesar and Abraham sets.[119] Carpets from Wolsey's collection were still at Hampton Court, too, and remained there until the Commonwealth Sale of 1649.[120]

The Henrician tapestries with which Elizabeth's court would have been familiar are invested with new meaning in relation to the new monarch. The Aeneas set discussed earlier would now be reinterpreted, with Venus and Dido taking centre stage instead of Aeneas, with whom Henry had identified (see fig. 29). The panels – on display at Westminster and Whitehall from 1530 to the late seventeenth century – depicted men upon their knees before the goddess Venus, with whom Elizabeth was often compared in art and literature (fig. 36). Elizabeth was Gloriana, Belphoebe (or Diana, the virgin huntress), Astraea, the virgin goddess of innocence, and Iris, the sun goddess.[121] Dido, too, was an important allegorical figure

at the Elizabethan court, exemplified in Christopher Marlowe's play *Dido, Queen of Carthage*, written with Thomas Nashe between 1585 and 1588 (fig. 37). Dido's downfall is her love for Aeneas; she relinquishes her authority and takes her own life after he deserts her. Marlowe's play can be read as a dramatisation of Elizabeth's virginity as the source of her power,[122] a message that would have been reaffirmed by the imagery of the court.

In Edmund Spenser's 1590 allegory of Elizabeth and the Tudor dynasty, *The Faerie Queene*, the inner room of Castle Joyeous (so called to represent decadence) was

> round about apparelled
> With costly clothes of Arras and of Toure,
> In which with cunning hand was pourtrahed
> The love of Venus and her Paramoure [. . .]
> A worke of rare device, and wondrous wit.[123]

FIG. 36 Hans Eworth (d. 1574), *Elizabeth I and the Three Goddesses*, 1569, oil on panel. In this reworking of the contest known as 'The Judgement of Paris', Elizabeth is cast as Paris to decide which of the three goddesses is the most worthy. But the competition is abandoned, as Elizabeth herself embodies all their collective virtues. Royal Collection, Windsor Castle.

FIG. 37 The court of Dido, Queen of Carthage, from a series illustrating the story of Dido and Aeneas, early 1530s, tapestry, wool and silk with gilt-metal- and silver-wrapped thread, woven in Brussels. Dido sits under a canopied cloth of estate with her courtiers in the background; Aeneas, concealed behind a pillar, looks on. The border is of arabesque design with classical medallions. Royal Collection, RCIN 1255.3.

The tapestries, stained glass and architecture of English art formed Spenser's aesthetic understanding.[124] Tapestries still provoked wonder, and yet in *The Faerie Queene* the mythological figures of these ancient tapestries are corrupting. They and their lustful imagery are a danger to the heroine; they threaten chastity, which is virtuous, worthy and heroic – a clear reference to the Virgin Queen, Elizabeth.[125] Henry's reign is compared to Elizabeth's, and is found wanting. For Spenser, chastity brings order: 'costly clothes of Arras' are the historic emblems of Henry's reign; Elizabeth's glory surpasses it.

A more prosaic consideration might be that Elizabethan travellers recalled 'in noble men's houses it is not rare to see abundance of [. . .] tapistrie [. . .] likewise in the houses of knights, gentlemen, merchantmen, and some other wealthie citizens'.[126] The proliferation of tapestries as status symbols might have been just one reason why another form of textile art took precedence at the Elizabethan court – embroidery.

Embroidery was undertaken by men in a professional capacity, but by noblewomen as a genteel amateur occupation.[127] Henry's daughters, Mary and Elizabeth, were expected to be proficient in the art, and worked a number of gifts for the king and other members of the royal family. Mary, in particular, seems to have enjoyed – or, at least, invested significant time in – embroidering cushions. In November 1543 she paid one John Hayes for 'drawing a pat'ne [pattern] for a qwyssion for the quene', at that time Queen Katherine Parr (1512–1548).[128] She paid for patterns, for feathers for stuffing, and for trimmings and buttons for a number of cushions.[129] At another time, she paid for gold thread to 'embraudre a qwyssion for m'Wriothesley', and for damaske lining and a fringe 'to the said qwission'.[130] Thomas Wriothesley was a secretary of state, and had been seeking an alliance between England and Spain.[131] This attempt to secure peace with her mother's homeland evidently disposed Mary well towards

FIG. 38 (LEFT) The embroidered cover of 'The Miroir or Glasse of the Synnefull Soul', gold and silver thread on blue silk ground, worked by the young Princess Elizabeth and given to Queen Katherine Parr in 1544 as a new year gift. Bodleian Library, Oxford, MS Cherry 36.

FIG. 39 (BELOW) The embroidered cover of 'Prayers of Queen Katherine Parr', gold, silver and coloured silk thread on red silk ground, worked by the young Princess Elizabeth and given to the queen in December 1545. It contains Katherine's *Prayers or Meditations* translated by Elizabeth into Latin, French and Italian. British Library, London, Royal MS 7 D X.

him, resulting in her gift of a gold cushion embroidered with her own hand. As queen, she would be able to assert her favour and power in more conventionally regal terms, but as a princess (in a precarious position in the succession and, often, her father's favour), embroidery was one of only a very few means available to Mary and the other young women of the nobility to express themselves creatively and intellectually.[132] Evidently it was used as a tool – a gift of thanks, favour or persuasion, but certainly meaningful.

Elizabeth's own embroidery demonstrates how the domestic pastime could become political. The 11-year-old Princess Elizabeth demonstrated her Renaissance education in a gift to her stepmother, Katherine Parr, at new year 1545. She presented a bound copy of 'The Miroir or Glasse of the Synnefull Soul' – her own prose translation of a French poem – with a book cover she had embroidered with interlacing strapwork in metal thread, with the letters KP in the centre and heartsease flowers (pansies) in each corner (fig. 38). It demonstrated a combination of scholarship and virtue, embodied in noblewomen by the genteel art of embroidery.[133] The skill shown here is still that of a novice; the canvas ground is indicative of the training stage rather than an accomplished needlewoman. Elizabeth embroidered a second book cover, for her own translation of Katherine Parr's *Prayers or Meditations* of 1545, written in English but translated by Elizabeth into Latin, French and Italian (fig. 39). It was a gift to the queen, dated 20 December 1545, but was dedicated to Elizabeth's father 'the illustrious Henry the eighth, King of England, France and Ireland'.[134]

Embroidery was an important means of expression for Mary, Queen of Scots (1542–1587), too. As queen, she employed professional embroiderers, and before her flight to England, while a prisoner at Lochleven Castle, she asked the Scottish lords, if she was not permitted to be moved closer to her infant son, James, for 'an imbroiderer to drawe forthe such work as she would be occupied about'.[135] Nicholas White, afterwards Master of the Rolls in Ireland, sent a report to Sir William Cecil, dated 26 February 1568:

> I asked hir grace howe she passed the tyme within? She sayd that all day she wrought with her nydill and that the diversitye of the colors made the worke seem less tedious, and contynued so long at it till the veray pain made her to give over [. . .] Upon this occasion she entred into a pretty disputable comparison between karving, painting and working with the nydil.[136]

Mary was well read and cultured – she set much store by 'her books and other weighty trumpery on which she placed much importance'. Her thoughts on embroidery and its value as compared to painting and carving, and the work she produced demonstrate that she was informed by the artistic ideals of the Renaissance.[137] Mary escaped from Scotland to England in 1568, at the age of just 27. She was placed in the custody of George Talbot, 6th Earl of Shrewsbury (c.1522–1590), at Hardwick Hall in Derbyshire, where she would remain until 1584. She occupied her time with embroidery in the company of Talbot's wife, Bess of Hardwick. In a letter dated 13 March 1569, Talbot gave a report of Mary's activities to Cecil, writing that 'this Queen continueth daily to resort unto my wife's chamber where with the Lady Lewiston and Mrs Seton [ladies-in-waiting] she useth to sit working with the needle in which she much delighteth'.[138] Along with members of the household, including grooms, women and boys, they created rich hangings of cutwork, using cloth of gold from copes and religious vestments, presumably from dissolved religious houses.[139] Their collaboration produced some of the most important surviving sixteenth-century domestic embroidery, including cutwork wall hangings featuring female rulers who included Artemisia, Cleopatra and Zenobia.[140] A large number of Mary's needlework

panels have survived (fig. 40). Many of their motifs can be traced to popular herbals and printed pattern books; some feature Mary's cipher, and some are thought to convey messages, both overt and hidden. One of the panels shows a phoenix rising from the ashes, alongside Mary's own cipher, a powerful symbol of her longed-for restoration.[141] In another, a ginger cat wearing a crown plays with a small mouse, reflecting Mary's own feelings about her incarceration at the hands of her red-haired cousin, Elizabeth. In another, even more subversive, panel, a heavenly hand holds a scythe and cuts away the barren branch of a grapevine, leaving the fruitful branch to grow. It is difficult not to interpret this panel as a metaphor for the childless Elizabeth next to the 'fruitful' Stuart branch. Mary had already borne a healthy son in James, who would, indeed, eventually succeed Elizabeth.

During Elizabeth's reign, embroidery took on ever more significant meaning. Elizabeth herself has been described as the 'quintessential embodiment of the artifice of secrecy'.[142] On more than one occasion, words attributed to her stated that her true self was always hidden. Famously, we know the boast 'I know I have but the body of weak and feeble woman; but I have the heart and stomach of a king'.[143] The poem 'On Monsieur's Departure' reads:

FIG. 40 Needlework panel by Mary, Queen of Scots, 1569–84, silk on canvas. The octagonal piece shows an interlaced monogram, with the lily of France and the thistle of Scotland, with a royal crown above. Royal Collection, RCIN 28223.

I grieve and dare not show my discontent,
I love and yet am forced to seem to hate.

Although it was written in the early 1580s, after the departure of her last serious suitor for marriage, the Duke of Alençon (1555–1584), some scholars have claimed that the poem might better convey her feelings for her long-term favourite, Robert Dudley, Earl of Leicester. Even here, her true meaning is not known.[144]

The bold assertions of martial ability, virility and heroism represented by the Field of Cloth of Gold gave way in Elizabeth's reign to something more inscrutable. The vast scale of royal display embodied by great tapestries and murals was replaced with the intimate, the private, the coded and the small. This aesthetic can be seen in the works of Sir Philip Sidney (1554–1586) and in the miniatures of Nicholas Hilliard (1547?–1619).[145] It can be read in Elizabeth's Petrarchan habit of addressing her courtiers by nicknames – William Cecil was her 'Spirit', Dudley her 'Eyes', and Sir Christopher Hatton her 'Lids'.[146] And tellingly, it can be seen in the things that Elizabeth herself considered important.

In 1564 Sir James Melville (1535/6–1617) visited Whitehall Palace. He was the Scottish ambassador to London, sent from Elizabeth's cousin, Mary Queen of Scots. Elizabeth promised 'to open a good part of her inward mind' to Melville, who recalled that 'she took me to her bed-chamber and opened a little cabinet wherein were divers little pictures wrapt within paper, and their names written with her own hand upon the papers'.[147] These miniatures included portraits of the Queen of Scots and of Robert Dudley, Earl of Leicester. The bedchamber, the 'little cabinet', and these 'little pictures' speak to the Renaissance fascination with *multum in parvo*, or 'much in little', which suggests that the smallest spaces are the most symbolically meaningful. Susan Frye writes that small spaces are 'more replete, and thus symbolically larger, than more expansive ones'.[148] Towards the end of the sixteenth century, ceremony and spectacle shifted from outdoors to indoors, where visual effects are more intimate and more easily controlled.[149] The court and the nobility commonly kept their miniatures in the bedchamber or the closet, and looked at them with their confidants and intimates, in marked contrast to the way that tapestries and murals were viewed.[150]

FIG. 41 (ABOVE) Nicholas Hilliard (1547?–1619), *Young Man among Roses*, portrait miniature, *c.*1587, watercolour on vellum, mounted on card. The young man, possibly Robert Devereux, 2nd Earl of Essex (1566–1601), wears the queen's colours of black and white, and stands leaning against a tree, hand on heart, among white eglantine flowers, also a symbol of the queen. Victoria and Albert Museum, London, P.163-1910.

FIG. 42 (OPPOSITE) Unknown artist (attrib. Marcus Gheeraerts the younger (1561–1636) or Isaac Oliver (1556?–1617)), the so-called 'Rainbow Portrait' of Elizabeth I, *c.*1600, oil on canvas. The portrait is full of emblematic imagery that would be meaningful to the Tudor observer. The rainbow in the queen's hand represents the celestial, her gown features eyes and ears to show that she sees and hears all, and the serpent on her sleeve represents intelligence. Collection of the Marquess of Salisbury, Hatfield House, Hertfordshire.

SINE SOLE
IRIS.

Miniatures were hugely fashionable during Elizabeth I's reign. The master of the art, Nicholas Hilliard, said: 'it is a kind of gentle painting [. . .] it is a secret'.[151] He was referring not only to the secrets of his craft, which he had developed from his training as a goldsmith, nor, indeed, simply to the fact that a miniature could be viewed only by an individual rather than a crowd, but also to the secret symbols he would deploy within the painting, for example in his *Young Man among Roses* (fig. 41). He would often back his portraits with playing cards – one miniature of Elizabeth was backed with the queen of hearts.[152]

These games and codes were highly favoured by Elizabeth and her court. They may have been born of political circumstance, for under Elizabeth – to protect her life from assassins' plots – a secret service of informants and spies was established under the auspices of her chief minister, William Cecil, his son and successor, Robert Cecil, and Francis Walsingham. Walsingham even employed teams of forgers and code-breakers within his own home.[153] At court, symbols and codes became a sophisticated puzzle to challenge and delight the viewer, and to demonstrate learning and culture. In 1586, Geoffrey Whitney (1548?–1600/01) dedicated *A choice of emblemes, and other devises* to his patron Robert Dudley. It contained an illustrated guide to symbols and their hidden meanings. Whitney wrote that emblems would provide delight once the code had been cracked: 'having some wittie devise expressed with cunning woorkemanship, something obscure to be perceived at the first, whereby, when with further consideration it is understood, it maie the greater delighte the beholder'.[154] He suggested that for the virtuous, the 'emblem' would provide encouragement, and for the wicked would provide admonishment and correction.[155] His book set out a language of symbolism – the spire represented the celestial, the arrow was martial loyalty, the serpent was intelligence or wisdom, and the heart mercy.[156] Each emblem appeared with a verse and an image. These symbols found their way into portraits and portrait miniatures, jewellery and, importantly for us, the embroidery of the court. Among Elizabeth's possessions in 1600 were petticoats and gowns embroidered with spires and snakes of venice gold, with clouds, seas, rainbows and diverse flowers and fruits (fig. 42).[157]

FIG. 43 Jacques Le Moyne de Morgues (c.1533–1588), medlar pear, 1585, watercolour, from an album of drawings on which Le Moyne based stylised woodcuts published in *La clef des champs* (1586). British Museum, London, 1962,0714.1.34.

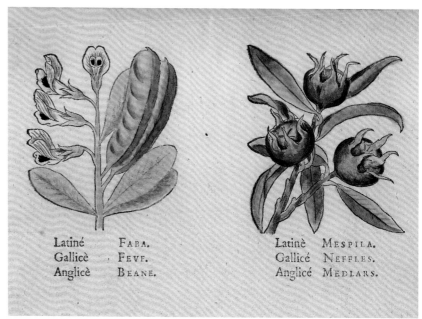

FIG. 44 Jacques Le Moyne de Morgues, illustration from *La clef des champs* (1586), hand-coloured woodcut on paper: broad bean (*left*), medlar pear (*right*). British Museum, London, 1952,0522.1.43.

In the same year that Geoffrey Whitney published his *Choice of emblemes*, Jacques Le Moyne de Morgues published his book of woodcuts *La clef des champs*.[158] The images are of plants and flowers found in English gardens. They include heartsease, columbine, apple, sweet pea, plum, rose, daffodil and strawberry, with insects and butterflies. Traditional religious iconography was frowned upon at this period as a result of the Reformation, and it might be that embroidering elements of the natural world was seen as a way to venerate God's creation.

As a Huguenot, Le Moyne suffered religious persecution and fled his homeland. He found patronage in London among influential courtiers such as Sir Walter Raleigh and the prominent Sidney family. He created intricate and naturalistic watercolours of botanical subjects (fig. 43), which were then simplified and stylised as woodcuts in *La clef* (figs 44 and 45). He dedicated *La clef* to 'Madame de Sidney'; while scholars still debate which Sidney this might refer to, it is likely to be Mary Herbert (née Sidney), Countess of Pembroke.[159] Even though she was married, she still often referred to herself as 'the Lady Mary Sidney'.[160] She was a well-known poet and artistic patron, and moved at

the heart of court life. She was the daughter of Mary Dudley, the maid of honour who had nursed the queen through smallpox in 1562. She was sister to the poet Sir Philip Sidney, who entrusted her with the control of his poem *Arcadia*, in language reflected in Le Moyne's dedication of *La clef* to her: 'since I know you favour the liberal arts, I have made bold to dedicate to you what I have prepared, for publication under the protection of your name'.[161]

In his dedication, Le Moyne wrote that his book had been devised to 'serve those to prepare themselves for the arts of painting or engraving, those to be goldsmiths or sculptors, and others for embroidery, tapestry and also for all kinds of needlework'.[162] The British Library copy of *La clef* shows signs of pricking, the process whereby small holes punched in a paper pattern are used to mark the outline of the design on to the fabric beneath.[163] A canvas slip in the collection of the Victoria and Albert Museum, one of a small group dating to c.1600, with floral motifs worked in coloured silks, is clearly copied from the pages of *La clef* (figs 45, 46). It features an embroidered blue and cornflower with the same – albeit simplified – composition as Le Moyne's woodcut. When the design

FIG. 45 Jacques Le Moyne de Morgues, illustration from *La clef des champs* (1586), hand-coloured woodcut on paper; cornflower (*left*), sweet briar (*right*). British Museum, London, 1952,0522.1.25.

FIG. 46 Cornflower, *c.*1600, canvas slip embroidered with silk. Victoria and Albert Museum, London, T.47-1972.

had been embroidered, the excess canvas of such slips would have been cut away, allowing the motif to be applied to various types of furnishing. This was a manageable way for domestic embroiderers to create attractive interior textiles, allowing them to work, a piece at a time, on a small embroidery frame. It was also a forgiving and cost-effective technique, allowing for easy correction and repurposing. The group of slips in the V&A were not cut out, but survive as wonderful material evidence of the type of embroidery undertaken by the noblewomen of the court. They survive with two notes, relating to their original commission by Anne Fitzwilliam (née Sidney; 1528–1602), the wife of Sir William Fitzwilliam (1526–1599), who, as governor of Fotheringhay Castle, presided over the execution of Mary Queen of Scots.[164] Anne was also the aunt of our Mary, Le Moyne's 'Madame de Sidney'.[165]

Le Moyne's motifs may well have inspired or served as patterns for slips worked by Bess of Hardwick, which survive on cushions, hangings and chairs at Hardwick Hall (fig. 47). Those on the chairs and canopy of the High Great Chamber have been reapplied to much later textiles, but the motifs themselves date from Bess's time.[166] They are embroidered slips, much like Anne Fitzwilliam's, but have been taken to the next step – cut out, and applied to rich furnishing velvets.[167] A similar aesthetic can be seen on the canopy depicted in a painting of Elizabeth I being carried in procession (fig. 48).

The same motifs can be found on the Bacton Altar Cloth.[168] Dating from around 1600, this embroidered textile served as an altar cloth for the small church of St Faith in Bacton, Herefordshire. The T-shaped cloth shows evidence of pattern cutting, and is pieced together in a way that suggests it was formerly an item of dress. It is made of an Italian white ribbed silk, with an additional weft of silver strip – a cloth known as 'silver chamblet' at the time it was made. The presence of silver marks it out as a court textile, as silver was reserved for the rank of lord or lady and above.[169] It features professionally embroidered botanical motifs in gold, silver and coloured silk, whose closest known patterns are to be found in the pages of Le Moyne's *La clef des champs* – pea-pods, roses, foxgloves, strawberries, cornflowers, acorns, honeysuckle, thistles, borage, heartsease and others. The motifs are wrought in an incredibly uniform seed-stitch, with plied

FIG. 47 (BELOW) Cushion cover, late 16th century, needlework slips on velvet, probably worked (or at least commissioned) by Bess of Hardwick. Hardwick Hall (National Trust), inv. no. T/192.

FIG. 48 (OPPOSITE) Unknown Anglo-Netherlandish artist (attrib. Robert Peake the elder (1551–1619)), the so-called 'Procession Portrait' of Elizabeth I, c.1600–03, oil on canvas. The painting has variously been seen as a procession of the Knights of the Garter and as the procession to the wedding of Anne Russell in 1600. The canopy over the queen's chair is decorated with embroidered slips. Sherborne Castle, Dorset.

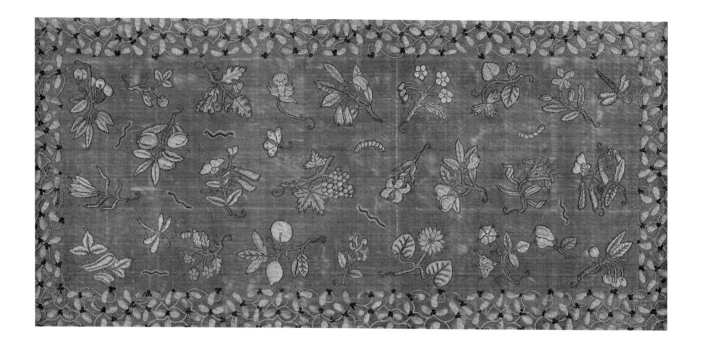

threads of different colours providing subtle variations of light and shade; varying densities of stitching provide further detail. It is a work of virtuosic needlecraft, as the embroidery is stitched directly through the silk ground, and is not worked on a slip or canvas of any kind. At the point of writing, this technique finds no parallel in major collections or catalogues, this being the case, the Bacton cloth has an importance relating to its technique (in the rarity of its survival) quite apart from any historical context.[170] A secondary contribution of domestic embroidery has been undertaken around the primary botanical motifs by an amateur embroiderer or embroiderers. This secondary work features sea creatures, caterpillars, a hunting scene, birds and butterflies; it is done in a variety of stitches and styles, and was perhaps carried out by a number of noble ladies at court.[171] All of these motifs are popular in embroidery pattern books and print books of the period (fig. 49). Several of the secondary motifs on the Bacton Altar Cloth have been traced to the engravings in a bestiary of 1594, *Animalium quadrapedum*, by the Antwerp-born Nicolaes de Bruyn (1571–1656), proving that ladies of the English court were familiar with, and took inspiration from, books and printed patterns.[172]

The cloth's status stems from its connection to Blanche Parry (1507/8–1590), a native of Bacton, chief gentlewoman of the Privy Chamber and an almost lifelong companion to Queen Elizabeth.[173] (She was also a friend of Bess of Hardwick.)[174] Blanche was in the queen's service from her infancy and remained, unmarried, by her side for fifty-seven years. Elizabeth gave her a number of her own clothes as a sign of favour, and when Blanche died the queen paid for a funeral befitting a baroness. Stylistically, the cloth post-dates Blanche's death in 1590 and cannot have been worked, or even seen, by her. However, the cloth's materials and techniques make it an elite court item, with precious few surviving parallels. That it could have found its way to the small hamlet of Bacton by other means than by association with Blanche is a difficult case to make.[175] It is highly likely that Elizabeth, out of affection for Blanche, donated the cloth to the church in memory of her long-serving gentlewoman. Or, indeed, those ladies

who had been close to her at court, might have sent it at the time of Elizabeth's own death. Janet Arnold suggests that her ladies were influential, and that 'the Queen and her ladies may have discussed among themselves who would be the most suitable recipient for the gift'.[176] Records show, for example, that the consent of the gentlewomen of the Privy Chamber was sought before an Irish gentlewoman was presented with a velvet safeguard, doublet and sleeves.[177]

Embroidery was a commodity that was within a woman's gift to proffer (fig. 50). The New Year Gift Roll, taken at Richmond Palace in January 1589, records gifts to the queen from her court. From the earls, the gifts were mostly of gold; from the bishops all were of gold; some of the lords gave jewels. But a different picture appears of the ladies of the court. From Elizabeth, Lady Lumley (d. 1617), the queen received 'a wastecoate of white taffety imbrodered all over with a twist of flowers of venis gold silver and some black silk'; from Dorothy, Lady Chandos (c.1524–1605), 'a stoole [. . .] the seate covered with murry velvet ymbrodered all over with pillers arched of venis gold silver and silk'; from the Lady Katheryn Constable (d. 1591), 'one longe cushion of black velvet ymbroidered all over with flowers of silke needlework of sundy cullors'; from Lady Walsingham (d. 1602), 'cloth of silver ymbrodered all over very faire with beasts fowles and trees of venis gold silver silke'; and from Lady Leighton (1549–c.1605), 'a wastecote of white sarsnett ymbroddered round about with a border of eglantine flowers and ymbrodered all over with a twist of venis gold'.[178]

Embroidery was more than just a commodity, however; it was also a device for communication – a language that women considered their own (fig. 51). During the summer of 1592, the queen stayed at Bisham

FIG. 50 (OVERLEAF, LEFT) Ladies in a garden, embroidering and lace-making, from Gervasius Fabricius, 'Album amicorum', 1603–37, watercolour. The ladies seated in the foreground are weaving bobbin lace (*left*), embroidering (*centre*) and sewing needle lace (*right*); to the right a lady accompanies a singer on the virginal, and in the background is a formal garden. British Library, London, Add. MS 17025, fol. 50.

FIG. 51 (OVERLEAF, RIGHT) Francesco del Cossa (c.1435–c.1477), *The Allegory of March*, 1470s, fresco, detail. The ladies are shown weaving and working embroidery; the latter, in particular, was the pursuit of young noblewomen. Palazzo Schifanoia, Ferrara.

FIG. 49 Medlar pear, detail from the Bacton Altar Cloth, c.1600, silk and silver camlet embroidered with silk and metal thread).

JANE ROSNOCKI 1598

ALICE·LEE·WAS·BORNE·THE·23·OF·NOVEMBER·BE
ING·TVESDAY·IN·THE·AFTER·NOONE·1596

Abbey in Berkshire for six days. Her hostess was Elizabeth, Lady Russell (1528–1609), sister-in-law to William Cecil. A play was staged for her, which some scholars contend may have been written by the hostess herself; it was certainly performed by her teenage daughters, Anne (d. 1639) and Elizabeth (d. 1600), who played virgin shepherdesses occupied with embroidering samplers (fig. 52).[179] In the play, they embroider roses, heartsease and eglantine – fashionable motifs of the Elizabethan court. The god Pan asks the content of their samplers, and the shepherdesses reply that they contain witty criticisms of men and praise of unmarried women. The queen's stitch is true, while men's tongues are 'wrought all with double stitche but not one true'.[180] They go on to praise virginity and claim that, by their chastity, women can become goddesses. Through the act of needlework, the Russell daughters demonstrated their wit and intelligence, and their shared female bond with the queen. The play evidently pleased Elizabeth, as the Russell girls became maids of honour just a couple of years later. Anne Russell married Henry Somerset, Lord Herbert (1577–1646), in June 1600. The painting of the queen carried in procession has traditionally been interpreted as an illustration of the wedding day (see fig. 48).[181]

The inventory of Queen Elizabeth's clothes and silks, taken in July 1600 and known as the Stowe Inventory, shows that her wardrobe was replete with embroidery.[182] The inventory lists items kept within the Wardrobes at the Tower, Whitehall (Westminster) and other royal residences. It contains a number of pieces identifiable with gifts to the queen from her court, and demonstrates the ubiquity of rich, symbolic embroidery within her wardrobe. One entry describes a mantle of 'blacke stitched cloth enbrodered allover with a border of Roses Cloudes and Daizeis of venice golde'. Other items are 'a Frenche gowne with a traine of silver chamblet wrought with trees and birds of venice golde, silver and silke of sondrie colours'; a 'french gowne of tawny satten embroidered allover with knottes sonnes and cloudes of golde silver

and silk'; 'a covering for a frenche gowne of lawne embroidered allover with Fountaines, Snailes, swords and other devices upon silver chamblet'; and 'one rounde [gown] of partridge colour taphata with a broade border enbrodred with golde and silver like peramides and cut and tackt up with a kirtle under it of silver chamblet painted in waves fishes and Rockes'.[183]

These records of gifts and accounts of the Great Wardrobe further assist us in dating the Bacton Altar Cloth to the 1590s or early 1600s, as the combination of floral embroidery upon silver chamblet occurs only after 1590. There is an entry for a 'canapie' of 'carnation chamblett' being 'stained [painted] with flowers'.[184] Other entries record silver chamblet sleeves or gowns, as above. Another listing is of a gift to the queen by Lady Chandos, for new year 1599, of 'one rounde kyrtell of silver chamlett [. . .] with flowers of golde, silver, and silke of sondrye colours'.[185] Within the records, this last entry most closely resembles the Bacton Altar Cloth.

The inventory includes some items that had belonged to Elizabeth's half-siblings, Edward and Mary. The descriptions of their textiles reveal rich fabrics – velvets and taffetas in blue, purple, crimson and green – but lacking embroidery as a distinctive feature (fig. 53). Much of the detail comes from intricate Italian weaving such as 'gold and silver tissue' (fig. 54) or 'clothe of silver chequered with red silk'.[186] Where there is embellishment it tends to be listed as a trim or border, or as 'purles of damaske golde' (twists of gold or silver wire).[187] There are no descriptions of emblematic or symbolic embroidery as we see in Elizabeth's wardrobe, though, given the passing of so many decades, it is unlikely that these items are representative of either Edward's or Mary's full wardrobes. We know that Elizabeth re-used and repurposed many of her predecessors' possessions, including Mary's coronation robe of cloth of gold. However, the distinctions between the styles of the mid-century and the later part of Elizabeth's reign are clear.

* * *

The changes observed in textile fashions from the beginning of the Tudor era to its end are illuminating. Textiles reflected the political and cultural milieu, and were key reflectors of taste, prestige and power. The textiles of Henry VII's reign were typically heraldic

FIG. 52 Sampler worked by Jane Bostocke of Shropshire, 1598, linen embroidered with coloured silk and metal threads, seed pearls and beads. This is the earliest dated British sampler, and records the birth of a child. Samplers served as reference pieces for experienced embroiderers, as well as for novices, and were worked by gentlewomen as well as noblewomen. Victoria and Albert Museum, London, T.190-1960.

– late-medieval, feudal and martial – they asserted Henry's lineage, his arms and his right to rule. His son, Henry VIII, projected a different image. He was the young, learned Renaissance prince. His tapestries expressed his learning through sophisticated classical narratives, and the tents of the Field of Cloth of Gold projected both his wealth and his chivalric self-image. Elizabeth, last (and arguably greatest) of the Tudors, ruled in a period of expanding horizons and global influences. The textiles of her court were shaped by the imagery of books and prints, and by the hidden meaning of small and inscrutable symbols and emblems. However, Elizabeth lived, as did all of Henry's children, in his shadow. Henry's expenditure meant that they could not afford the major commissions that he undertook, but, more than that, they actively used the visual culture of their father's court to assert their legitimacy as his heirs. Hampton Court retained much of its Henrician legacy well into the Stuart period.

FIG. 53 (OPPOSITE) Fragment of pile-on-pile velvet, 1500–50, Italy. The long and short piles of this silk velvet contrast to create a pattern. Victoria and Albert Museum, London, 1073-1901.

FIG. 54 (ABOVE) Cloth of silver tissue, detail of Antonis Mor (d. 1576?), portrait of Mary I, 1554, oil on panel (see fig. 124). Museo del Prado, Madrid.

3 PRIVATE SPACES

The Textiles of the Privy Chambers

In the early sixteenth century, the majority of linen tablecloths in the royal inventories were 4 ells wide. As the century progressed they reduced in width, to just 3 ells. This seemingly insignificant detail heralds the move of the monarch to dining in relative privacy, as compared with the late medieval period.[1] Simply put, the tablecloths were narrower because the tables – and the spaces they occupied – were smaller. Throughout the Tudor period there was a conscious withdrawing from the medieval hall to the privy chamber and beyond; by the end of Henry VIII's reign, an area had been identified as the 'Secret Lodging' where only the groom of the stool might attend him.[2] Indeed, the Renaissance concept of *multum in parvo*, or 'much in little', regarded smaller spaces as symbolically more meaningful than larger spaces (as discussed in chapter 2, see p. 60).[3] The sovereign, it seems, wanted some privacy.

FIG. 55 Unknown artist, Henry VIII dining in his privy chamber, late 1540s, pen and ink on paper, possibly after a sketch by Hans Holbein the younger (1497/8–1543). Attended by courtiers, the king sits at a table on a dais, beneath a cloth of estate. The table is laid with a linen cloth, and a cloth also adorns the cupboard to the right, on which plate is arranged. British Museum, London, 1854-6-28-74.

We know that a number of rooms were considered part of the royal privy lodgings. A book of ceremonies at Henry's court, written by one of his gentleman ushers, John Norris (*c.*1481–1564), stated that ideally the 'kinge ought to have Foure chambers prepared for him selfe', but that at the very least he should have three. One chamber was required for the king's bed, a 'second chamber to make the kinge ready in', and the 'thirde chamber for the kings dyninge and ther the cloth of Estate shall hange' (fig. 55).[4] These directives were instructive not only for the royal court, where the king had more rooms at his disposal, including his private study and bath-house, but also on progresses or in the construction of temporary spaces or lodgings.

From 1530, Hampton Court Palace featured a sequence of five rooms in the King's Lodgings. Beyond the guard room, there was a presence chamber, wherein were located the cloth and chair of estate, a separate dining chamber (though elsewhere the presence and dining chambers were one and the same), a withdrawing or privy chamber and a bedchamber. There was also a closet, a small room for private study or prayer. Within the Bayne Tower – Bayne coming from French *bain*, 'bath' – there was, indeed, a bath, and also a private library and study.[5]

However, we know little about the appearance and décor of the royal private apartments, in comparison to the relatively more abundant descriptions of the public areas of the court. Indeed, the nature of 'private' and 'public' spaces as it relates to the Tudor court is fraught with difficulty as, arguably, the Tudor monarchs lived their lives attended by others. The household code of conduct issued by Cardinal Wolsey in 1526, known as the Eltham Ordinances, stated that two esquires 'shall nightly lie on the pallet within the King's said privy chamber'.[6] Consequently, there has been much debate about the social and political implications of Tudor 'privacy', with the suggestion that privacy, as understood by a modern audience, did not exist.[7] Yet there was a significant hierarchy of chambers, and restrictions about who had access where. We see this in the appointment of Henry Norris (d. 1536) to the service of Henry VIII: 'It is the king's pleasure that Mr Norris shall be in the room [. . .] not only giving his attendance as groom of the stool but also in his bedchamber and other privy places as shall stand with his pleasure.'[8] Access to the privy chambers was highly privileged, and only by permission or favour of the monarch. This serves as an acceptable definition of the distinction between public and private, and provides the basis for attempting to identify differences in the use of decorative objects within the monarch's private spaces.

THE PRESENCE CHAMBER: CLOTH AND CHAIR OF ESTATE

The cloth of estate was a vital representation of monarchy during the Tudor period. It was the cloth that hung behind the chair of estate in the presence chamber, and under which the monarch sat to receive visitors. It consisted of a celure (roof piece) that created a canopy over the chair, and a tester (a back piece, hanging down from the celure behind the chair). Even when the monarch was not present, members of the household were required to doff their caps to the cloth and chair of estate.[9] A canopy represented the cloth of estate when the monarch was in procession (see fig. 48).

John Norris, gentleman usher to Henry VIII, described his duties relating to the maintenance of the cloth and chair of estate, including commanding that a page of the chamber 'make cleane and playne the carpett that lyeth under the kings chaire and cloth of Estate and to see that no rushes nor foule thinge shall rest on it'.[10] Additionally, when the court moved, it was imperative that the king or queen was furnished with a cloth and chair of estate. Norris explained that when the monarch moved to a new location, the lord chamberlain should 'warne the Grome of the warderobe aforesaid to bringe in arras to hange the chambers [. . .] and to bringe also a cloth of Estate with a Chaire and Cusshions and then the yeoman of the

FIG. 56 The king's arms, embroidered on a cloth of estate, detail of *The Family of Henry VIII*, c.1545, oil on canvas (see fig. 5). Royal Collection, Hampton Court Palace.

Chamber shall hange the saide chambres'.[11] When a queen went into labour the nursery was furnished with 'a silour and testour with dobull valaunces and three curteynes large and long of blewe and dobull sarcenet accordingly to hang over the cradell of estate'.[12]

Cloths and chairs of estate are prominent in Tudor portraiture, representing as they do the symbolic majesty of monarchy. The 1547 Inventory lists around twenty tapestries with heraldic devices, dating from the fifteenth and early sixteenth century – that is, the reign of Henry VII and possibly his predecessors.[13] It is difficult to ascertain whether or not the various celures and testers listed in the inventory belonged to cloths of estate or beds, as they shared the same nomenclature. The surviving tapestry at Haddon Hall (see fig. 23) offers a glimpse of these tapestry-woven heraldic cloths of estate. The reign of Henry VIII saw a shift towards embroidered armorials on rich silks. One cloth of estate is described as 'conteyning a ceeler and a tester of purple velat embrawdered with golde [. . .] and garnished in sondrie places with ragged perles [. . .] garnettes, a white sapphire [. . .] the saide tester having the kings armes crowned with a Garter and a garlond embrawdered upon it' (fig. 56).[14]

The cloth of estate was symbolic, and so varied with favour and status. The 1535 inventory of Katherine of Aragon's Wardrobe at Baynard's Castle records 'a rich cloth of astate of crymsene cloth of tissue enbrowdered with the armes of England and Spayne, as welle in the ceelour and testour [. . .] lined with grene bokerhame, havinge doble valaunce fringed with crymsene silke and Venysse golde'.[15] Henry's heir, Edward, was provided with three cloths of estate. His illegitimate son, Henry Fitzroy (1519–1536), was provided with one, of cloth of gold but bearing no coat of arms. Princess Mary had two cloths of estate, but Elizabeth – after she was declared illegitimate in July 1536 – had none.[16] Within the inventory of Cardinal Wolsey's possessions, taken following his fall from grace in January 1530, were 'six cloths of estate of cloth of gold and velvet, two with my Lord's arms'.[17] Wolsey also had five chairs of estate in his possession, with upholstery of cloth of tissue and cloth of gold, and a significant number of cushions of rich fabrics such as cloth of gold and violet satin, embroidered with crosses, gold flowers, birds, a pelican, roses and lions.

The Black Book of the Garter (so called because of its black velvet cover), a register of the Order of the Garter, was commissioned by Henry VIII and begun in 1534. An illumination within it shows Henry kneeling on a golden cushion at a prie-dieu draped with red cloth, on which rests a cushion that holds a prayer book, itself probably bound in fabric (fig. 57). The prie-dieu is in front of an altar adorned with cloth of gold in a Renaissance pomegranate design, with an embroidered linen cloth draped over it. In the background is a blue cloth of estate with embroidery of gold reading 'Dieu et mon droeit' ('God and my right').

Sixteenth-century visitors to Hampton Court recorded an intriguing room, known as 'Paradise'. It was created by Henry VIII in 1534 at the end of the king's Long Gallery, and both were destroyed as part of the development of the Baroque palace by William and Mary in the late seventeenth century. In the building accounts of 1567–70, a clerk described Paradise as a privy chamber.[18] It was in regular use, as it was re-matted with rush matting in 1584–5 and 1589–90.[19] During Elizabeth's reign, a small apartment hung with silk hangings, said to be a gift to the queen from the Earl of Leicester, led to the Paradise Chamber,

> where the ceiling is adorned with very beautiful paint-
> ings and an extremely costly canopy or royal throne,
> from which amongst other precious stones, pearls,
> large diamonds, rubies, sapphires and the rest shine
> forth, like the sun amongst the stars. Beneath this the
> queen is accustomed to sit in her magnificence, upon a
> very stately chair covered with cushions [. . .] The royal
> arms are on the wall on a very fine tapestry with an
> extremely large square diamond.[20]

The canopy featured the royal arms of England and 'was made to the order of Henry VIII'.[21] The luxury of Henry's commissions, it seems, still impressed with their magnificence, and Elizabeth made a conspicuous display of showcasing his legacy, and her inheritance, even to the end of her own reign (fig. 58).

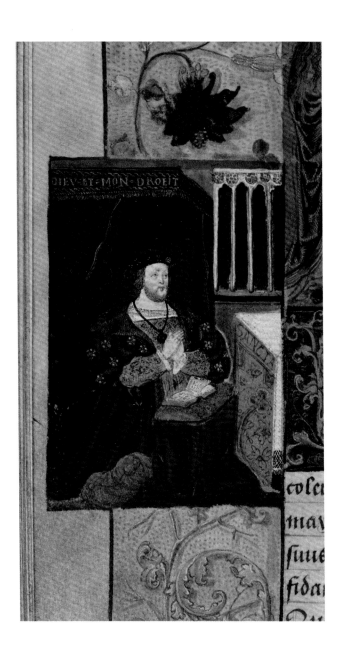

FIG. 57 Unknown artist (attrib. Lucas Horenbout (1490–1544)), Henry VIII at prayer in his closet, detail from the Black Book of the Garter, 1534–51, manuscript painting. Even at his devotions, the king is surrounded by luxurious textiles: the altar is dressed in cloth of gold, and a rich cloth of estate behind him is embroidered in gold with his motto. College of St George, Windsor, MS Doc. 162a.

FIG. 58 Unknown artist (attrib. Steven van der Meulen (*fl.* 1543–68) or Steven van Herwijck (*c.*1530–1565/7)), the so-called 'Hampden Portrait' of Queen Elizabeth I, *c.*1563, oil on panel. The portrait is replete with luxurious textiles. A cloth of estate of cloth of gold is embellished with embroidery, fringing and jewels; the X-frame chair holds a large cloth of gold cushion, and a verdure tapestry lines the wall behind the cloth of estate. The queen herself is dressed in crimson silk satin or velvet. Hampden House, Buckinghamshire.

DINING

Table linen, or napery, included tablecloths, towels and napkins (fig. 59). The terminology relating to fine figured linen changed through the Tudor period. Records in the earlier sixteenth century refer to 'fine diaper', but from the start of Elizabeth's reign it would have been described as 'of damask', and 'diaper' was used only for smaller repeating patterns.[22]

Napery was a formal part of dining, and a ritualised part of the monarch's dining-in-state. Long linen 'arming towels' were worn by the carver and the sewer (server). When serving royalty, and lords temporal or spiritual, the sewer wore the towel over one shoulder and the carver wore it around his neck, reflecting the way that a deacon and priest wore their stoles for Mass (fig. 61).[23] This semi-religious process surrounded the monarch with an aura of divinity and mystique.

First, the king washed his hands and dried them with a linen towel. The towel was passed from the gentleman usher to the 'prince or lord of the highest estate' (that is, rank), while the nobleman of the second highest rank held the basin under the king's hands. When the towel was returned to the gentleman usher, the part 'in which the king hath wiped was carried by the usher above his head'. Once the king was seated at the table, the tablecloth was lifted over his lap. He was given a napkin, and the servant waiting upon him held another on his arm.[24] A 'fynne square clouth of cambrick', called a coverpain, was to cover the bread until the meat was placed on the table, at which point the coverpain was removed.[25]

A surviving figured napkin reveals how napery was woven for the practicalities of use. A linen damask napkin, woven for the court of Queen Elizabeth features vertical repeats of an image and its mirror image, which complement each other once the napkin is folded (fig. 60). Another curiosity about the image on the napkin is that it features a woman in the fashionable dress of *c*.1560, St George, the Tudor royal arms, the Tudor rose, and the falcon badge of Anne Boleyn. It has been suggested that this provides evidence of Elizabeth's affection for her late mother, revealed in the objects of her privy lodgings. Indeed, Elizabeth privately used Anne's falcon badge for small items such as the covers of books.[26] Another suggestion is that Henry VIII commissioned table linen for Anne, and that years later, following the coronation of her daughter, the same Flemish weavers considered the emblem suitable to honour the new queen.[27] This idea is supported by the fact that the design was probably based on an engraving by Frans Huys, dating to 1559, the year of Elizabeth's coronation.[28]

FIG. 59 (OPPOSITE, LEFT) Linen napkin with inserted bands of woven linen and silk, early 16th century, Italy or Spain. Such cloths had various functions: they might be used to dry the hands, to cover a cupboard on which vessels were placed, or as coverpains to cover bread on the table. Victoria and Albert Museum, London, 234-1880.

FIG. 60 (OPPOSITE, RIGHT) Linen napkin, mid-16th century, woven with repeat motifs and bands of lettering, in direct and mirror image, including (*top*) the falcon badge of Anne Boleyn and (*bottom*) the royal arms. Victoria and Albert Museum, London, T.119-1927.

FIG. 61 (ABOVE) Master of the Catholic Kings (*fl. c.*1485–1500), *The Marriage at Cana*, *c.*1495/7, oil on panel. The carver (*left, foreground*) wears his linen towel around his neck, while the sewer (server, *right*) wears the towel over one shoulder. The linen tablecloth is embroidered and fringed at the edges, a cloth of estate is suspended from the ceiling, and in the room behind is a richly furnished bed. National Gallery of Art, Washington, DC.

FIG. 62 Unknown artist, *King Edward VI and the Pope*, *c.*1575, oil on panel, detail. Henry VIII is depicted passing power, both temporal and spiritual (hence the allegorical presence of the pope), to the young Edward; Henry sits in a bed furnished with crimson cloth of gold, with linen sheets and pillows embroidered with gold, and gold tassels. National Portrait Gallery, London.

THE BEDCHAMBER

The most obviously intimate or private item within the privy chambers was the monarch's bed, and yet, as with most things at the Tudor court, this too was an opportunity for the demonstration of social status. Furnished with a full set of textiles, it was arguably one of the most important royal objects.[29] It represented proximity to the royal person, and an intimacy suggesting private counsel and confidences. As such, it was an inherently political item.[30] Indeed, the cloth of estate was imbued with ceremonial meaning precisely because it evolved from bed hangings.[31] They may even have been interchangeable in some instances. The inventory of Katherine of Aragon's textiles in the Wardrobe at Baynard's Castle in London (the Wardrobe store of the queens consort) describes the cloth of estate embroidered with the royal arms of England and Spain mentioned above (p. 77), together with a separate panel, which –as the record explicitly states – belonged to the saide clothe of astate whatte tyme it was a bedde'.[32]

Bed hangings consisted of a celure and a tester (as for a cloth of estate), accompanied by valances, curtains and a quilt or counterpane.[33] Fine linen sheets and pillowcases, embroidered with silk and gold, are clearly visible in paintings of the time (fig. 62), and are verified by the inventory of Henry VIII's possessions – for example, 'viii pillowberes of holland with broade seams of silke of sundrie collors needle work'.[34]

Detailed specifications for royal beds are given in the household ordinances of 1493.[35] The instructions for how to make the king's bed were exacting. A gentleman usher, two esquires of the body and two yeomen of the crown were required to make the bed, each standing in a specific position and having a specific role. Once the old linen was removed, a yeoman was to beat the feather mattress to make it even and smooth, then 'shall the yeoman of the stuffe take a fustian [brushed linen sheet . . .] then shall esquires of the body lay hands thereon, and lay it straight on the bed without any wrinkles [. . . and] gather the sheete round together in ther hand and eyther side of the bed'. The yeomen were also to beat the pillows well with their hands, and then cast them up to the esquires 'and let them lay them on, as it pleaseth the Kinge best, highe or lowe'.[36] The queen's bed was to be provided with two pairs of sheets of fine linen, two long pillows and

FIG. 63 John Carter (1748–1817), drawing of a late 16th-century Flemish tapestry, *c*.1790–1810, pen and ink. The tapestry formerly hung in the Prince's Chamber in Westminster Palace. It shows the birth of a royal infant, said to be the Princess Elizabeth. The queen sits in bed, propped up by pillows; a decorative valance surrounds the top of the bed frame and the bed curtains are pulled back. A tapestry on the back wall shows a pastoral scene. Victoria and Albert Museum, London, E.2252-1924.

16. 10

la louenge de dieu & de la
vierge marie souueraine
et de tous les saintz et sain
tes de paradis A ceste histoi
re este escripte de la passio
de Ihesus nostre sauueur ☙ Et pour auoir

two squares of fustian filled with down, a pane [blanket] of fine scarlet, wool furred with ermine and 'boredered with velvet or cloth of gold'.[37] 'Scarlet' was a highly prized soft wool cloth, which in the late Middle Ages was worn extensively as clothing, but by the date of the ordinances was used mostly for bedding and fifty years later for underblankets.[38]

A detailed account of the creation of 'the riche bedde' for Elizabeth of York in December 1502 records payments to 'Robynet the Quenes brawderer', for expenses incurred by him for his team's wages and board. Artisans Anthony and William spent seven weeks working on the bed, along with two women called Joan (Johne) and one 'Margrette Stokes', who worked on the bed for five and two weeks respectively. Payments were also made for 'the white and red rosys and clowdes' and for tawny thread to work the edge of the red satin fabric.[39] Elizabeth of York would die in childbirth just a few months later, in February 1503. A presentation miniature from the illuminated manuscript known as the Vaux Passional, is reputed to depict Henry VII in mourning, receiving the manuscript, while his daughters sit by the fire, and his son – Henry – grieves besides his mother's empty bed (fig. 64).

Royal childbirth necessitated a considerable array of textiles, both to establish the dignity of the infant but also to insulate the room from any drafts and vapours that were thought to be harmful to both mother and unborn child during the confinement (fig. 63).[40] Confinement was the ritualised isolation of the mother-to-be from the rest of the court, along with her ladies and midwives, for around one month preceding the birth. The 1493 ordinances stipulate that the chamber 'must bee hanged with rich arras',[41] though it must not be woven with vivid imagery that might overwhelm the mother-to-be. For her confinement in 1486, Elizabeth of York's chamber was hung with blue cloth of arras with gold fleurs-de-lis.[42] The tapestries were to be hung around 'the roofe, side and windows, all except one windowe, and that must

FIG. 64 The presentation page of the Vaux Passional, c.1503–4, manuscript painting, showing Henry VII in mourning for his wife, Elizabeth of York. Henry sits under a cloth of estate, while his children are shown in the background (left). It is supposed that Prince Henry is depicted kneeling at his mother's empty bed, now shrouded in the dark fabric of mourning. National Library of Wales, Peniarth MS 482D.

bee hanged that shee may have light when it pleaseth her'. The floor was 'laid with carpets over and over'. The bed was to be arranged with great pillows and sheets of fine linen, made of imported 'lawne' (from Laon) or 'rayne' (attributed to Rennes or Reims). It should have a cover of ermine fur embroidered with cloth of gold. There was also to be a pallet bed, and it was this smaller bed that the queen would actually use during the birth. The reason for having two beds is probably twofold: the furnishings of a great bed were probably too expensive to be risked in labour, and the ministrations of midwives and attendants were probably logistically easier on a more functional pallet bed. The pallet bed was to consist of a mattress stuffed with wool (not down), plenty of linen sheets and pillows, and a blanket of scarlet wool 'furred with ermine and bordered with velvet or cloth of gold', which was probably removed during labour. The hangings of the pallet bed were, however, very richly decorated. There was to be a 'sperne [canopy] of crimson sattin, embrothered with crownes of gould, the Queen's armes and other devices [. . .] garnished with a fringe of silke, and gould, and blewe, and russet'.[43]

The 1547 Inventory of the king's goods at Hampton Court offers us a glimpse of the rich bed furnishings of Henry VIII's court. A bed that once belonged to Anne Boleyn was listed as 'one bedstead [. . .] curiouslie wrought and carved with the late Quene Annes ciphers'.[44] It comprised a celure, tester, valances and three lower valances of needlework in silk and gold, also showing Anne's ciphers and fringed with venice gold. The celure, tester and bases were lined with yellow sarcenet, and upon the celure and tester was 'one greate roundel bordered aboute [. . .] with the kings armes and the said Queen Annes armes'. The valances were double fringed with a deep fringe of venice gold and red silk, and there were five curtains of green damask, fringed on both sides with venice gold. A 'counterpointe' (quilt) of cloth of gold was embroidered all over with Anne's ciphers and applied works of green and crimson velvet, with a great embroidered roundel featuring the arms of the king and 'the saide Quene Anne'. For warmth there was a piece of fustian filled with down and four quilts of fine linen filled with wool.[45] The bed was clearly luxurious and opulent – designed not only for comfort and warmth, but for the tangible assertion, or legitimisation, of a royal claim.

And this bed was not an isolated example. As many as eighteen sets of bed furnishings were recorded at Hampton Court, and fifteen of those were embroidered, many with the king's arms.[46]

Some objects also survive to offer an insight into the fashionable aesthetics of Henry's 1530s bedchamber. A valance of cream silk taffeta features black silk velvet cutwork motifs, with the cipher 'HA' for Henry and Anne, surrounded by the acorns and honeysuckle that were their private emblems (fig. 65), and which were also recorded on other objects in the 1547 Inventory, including a carpet of gold, silver and silk needlework.[47] Another 'A' – this time for Anne of Cleves – appears as part of an inscription on a ceremonial bedhead made for her marriage to Henry in 1539 (fig. 66). Both objects feature the scrolling arabesque designs fashionable at this time (see fig. 67).

The 1530 inventory of Cardinal Wolsey's possessions lists bedding textiles that allow us to see the more prosaic steps taken for the comfort of the bed's occupant. In addition to the ornate coverings of 'rich tissue', satins and velvets, he also had thirty-two woollen mattresses covered with fine linen cloth for his own bed, three feather mattresses, and bolsters, cushions, and quilts of fine linen and fustian filled with feathers. He had two blankets furred with fine white lambskin fleece. Interestingly, listed alongside Wolsey's counterpoints of satin, damask and baudekin, some of which were embroidered, are some of 'tapestry and veerdurs with various devices', demonstrating the use of tapestry weaving as a bed cover.[48]

Surviving textiles of a slightly later date, but of a classical style, offer a glimpse into aspects of Henry's personal taste. As shown in chapter 2, we know from Henry's tapestry commissions that he enjoyed, and perhaps even identified with, classical heroic narratives and aesthetics. Indeed, the proportions of his classical tapestries suggest that they were reserved for his more private chambers (see p. 48). We might conjecture that he enjoyed similar designs for other textiles, such as bed furnishings. A 1550s tester of yellow silk strapwork applied to a blue satin ground shows the classical 'grotesque' style (fig. 68).[49] A surviving set of panels from a bed valance of the 1560s shows the story of Pyramus and Thisbe, two young lovers whose romance was forbidden, embroidered on a red satin ground (fig. 69). That these

FIG. 65 (OPPOSITE) Valance, c.1532–6, light cream silk taffeta with linen canvas backing, decorated with arabesque black silk velvet cutwork motifs of acorns and honeysuckle, with the cipher 'HA' for Henry VIII and Anne Boleyn. Burrell Collection, Glasgow Museums, 29.178a & b.

FIG. 66 (BELOW) Ceremonial bedhead, 1539, oak. Made for the marriage of Henry VIII to his fourth wife, Anne of Cleves, it is carved, painted and gilded with arabesque decoration that reflects embroidery and cutwork designs. Male and female figures at either side, representing fertility, symbolise the hope for the conception and birth of a second male heir for Henry. Burrell Collection, Glasgow Museums, 14.236.

textiles were of high status is confirmed by a similar example that survives in the Louvre, with the monogram of the French king, Henri II (1519–1559).

As queen, Elizabeth conspicuously displayed her father's possessions, and highlighted her lineage and history. When Francis, Duke of Anjou and Alençon (1555–1584), arrived on his last visit to England to court Elizabeth in late October 1581, she supervised the décor and furnishings of his chamber at Richmond herself. She had a 'crimson bed' placed within the chamber and suggested that the duke might recognise it.[50] It has been suggested that this was the so-called 'Alençon bed', referred to in the 1547 Inventory as the 'bedde of allaunson' and described as having a celure, tester and counterpoint 'richelye embrawdered upon Crimsen vellat'.[51] This bed was in Anne Boleyn's chamber for Elizabeth's birth in September 1533, when it was already more than a hundred years old, for it had been seized by John of Lancaster, in part payment of the ransom for the second Duke of Alençon in 1424.[52] Thus the bed was a reference to Elizabeth's own past and to the history of the Duchy of Alençon, but its use for Francis's visit may have hinted at a more intimate connection, and a form of delicate fliration on Elizabeth's part. Another contender for identification with the 'crimson bed' might be the bed given by the duke's grandfather King Francis I

to Elizabeth's father, Henry, during his visit to France in 1532. On that occasion, Francis I 'gave the English King a suite of bed furniture, wrought throughout with pearls on crimson velvet, which he purchased lately in Paris of an Italian merchant for 10,000 golden crowns'.[53]

Elizabeth's own bed was apparently markedly different from those of her forebears, as witnessed by a visitor to Windsor Castle. A chamber there contained 'the Royal beds of Henry VII and his Queen, of Edward VI, of Henry VIII, and of Anne Bullen, all of them eleven feet square and covered with quilts shining with gold and silver; Queen Elizabeth's bed', on the other hand, featured a 'curious covering of embroidery, but not quite so long or large as the others'. The same visitor also noted a 'cushion most curiously wrought by Queen Elizabeth's own hands'.[54] One wonders if the 'curious' embroidery that attracted his interest was the result of the fashion for emblems and symbols that captivated the late Elizabethan court, or even the kinds of botanical motif that are so distinctive of the late sixteenth and early seventeenth centuries (fig. 70), such as those seen on the Bacton Altar Cloth. It certainly suggests that the embroidery of Elizabeth's court was unlike any visitor had seen before, and that – in some aspects, at least – personal taste or fashion was allowed to encroach upon her bedchamber.

FIG. 67 (ABOVE) Detail of arabesque decoration on a valance, mid-16th century London, dark red velvet with cutwork of cloth of gold and gold embroidery (see fig. 119). Victoria and Albert Museum, London, 4513-1858.

FIG. 68 (OPPOSITE) Tester, c.1550, school of Fontainebleau, France, satin cutwork on silk satin embroidered in silk thread. The strapwork design frames musical, floral and animal motifs in the grotesque style. Victoria and Albert Museum, London, T.405-1980.

FIG. 69 One of a set of panels, probably for a bed valance, 1560s, France, red satin embroidered in silk. The panel shows part of the story of Pyramus and Thisbe, from Ovid's *Metamorphoses*. Pyramus, thinking that Thisbe is dead, has killed himself by falling on his sword. The surrounding motifs are typical of the fashionable grotesque style. Victoria and Albert Museum, London, T.21b-1981.

FIG. 70 Curtain, early 17th century, England, linen embroidered in silk. Flowers, fruit and insects were much favoured as embroidery motifs in this period: readily identifiable are rose, cornflower, strawberry, pomegranate, snail, butterfly and spider. Victoria and Albert Museum, London, T.63-1933.

WALLS AND FLOORS

Bedding was elaborate, made with damask silks, cloth of gold and velvets, fringed with gold and embroidered with ciphers and arms. However, we know that the privy chambers abounded with other elaborate textiles in a riot of colour and textures.

The walls were hung with arras and tapestry. A Wardrobe account for 1543 records a payment for lining twelve pieces 'of good tapestry for the King's private apartment' at Hampton Court.[55] These pieces may have been verdure or millefleurs tapestries, which were often used in more private spaces, as may be seen in a painting of the 1570s depicting Elizabeth receiving Dutch ambassadors (fig. 71).[56] This painting depicts a number of such tapestries, arranged or cut to fit every inch of the presence chamber wall, with spaces only for the windows and doors.

Figurative tapestries also hung in the privy apartments. While more religious subjects hung in the Great Hall, the dimensions of a number of classical or mythological narratives suggest that they were intended for smaller, more private spaces.[57] The Dido and Aeneas set, purchased by Henry in the 1530s, and discussed in chapter 2 (pp. 46–8, 56), were probably of this kind. Another set that may have been destined for the king's private apartments is the one produced for Hampton Court by Pieter van der Walle in the 1540s, featuring Romulus and Remus, the founders of Rome. We might extrapolate that these classical heroes were especially admired by Henry, or even that he identified himself as belonging to the line of these heroes and founders of empires.[58]

The 1547 Inventory lists only a few items of figurative embroidered hangings (that is, not of tapestry or arras), including two at Nonsuch Palace, one 'olde embrawdered with horsemen', and a piece at the Tower stained (painted) with 'thistorye of Josephe brodred rounde abowte with cloth of golde'.[59] An embroidered hanging can be seen in the portrait of Margaret Beaufort at prayer, where it lines the walls around the cloth of estate (see fig. 24).

It may be that the silks *not* embellished with embroidery (fig. 72) were not all itemised as wall hangings, but numerous costly silk hangings can be seen in Tudor portraits, including Hans Holbein's *The Ambassadors* of 1533 (fig. 73). Similarly, a blue silk damask lines the wall in Holbein's portrait of Thomas Cromwell of the same year,[60]

and a voluminous green curtain hangs behind Sir Thomas More in Holbein's 1527 portrait of him.[61] Listed in Wolsey's inventory are '6 window curtains of changeable sarcenet, and 6 of red, orange, and blue sarcenet'.[62] For the most part, however, windows were not hung with curtains. Shutters, or even large window cushions, might keep out the draughts. Curtains and hangings were used, as we have seen, to line walls or used on rails to subdivide spaces (fig. 74).

The title page of Edward Hall's *Union of the two noble and illustre famelies of Lancastre & Yorke* (1548) shows Henry VIII sitting in his council chamber (fig. 75). The chamber walls are completely hidden behind draped fabric, decorated with a flower that may be the Tudor rose. The cloth of estate features the Tudor arms, above the king, on what appears to be a fabric bearing a large Renaissance pomegranate motif. A different version of the image, later in the book, shows more pronounced drapery, with fleurs-de-lis alongside the flowers and a motto reading 'King Henry the eyght'.[63] Similarly, the frontispiece to *Christian prayers and meditations*, published by John Day in 1569, shows Elizabeth I at the centre of a stylised array of elaborate textiles, including what appears to be a patterned green textile lining the walls of the alcove, trimmed with fringing at the bottom and cut away at the windows (fig. 76).

The 1547 Inventory lists 800 carpets, most of which were imported, hand-knotted Eastern carpets, from the Islamic Middle East and north Africa. Such carpets were luxury commodities, and were not generally placed on the floor. Around 500 or 600 of them were described as cupboard or window carpets. Measuring around 2 metres long, they decorated the tops of dressers, coffers, window ledges, seats and cupboards, as seen in *The Ambassadors* (see fig. 73). Another hundred pieces were 'great carpets' of roughly 5–10 metres long. They were used to cover tables or, sometimes, high-status floors, such as the area under a chair of estate or around a royal bed. Another hundred or so carpets of 'di' or 'demi' size, around 2–5 metres long, served as smaller foot or table carpets, or larger cupboard carpets.[64]

At least 200 carpets were located at Hampton Court Palace.[65] They were procured by Wolsey before 1530, or were given to him by merchants eager for business, and remained there until the middle of the seventeenth century.[66] Wolsey's inventory also included cushions of carpet work, probably knotted pile.

FIG. 71 Unknown artist (attrib. Levina Teerlinc (1510s–1576)), *Elizabeth I of England Receiving Dutch Ambassadors*, 1570–75, gouache on card. The queen is shown standing in front of her cloth and chair of estate; her ladies sit on the floor, probably on large cushions. The floor is carpeted with bright rush matting, and the walls are lined with millefleurs tapestries. Neue Galerie, Kassel.

FIG. 72 (OVERLEAF, LEFT) Pale blue silk damask, mid-16th century, Italy. This stylised plant design, with scrolling patterns encircling motifs that resemble pomegranates or artichokes, was fashionable for velvet and silk hangings in the Tudor period. Victoria and Albert Museum, London, 946-1877.

FIG. 73 (OVERLEAF, RIGHT) Hans Holbein the younger (1497/8–1543), *The Ambassadors*, 1533, oil on panel. Jean de Dinteville and Georges de Selve are shown with the accoutrements of sophistication and learning, including an Eastern ('Turkey') carpet and a background of rich damask silk. National Gallery, London.

An abundance of different types of cushion were also recorded in the royal inventories (fig. 77). The 1547 Inventory showed fifty-three cushions at Westminster, almost a hundred at Hampton Court, forty-six at Greenwich and eighty at the Tower.[67] They provided comfort and decoration for chairs, benches or window seats. Some were large and were backed with leather for use as footrests, prayer kneelers or floor cushions, such as the twelve 'square cushions of nedleworke of dyvers coolors works and bignesse, the backs of x [10] lined with leather'.[68] In the image of Elizabeth receiving the ambassadors (see fig. 71), the queen's ladies appear to be sitting on the floor, but would have been seated on large cushions. The ladies of the court, including members of the royal family, may well have worked some of the smaller cushions listed in the inventories. The Princess Mary's accounts from the early 1540s record payments for embroidery patterns, rich fabrics such as damask, and stuffing and fringes for a number of 'qwssions', which she gave as gifts.[69]

FIG. 74 (OPPOSITE) Hans Holbein the younger, portrait of Sir Henry Guildford (1489–1532), 1527, oil on panel. Guildford wears tissue of cloth of gold with a bold pomegranate design. A silk hanging is suspended from a rail in the background. Royal Collection, Windsor Castle.

FIG. 75 (ABOVE AND DETAIL BELOW) The king's council chamber, title page of Edward Hall, *The union of the two noble and illustre famelies of Lancastre & Yorke* (1548), engraving. The king sits under a cloth of estate, in a chamber that appears to be lined throughout with wall hangings. British Library, London, G.6004.

FIG. 76 (OPPOSITE) Queen Elizabeth I at prayer, frontispiece to *Christian prayers and meditations* (1569), hand-coloured woodcut on paper. The room is hung with rich textiles, and the queen kneels on a large tasselled cushion, set on a linen cloth that covers her prie-dieu and flows onto the floor. Lambeth Palace Library, London, 1569,9, fol. 2v.

FIG. 77 (ABOVE) Cushion, *c.*1600, England, silk satin embroidered with silk, metal thread and metal strip. Each heart-shaped compartment contains a different plant motif – including borage, marigold, lily, bluebell, columbine and pansy; that they can easily be identified testifies to the common use of botanical books as models for embroidery designs. Victoria and Albert Museum, London, T.21-1923.

It seems that, in all things, textiles provided comfort and a bit of luxury. They are found on even the least glamorous items of the privy apartments. The inventory of Wolsey's possessions, taken in January 1530, included thirteen 'close stools' – that is, toilets – 'covered with scarlet and black velvet' (fig. 78).[70] The word 'scarlet' in this description might be refer to the colour of the 'velvet', but might alternatively refer to the fine woollen cloth, known as 'scarlet' since the Middle Ages.[71]

Many other items at court were decorated with textiles or were made from luxury textiles. Books, in particular, were covered or wrapped in luxurious silks and velvets and often embroidered (fig. 79). A surviving book binding of purple velvet features the applied motifs of the royal arms and Tudor roses, worked in silver-gilt thread, silks and pearls; it represents typically costly and elaborate work (fig. 80). Other items were decorated, too, revealing the private pursuits and pastimes of the Tudors. Tennis rackets featured embroidered handles, flutes and recorders were kept in velvet cases, as were quivers for arrows, one being described as being of green velvet 'enbrodred over with gold and the kynges armes with one bowe'.[72]

Within the 1547 Inventory of Henry's possessions, small items that make up a sewing kit are recorded, including threads, needles, scissors, thimbles and loose seed pearls.[73] These were not the stocks of the Wardrobe staff, but itemised royal possessions. Samplers too are recorded in the inventory, and are evidence of the training in embroidery skills that royal and noble women learned and practised as a genteel pastime at court.[74] Could they have belonged to one of Henry's wives or daughters, kept by him for sentimental reasons, or maybe forgotten about amid other items? Some items were kept in prominent places, suggesting an emotional attachment. For example, small boxes containing an infant's gold-fringed taffeta swaddling band, and other small children's clothes, were itemised in Henry's private study, next to his bedchamber at Whitehall Palace.[75] We cannot know by whom these items were worn. One might assume that they belonged to his yearned-for son and heir, Edward, but – as well as Mary, Elizabeth and Edward – Henry fathered an illegitimate son, Henry Fitzroy, and a son by Katherine of Aragon who died in early infancy.[76] How different Henry's reign would have been if that first son, Henry, Duke of Cornwall, had not died in February 1511 at less than two months old.

* * *

The textiles of the privy chambers occupied relatively small spaces and were seen by a limited audience; yet, strangely, this increased their importance. Proximity to the monarch was a matter of prestige, and the décor of the privy chambers reflected this. These chambers contained some of the most luxurious textiles at court, particularly those that were considered symbolic of the majesty of royalty, such as a cloth of estate and bed furnishings. Hidden, too, in some of the descriptions of the textiles of the privy chambers may be indicators of personal taste or biography. Fashionable motifs, for example, recur with tantalising frequency in some private locations, suggesting a preference for particular styles. What is clear, however, is that standing in attendance in the privy chambers of a Tudor palace, one would have been surrounded by the most costly fabrics and ornate embroidery. That these textiles were seen only by a select few was a daily reminder that the monarch's power and wealth knew no bounds and was beyond anything the average Tudor subject could imagine.

FIG. 78 (OPPOSITE) William III's close stool, late 17th century, wood, metal and velvet. Although this commode, upholstered in red velvet, dates from a hundred years after the Tudor period, it may be assumed to resemble those listed in Wolsey's inventory of 1530. Hampton Court Palace, RCIN 1039.

FIG. 79 (BELOW, LEFT) Henry VIII reading in his bedchamber, c.1540, manuscript painting, from Henry VIII's psalter, commissioned for his own use and still bound in its original red velvet. In the background, his bed is furnished with a blue hanging fringed and tasselled with gold. Other images in the psalter depict Henry as the biblical King David, one with Goliath, and another playing David's harp. British Library, London, Royal MS 2 A XVI, fol. 3.

FIG. 80 (BELOW, RIGHT) The armorial binding of Martin de Brion's description of the Holy Land, c.1540, purple velvet embroidered with silk and metal thread and pearls. The manuscript is dedicated to Henry VIII, and the embroidered binding shows his arms, the motto and device of the Order of the Garter with the initial 'H' to either side, and Tudor roses in the corners. British Library, London, Royal MS 20 A IV.

Bow

Olde baily

Black fryers

lud gat

Poles church

Carter lane

Knight Ryder streat

Watlinge streat

Maidenhed lane

Pissingla: Basing la:

S. Andrewes hyll

The wardrop

S. Peter hyll

Lambert hyll

S. Peter

S. Mary Somerset

Tames streate

Breadstreat

Hugbin lane

Black F

Baynardes Castel

Poles Wharfe

Boss alley

Trygdane

Broken Wharfe

Querenbyth

The Banck

The bolle bayting

4 THE GREAT WARDROBE

The Administration of Royal Textiles

The Great Wardrobe of Robes and Beds was a department of the royal household under the authority of the Privy Chamber.[1] It included three sub-departments: the Removing Wardrobe of Beds (responsible also for cushions, carpets and tapestries), the Stable and the Wardrobe of Robes.[2] The Great Wardrobe was often referred to simply as 'the Wardrobe'. It was the department that ordered, paid for, managed and maintained the stocks of cloth, dress and furnishings for the royal family and the court, with a hierarchy of officers and procedures. Since 1360, its main store had been located in the parish of St Andrew in the City of London, just to the north of Puddle Wharf (fig. 81). It was here that the artisans and craftsmen of the Wardrobe were based, serving the monarch and the court. The Wardrobe of the Queens Consort was a dedicated subsidiary store, at Baynard's Castle, on the river just to the south of the main premises. Baynard's Castle had been the London residence of the house of York, but was refurbished by Henry VII in 1500. Both sites were completely destroyed in the Great Fire of London in 1666.

There were also permanent stores for the Wardrobe's holdings at the Tower of London, Whitehall Palace (Westminster) and other royal residences, including Somerset Place.[3] The Wardrobe Tower at the Tower of London is now a ruin, but a visitor in 1598 recorded seeing 'above one hundred pieces of arras [. . .] made of gold, silver and silk [. . .] and immense quantity of bed furniture [. . .] some of them most richly ornamented with pearl'.[4] There were also the Removing Wardrobes, or rooms in each palace to which the coffers of clothes and furnishings could be delivered as the court moved from one location to another.

At the time of Henry VIII's death in 1547, the value of the stocks of silks and cloths of gold alone came to £33,000. This represented a fortune.[5] Today it would be worth over £9 million, and at the time the sum would have bought 7,000 horses or paid the daily wage of over a million skilled craftsmen.[6]

FIG. 81 A section of the map of London by Ralph Agas, printed in 1561 from woodblocks. It shows the area around the Great Wardrobe (which consists of the buildings labelled 'The wardrop' at the top of 'S. Andrewes hyll'). Baynard's Castle, the Wardrobe of the Tudor queens consort, can be seen on the river; to its left is Puddle Wharf. London Metropolitan Archives.

Merchants affiliated with specific craft guilds were the main conduits of luxury items to the court.[7] Indeed, sometimes the boundaries blurred between guildsmen and courtiers. Richard Gibson (1480–1534), a Merchant Taylor of London and sometime master of the company, was also, for more than thirty-three years, an official of the royal household. He rose to become a sergeant-at-arms, in direct attendance upon the king, and throughout his career provided the court with textiles and garments for the tents and revels, including textiles for the Field of Cloth of Gold.[8] He held the office of yeoman of the revels (1510–34) and first yeoman, then sergeant, of the tents (1513–34).[9] The accounts of the revels show that he procured fabrics from London merchants as required, in addition to receiving quantities from the Wardrobe.[10]

English merchants often acquired imported silks from Italian merchants. The records of the London-based Italian company of Giovanni Cavalcanti and Pierfrancesco de' Bardi show that they sold to English merchants, who in turn provided cloth to the court.[11] The Italians mainly supplied the finest silks and cloths of gold from Florence.[12] They regularly supplied 'Gianni Aparker' (John Parker, a yeoman of the king's robes), 'Riccardo Gressam' (Richard Gresham, merchant) and 'Guglielmo Lok' (William Lock, merchant).[13] Records from the privy purse expenses of the early 1530s show several payments to these men.[14] Cavalcanti and Bardi also regularly supplied cloth directly to the royal court themselves. In April 1522, 'Jean' (Giovanni) Cavalcanti was granted 'licence to import cloths of gold, silver and damask, gold cloths of "tynsyn saten" with gold, and all other cloths wrought with gold. The King to have the first choice. A copy of this licence, signed by the duke of Norfolk, treasurer, to be a sufficient warrant'.[15] The king's right to a 'first choice' of luxury fabrics was a well-established tradition and ensured that the monarch was most fashionably and finely furnished. Ideally, the merchant would present the goods to the king or queen in person, for which purpose merchants like Cavalcanti were allocated the privileged title of 'gentlemen usher'.[16] A successful audience was afterwards followed up by a meeting with the officers of the Wardrobe, with whom measurements and payment could be exchanged and recorded.[17]

An audience with the monarch or a member of the royal family could not always be secured, and the frequent movements of the court often complicated the process. Merchants had to carry bulky wares to different palaces. An entry in the records of the Cavalcanti and Bardi company shows that in 1529, in the course of one sale, one of the company's agents, Anthony Carsidoni, was summoned to Greenwich, then several times to Westminster, and then again to Hampton Court, where the fabrics were taken by barge. Henry Norris, groom of the stool, received the cases and took the goods to the king's chamber. It seems that Carsidoni did not present his wares in person, but instead waited five days for the king to make his choice. Only then did he collect the goods that were not required and receive payment for those that were. Expenses incurred for travel and lodgings were charged back to the manufacturers of the goods.[18]

Sometimes a loss-leader was deemed expedient. When Cardinal Wolsey asked Sebastiano Giustiniani, the Venetian ambassador in London, if he might be able to secure around sixty Damascene carpets for him, the ambassador wrote to the Venetian Senate that it might be worth offering the carpets as a gift, to secure Wolsey's goodwill and future trade, 'by reason of the supreme authority and favour enjoyed by him with the King of England'. They were duly sent, via Antwerp.[19]

For the privilege of these licences, the king was clearly allowed to run up significant debts for payment. Among a collection of loose papers in Thomas Cromwell's hand, is a note to remember the king's debts to the merchants 'Master Gresham' and 'Antony Bonvyxye' (Bonvisi).[20] The debts may have been incurred by Cromwell himself on the king's behalf. Wolsey, for example, is known to have managed purchases and credit for the king. Following Wolsey's death, Cavalcanti and Bardi petitioned the king for payment for '2 pieces of cloth of gold [. . .] 2 pieces of crimson silk camlet [. . .] 311 yards rich cloth of gold for the church, of divers colours, and 195 yards of a coarser cloth of gold'.[21] The total came to over £1,000. Cavalcanti's agent stated that Wolsey had promised to appeal to 'the King for payment; and undertook that if the King would not pay it, he would do it himself'.

It seems that credit ran both ways in some instances. One Avery Rawson, a mercer of London, was a merchant to Cardinal Wolsey.[22] He had sold him eighty-five coverlets

FIG. 82 Seal burse (or bag) for the Great Seal of England, 1596–1603, velvet and satin embroidered with silver and gold thread. Sir Thomas Egerton was appointed Keeper of the Great Seal on 6 May 1596; he gave this burse to his servant Henry Jones, whose family transformed it into a cushion cover. Such repurposing of textiles was common during the Tudor period. British Museum, London, 1997,0301.1.

of Norfolk wool, as listed in the 1530 inventory of Wolsey's possessions.[23] It seems, however, that he had not met all his obligations to the cardinal, and Thomas Heneage (c.1480–1553), later a gentleman of the Privy Chamber but at that time a servant of Wolsey's, confiscated the beams, scales and weights necessary for Rawson's business, while Rawson himself fled the city and sought sanctuary.[24]

It is likely that the monarch was personally involved in certain commissions or orders. A 'to-do' list drawn up by Cromwell in October 1533 included writing indictments for treason and a reminder 'to show the king the patterns for the embroidery for the Queen'.[25] Also, as we have seen in earlier chapters, Henry VIII had a personal interest in the narrative content of his tapestries, and the sheer cost of the exercise probably necessitated his involvement and sign-off. The King's Book of Payments for 1517 records a payment to 'Peter van Enghien' (that is, Pieter van Aelst of Enghien) by the Earl of Worcester, Henry's lord chamberlain.[26] The payment is for close to £1,500, the equivalent cost of over a thousand horses or fifty thousand days' wages for a skilled craftsman (some 136 years' worth of time).[27] When he was personally interested,

Henry would initiate orders himself. On 23 August 1520, the king sent for Richard Gibson, and ordered letters written to William Botre, mercer, for 'the provision of silks and other stuffs' for the revels on 3 September.[28]

The intrinsic value of textiles and the resources and time required to create something of worth, meant that they were often handed down and repurposed, even among the wealthy elite (fig. 82). As extravagant as Henry VIII was, even he was not beyond repurposing some items. The value of gold and silver in textiles, for example, was carefully measured. Entries itemising goods in the care of the clerk of the Stable for 1519 show that some horse harnesses and trappers embroidered with 'goldsmiths' work' were delivered 'by the King's orders to George Senesco and John Burton, gold-wire drawers' for the removal and re-use of the metal thread.[29] Other embroidered motifs, such as 'the lion of England [...] with crowns imperial, clouds and suns [...] with several others' were sent to Richard Gibson, 'to rip and put upon russet and white'.[30]

Wolsey acquired a significant number of textiles from former clerics. For example, he purchased a number of hangings from the 'executors of my lord Durham' (Thomas Ruthall, Bishop of Durham (d. 1523)), 'containing the triumphs of Time, Death, Chastity, Eternity, Cupid and Venus and Renown or Julyus Cisar [...] Some of these served for the hangings of Durham Hall'.[31] A fall from the king's favour and any subsequent act of attainder were also useful sources of acquisition.[32] Wolsey's own fall resulted in Henry's receipt of all his possessions and property. Similarly, the dissolution of the monasteries from 1536 provided further opportunities. Thomas Cromwell's officers were instructed to seize any suitable tapestries for the king's use. Indeed, when Cromwell was imprisoned in 1540, his own tapestries were seized for the king.[33] His goods were distributed to members of Henry's inner circle at Hampton Court the day *before* his execution.[34]

Peter Heylyn's *Ecclesia restaurata; or The history of the reformation* (1661), stated that

> many private men's parlours were hung with altar cloth, their tables and beds covered with copes [...] it was a sorry house and not worth the naming which had not somewhat of this furniture in it, although it were only a fair large cushion made of a cope or altar cloth.[35]

The inventories of Mary, Queen of Scots, made in December 1562, detailed ten items of ecclesiastical vestments, including copes and chasubles. The Bishop of Aberdeen had given them to George Gordon, Earl of Huntly (1514–1562), for safekeeping in 1559, so as to avoid the general destruction of Catholic property and materials following the Protestant Reformation. After the earl's defeat at the Battle of Corrichie in October 1562, they had been seized and taken to Holyrood. A later note in the margin adds that in March 1567 Mary used the 'fairest' of these to make a cape for herself and to 'make a bed for the king', her infant son, James (1566–1625). The vestments were 'all of claith of golde', three figured with red, and the rest with white and yellow.[36]

Elizabeth, in particular, was obliged to repurpose textiles much more judiciously than her father, mainly because his profligate spending had depleted the treasury. Elizabeth had to maintain the appearance of magnificence with fewer resources, and the records of the Wardrobe show that her clothing was frequently altered. From September 1587 to March 1588, William Jones, her tailor, altered forty of her gowns.[37] The queen also made it clear that she liked to receive gifts of jewels, cloth and clothing at new year, rather than the plate and money favoured by her father and half-siblings.[38] Such gifts were an important source of new acquisitions for Elizabeth: in 1562, for example, she received bolts of linen, pieces of fine cambric, a needlework carpet with gold and silk, embroidered cushions, handkerchiefs, and from her gentlewoman, Blanche Parry, 'a square pece of unshorne vellat [velvet] edged with siluer lase'.[39] Fewer major acquisitions of tapestry were made under Elizabeth, and the decorative scheme – particularly of Hampton Court, as we have seen – stayed very much as it had been in Henry's time. The Paradise Chamber (see p. 77), which featured Henrician tapestries, embroidered carpet and cloth of estate, was, however, also adorned with silk hangings, reputedly given to the queen as a gift by her favourite, Robert Dudley.[40]

MANAGEMENT OF THE STOCKS

It was the duty of the keeper of the Wardrobe to maintain thorough records and accounts. Sir Andrew Windsor (1467–1543; keeper from around 1504/5 until his death) kept a yearly record of all the warrants, deliveries, payments to officers of the Wardrobe and expenses, and the full details of the quantity and price of 'stuff delivered', together with the names of the merchants who supplied it all.[41] ('Stuff' was a general term for woven textiles.)

Nicholas Bristowe (1494–1584),[42] clerk of the Wardrobe under Sir Anthony Denny (1501–1549), keeper of the Palace of Westminster, recorded the following twelve-point system for the delivery of silk in 1538, entitled 'An order to be taken, by Mr Denny touching his business at Westminster devised by Bristowe':

1. No silks to be delivered without Bristowe's presence. 2. The clerk to note whether silks thus delivered are of the old store or of the new. 3. Silks must be marked with the contents and the name of the person from whom bought. 4. At the delivery of silks a clerk must write the name of the person to whom delivered, to what use, and of what piece, upon the bills of content and in the book of silks with Mr. Denny, and a copy to be given to Bristowe. 5. The price of silks bought by the King must be put upon the labels. 6. Bills for money brought in by any persons must be comptrolled to Bristowe. 7. Such bills are not to be paid without Bristowe's presence, and he is to enter them in the journal book. 8. All manner of warrants are to be made by Bristowe. 9. Immediately upon the receipt of a bill he must make a remembrance of it and in what title he is discharged. 10. That no stuff be delivered by Hewetson, Mrs. Vaughan, Mr. Lok, or any other which ought to be allowed by Mr. Denny without a bill signed by Denny or his deputy, which the clerk is to enter in his book of remembrance. 11. The clerk is to have a receipt for all money delivered to his master's use. 12. No man shall have a key to the clerk's study except his master or his deputy.[43]

The above points make clear that security and accountability were of utmost importance in the maintenance of the valuable Tudor stocks of silk. Point 10 indicates that even (or perhaps especially) those mercers and artificers well known to the court required the correct entry records. 'Mrs. Vaughan' probably refers to the queen's silk woman, Margery (or Margaret) Vaughan, first wife of merchant and royal agent Stephen Vaughan (d. 1549).[44] The role of silk woman was to make ribbons, braids and trimmings, in addition to some laundering and

starching of items of linen. This was one of the only trades in which a woman might transact business independently, with the legal right to take apprentices.[45] William Hewetson and William Lock were well known mercers.[46] Hewetson is described as one of the 'chief tradesmen who supplied velvet and other materials for the Wardrobe'.[47] Lock (1480–1550) had endeared himself to the king by tearing down the pope's bull of excommunication against Henry while in Dunkirk in 1533, for which he was made a gentleman of the Privy Chamber and won an annual pension of £100.[48]

Bristowe took receipt of regular orders, such as linen for tablecloths and napkins, exported into England from the Low Countries by the loom piece. An inventory taken in 1542 records a parcel of loom pieces, with annotations in the margin, duly signed by 'N. Bristowe'; in one case he notes that a certain 'towel [9 metres long] [. . .] is cut by the kings comaundment to make three towels'.[49]

The upkeep of the table linen, particularly that which graced the king's own table, was managed closely and was under the supervision of the Ewery.[50] An order drawn up by Sir John Gage, knight comptroller of the household, and other officers of the Green Cloth (those responsible for administering the finances of the royal household),[51] dated 'the 18th Day of January 1543', detailed the washing and 'cleane keeping of the Napery' (fig. 83) by one Anne Harris, the king's laundress. It outlined her responsibilities for maintaining the king's napery, all of 'fine Diaper [and . . .] Damascue worke'. Her stock totalled 'four great pieces, 28 long Breakfast-clothes, 28 short ones of 3 yards the peice, 28 Hand towels, and 12 dozen of Napkins to be by her sasht [folded] and sweet kept'. She was required to 'dayly deliver as much [. . .] as shall be necessary to serve the King's Majesty withal', to the sergeant or yeoman of the 'king's mouth' of the Ewery. The rest was to remain with her 'to be kept sweet'.[52] Anne was also to collect any used napkins and towels for washing, and if any were too badly worn, she should approach the 'Officers of the Compting house' to renew her stocks. She was provided with '2 Standard-Chestes [. . .] for the keeping of the said Diaper, the one to keep the cleane stuff, and th'other to keep the stuff that hath been occupied'. She was, however, to provide her own 'sweet Powder, sweet Herbes, and other sweet things [. . .] for the sweet keeping of the said stuff'. Initially she was paid £10 a year. However, recorded on the same page of the order of 1543, but a couple of years later, and following a dispute with the knight comptroller, the officers of the Green Cloth 'granted unto the said Anne Harris' an annual sum of £20 and 8 ells of canvas for bags. It seems that Anne Harris had fought for, and won, a massive increase in her salary and supplies.[53]

The sergeant of the Ewery was able to claim for himself the 'tableclothes, napkings and cupboard cloths [...] when they are dampened and unfit for [...] use any more'.[54] These perquisites were not an isolated case. During her husband's tenure as governor of Calais, Lady Lisle (c.1493–1566), wrote to her agent, the merchant John Husee (d. 1548), enquiring if he could procure old arras and carpets from the Great Wardrobe for her. (Her husband, Arthur Plantagenet, Viscount Lisle (d. 1542), was the illegitimate son of Edward IV and therefore uncle to King Henry, and perhaps she felt that regal splendour was appropriate for his household. Certainly, it was not her only attempt to secure things from the Wardrobe.)[55] Husee wrote back that she should not hope for success in this, as the Wardrobe was not reviewed often – 'not once in 30 years' – and even then 'the Lord Chamberlain and the head officers have the best stuff, and the worst remain for the mean and inferior officers'.[56]

As with napery, we know that tapestry underwent maintenance as required. Accounts show that 'old hangings of counterfeit arras and tapestry [...] were shorn and new dressed on the wrong side' – that is, lined with buckram – 'and made meet for the hall in Hampton Court'.[57] In 1502, the Fleming Cornelius van de Strete (d. 1509) was appointed 'royal arras-maker' to Henry VII, which was a new position, in line with Henry's interest in tapestry.[58] Van de Strete was a skilled weaver but did not weave new sets; rather, he repaired existing pieces, or made minor additions such as badges or borders.[59] (Flemish weaver–merchants such as Pasquier Grenier, and thereafter Pieter van Aelst, were appointed actually to provide the tapestries.) Following van de Strete's death, his former deputy, one 'John Mustyng' (Jan Mostnick) was appointed as 'chief arras-maker to the King', with an annual salary of £10.[60] The same grant shows that he had previously been in the employ of the king's late grandmother, Margaret Beaufort. Mostnick hailed from Enghien, the same Low Countries centre of tapestry production as Pieter van Aelst,[61] by which might be

inferred that he possessed considerable skill; but it is likely that Mostnick, like van de Strete before him, was tasked with the repair and upkeep of the tapestry stock rather than with much, if any, new weaving.

A priority for modern conservation specialists is mitigating the amount of harmful ultraviolet light that historic textiles are exposed to, as it fades colours and degrades the structure of the fabric. One might think that this was a recent concern, but Tudor correspondence shows that people of that period were fully aware of the damaging effects of light. Sir Thomas Cecil (1542–1623), Lord Burghley's eldest son, wrote to his father in September 1578 about whether to opt for a decorative plaster ceiling or textile hangings in the new Burghley House, still under construction. He wrote that, in his opinion, 'it were better to ceil it with a fair ceiling, because hangings are so costly [...] and besides, the place itself is subject much to sun and air, which will quickly make them fade'.[62] This demonstrates that not only was the cost of textiles higher than more permanent architectural décor, but also that the resource required to keep them looking at their best or the ability to buy replacement hangings at various intervals was a serious consideration. It suggests that the ability to support the care and upkeep of textiles was as much a sign of wealth and prestige as the textiles themselves.

Similarly, as with modern dress and textile stores, damp and pests were a worry. All the stores were regularly checked for damp, mould, pests and vermin. A yeoman would regularly air and beat the textiles to guard against mildew, dust and insects, and fires would be lit in the stores to fight the damp.[63] Textiles were also carefully wrapped in linen or canvas bags before being stored in chests or shelved cupboards.[64] In 1547, thirty-nine canvas bags, in which to 'putte fine arras', were listed at the Wardrobe Tower.[65] Arras was probably brushed to keep it clean. There are also references to a technique which – though not identified – was clearly effective. A grant issued to James Burton and Segar Drase, 'scowrers of Arras', in January 1585, specified that they had 'of late invented and devised a new kinde of making cleene of

FIG. 83 Napkin, 1520s, Flanders, linen damask woven with the royal arms of Henry VIII. Victoria and Albert Museum, London, 169-1869.

hangings and carpets much fayrer than heretofore hath bynne donne by any other'. This impressive new technique won them the sole right to clean the queen's arras, other tapestries and 'Turkey worke' carpets, on a handsome retainer for at least twelve years. The grant required all officers of the realm to aid them or incur the queen's 'highe displeasure'.[66]

PREPARATION AND TRANSPORTATION: THE LOGISTICS

For his coronation in 1485, Henry VII paid ten men for 'hangyng of arras at Westm'.[67] Another group of men were also paid for hanging arras, indicating that various areas of the palace, the abbey or surrounds were lavishly decorated: 'item, to iiii men by iiii dayes, at the coronacon and after, for hangyng and taking down of the kings arras'.[68] These items comprised payment to cover the expenses of one 'Piers of Wraton', who had also paid for hooks, hammers, 'bote hire frome Westm[inster] to the warderobe at diverse tymes', and 'for the wges of iii men by vi dayes to watche & attende upon the stuff of the warderobe'.[69] Piers Wraton had served as yeoman of the beds to Edward IV, and his experience was evidently being put to good use by the new king.[70]

When it came to arrangements for the many rituals and ceremonies of court, the duties of the Wardrobe officers were ordained in advance. A 'Book of Ceremonies' specified that 'the night before Ashwednesday, after the king has departed, the gentilman ussher shall comaunde the yeoman ussher [. . .] to give warning to the wardrobe of the beddes to change the cloth of estate, the chairs, the cushions that be in the kynges dyninge chamber on Ashwednesdaie in the morning. And that all thinges be pressed and ready in tyme'.[71] This particular directive was for the décor of the king's privy dining chamber, but the preparations extended around the court, and particularly to the chapel royal. It was, for example, directed that on Ash Wednesday (the first day of Lent), the yeoman usher should make sure that the ceremonial textiles were blue. He should prepare 'the chapels with a carpet and a blew coshion for the kinge to kneale upon when he shall come thether'. The chain of instruction was complicated: the gentleman usher was to command a yeoman usher to warn the sergeant of the vestry, or the dean of the chapel, and the clerk of the closet 'to make ready the chappell, church or abbey where ever the king shall fortune to be

that daie'. The gentleman usher also had to prepare a stool and a cushion to be ready for the king while he listened to the sermon.[72]

For other, less ritualised events, such as diplomatic meetings, there was an imperative to demonstrate magnificence, and a small army was quickly put to work. In October 1518, Cardinal Wolsey entertained the French ambassadors at Hampton Court, following the reading of the articles of the Treaty of London. The entertainments were lavish, and Wolsey's gentleman usher, George Cavendish, detailed the preparations involved. Once the reading was complete, Wolsey summoned all his chief officers – the stewards, treasurers, clerks and comptrollers – and having made known

> his Pleasure, to accomplish his Command, they sent out all the Carriers, Purveyors and other Persons to my Lord's Friends to prepare [. . .] The Yeomen and Grooms of his Wardrobe were busied in hanging the Chambers with costly Hangings, and furnishing the same with Beds of Silk and other Furniture for the same in every degree. Then my Lord sent me, being his Gentleman-usher, and two other of my Fellows to foresee all things touching our Rooms to be richly garnish'd.[73]

Cavendish's duties to supervise the 'garnishing' of the chambers with costly textiles and furnishings were clearly not light, and one can almost imagine his tired feet as he wrote, 'our Pains were not small; but daily we travell'd up and down from Chamber to Chamber to see things fitted [. . .] There were also provided 280 Beds, with all manner of Furniture to them, too long here to be related'.[74]

When Henry VIII met with Charles V in July 1520, a list of 'remembrances' was drawn up to itemise all that had to be done. Richard Gibson, sergeant of the king's tents, was to erect a pavilion. The lord chamberlain was to 'appoint officers of the wardrobe to furnish the lodgings [. . .] with apparel [. . .] The garnishing of the cupboards with plate is assigned to Sir Henry Wyat', and provision was also made for 'torches [. . .] fruit, wafers, hippocras, and other [dainties]'.[75] Similarly, when Elizabeth I heard disputations in St Mary's Church, Cambridge, in 1564, her own servants equipped the space within: 'In the east end was made a spacious and high room for the Queen's Majestie, which was, by her own servants, richly hanged with arras and cloth of state, and all other necessaries, with a cushion to lean upon.'[76]

The officers of the Wardrobe were not only practised at managing the setting up of chambers, ceremonies and pageants, they also had to be equipped to transport the necessary textiles from palace to palace or to different locations on progress – a logistical feat in itself. Textiles were eminently transportable. They could be rolled, cased and carted, and could easily be hung in new surroundings. The frontispiece to the Duke of Montmorency's translation of Cicero's 'Four Orations' (1531–3), shows the French duke surrounded by his courtiers in front of a display of gold and silver plate and millefleurs tapestries (see fig. 3). The tapestries hang on wall-mounted hooks, demonstrating both their portability and the logistics of how they were hung.[77]

Medieval courts had always travelled, but the peregrinations of Henry VIII and Francis I were accomplished at a speed and involved a complexity of organisation not previously seen.[78] The Venetian ambassador to the French court, Mariano Giustiniani, complained that 'during the forty-five months of my embassy, I was almost always travelling [. . .] Never [. . .] did the court remain a whole fortnight at the same place.'[79] Giustiniani complained that the constant travelling was a financial burden for 'even the richest of the nobility'.

This burden can be seen clearly in the household accounts of Robert Dudley, Earl of Leicester. Dudley was one of the wealthiest men at the Elizabethan court and his apartments were of high status, being close to the queen's, though their exact location is unknown. This meant that he required a lot of appropriately luxurious furnishings, worthy of his position; these would have included his clothing, tapestries, hangings, carpets, bed furnishings and furniture.[80] When the court moved from Hampton Court to St James's Palace in November 1584, Dudley needed eight men to spend two days moving his goods in nine carts.[81] It took a further two days to set up his rooms.[82] He also had to accommodate his retinue. During 1560, he paid for the lodgings around Hampton Court of four gentlemen and eight yeomen for seven weeks.[83]

Moving the court itself was an altogether larger affair. Around three hundred carts were required to move the monarch's goods and furnishings from one location to

another, as frequently as every fortnight (fig. 84).[84] In addition, significant numbers of canvas covers, bags and leather-bound wooden coffers were required to make sure that the household goods could be transported efficiently and safely. The 1530 inventory of Thomas Wolsey's possessions lists a number of these, including '8 leather cases for trussing beds [. . .] 11 cart canvases [. . .] 4 chests at Hampton Court and 10 at Westminster'.[85] Officers of the Wardrobe would ride ahead of the monarch and his or her courtiers to make sure that the lodgings were suitably furnished, travelling with the covered carts and a full inventory, which was checked upon arrival. The expense accounts of August 1576 for Anthony Wingfield (d. 1593), yeoman usher to the queen, show that he paid:

> The allowance of himself [. . .] three yeomen of the chamber, two grooms of the chamber, two grooms of the wardrobe, and one groom porter for making ready for her Majesty at Mr Althams by the space of eight days. To Ralph Hope, yeoman of the robes, for the charges of himself his man and horses in riding before to make ready the office of the robes in the time of the progress.[86]

In addition to moving the household from one palace to the next, the peripatetic nature of the court sometimes required more temporary accommodation. The Office of the Tents organised the provision of tents, pavilions and timber lodgings, managed by a sergeant who was assisted by a yeoman and groom. In the 1540s the office became more structured – the old monastic site of Charterhouse became a store for the tents, and in 1545 Sir Thomas Cawarden (d. 1559), already master of the revels, became 'Master of the King's pavilions, hales and tents'.[87] Nicholas Bristowe acted as clerk to the Office of the Tents and oversaw preparations for the visit of Claude d'Annebault (1495–1552), Marshal and Admiral of France, sent to England to sign a peace treaty. Bristowe organised the transfer of tents from London to Hampton Court, overseeing their setting up and duly compiling his accounts and inventories.[88] This makes it clear that tents were used not only for events held at a distance from the available accommodation of the court, but also to augment court spaces. Given the status of the visitor and the occasion, this must have been a way to ensure some

FIG. 84 Antoine Caron (1521–1599), drawing of the Château d'Anet, 1565–74, pen and ink. This depiction of a royal procession gives a sense of a court on the move, with an enormous convoy of carts and horses, along with tents for storage and cooking. Musée du Louvre, Paris, RF30624.

spectacle and pomp. It was recorded that 'great preparation is made for him at Hampton Court'.[89]

Very occasionally, the careful preparations and plans of the officers were thwarted by the wish of the monarch. In the summer of 1599, George Carey (1547–1603), then lord chamberlain of the royal household, wrote to Robert Cecil to say that the queen 'stands stiffly to her determined removing on Monday next, and will go more privately than is fitting'. Her lodgings at Hampton Court were not ready and so provisional arrangements were put in place. Lady Scudamore's lodgings acted as the queen's presence chamber, while Mrs Radcliffe's acted as her privy chamber, meaning that Carey had to lodge in the chambers he had appointed for Cecil.[90]

* * *

The logistics of procuring, storing and moving textiles at the Tudor court were complicated and impressively efficient. The merchants who imported and sold the textiles were prominent and influential, but equally important were the (often) unsung officials of the Great Wardrobe, who were pivotal to the ordered running of the royal household. They maintained efficient procedures for recording the entry and exit of their stocks, and managed the collection in their care, making sure that it was kept secure and in good condition. They organised the movement and distribution of the appropriate textiles to the allotted chambers at the correct time – a logistical feat that might also involve co-ordinating the timely transportation of dozens of carts and caskets from one palace to another.

Present-day collections managers and conservators, who monitor and preserve the objects at Hampton Court Palace, now carry out many of the duties of the Great Wardrobe, albeit with modern techniques and to modern standards. But Tudor officials were subject to an ultimate authority that was not always predictable, for their best-laid plans were always, and inevitably, subject to the notorious whims of the Tudor monarchs themselves.

5 TUDOR TEXTILES

Materials and Techniques

The preceding chapters have explored the role of textiles at the Tudor royal court, and their place in the visual and social culture and the value system of the people who inhabited the palaces (and the temporary structures) in which textiles were kept and displayed. This chapter takes a different approach, by summarising the fundamental materials and techniques involved in the making of textiles in this period. The first part of the chapter explores how raw materials such as fleece, flax, silkmoth cocoons and precious metals were transformed into yarns and thread, to be woven into cloth or used to embellish it, and how vegetable and animal ingredients were used for dyes. The second part of the chapter turns to the contextual history of the trades involved in creating textiles, and the processes and techniques used in their manufacture; it briefly covers weaving – including cloth of gold, carpets, tapestry, napery (linen) and lace – and surveys the important decorative art of embroidery.

FIG. 85 Pieter Bruegel the Elder (1526/30–1569), *Die niederländische Sprichwörter* ('The Dutch proverbs'), 1559, oil on panel, detail. Amid the bustle of a busy market square, a spinster sits spinning with a distaff between her knees and a spindle and whorl in her right hand. Gemäldegalerie, Staatliche Museen, Berlin.

MATERIALS

WOOL

Wool was Tudor England's primary export, and was vital to the fortunes and finances of the crown. The later medieval and the early Tudor court made heavy use of English broadcloth for dress and furnishings. In the fourteenth and fifteenth centuries, English kings wore formal robes of scarlet, a high-quality woollen cloth often imported from the Low Countries. As the Tudor period progressed, however, silk displaced scarlet as the mark of fashionable dress, though Henry VIII continued to wear wool for hunting.[1] Similarly, tapestries of wool alone came to be considered of relatively low status, even though the cost was still beyond the reach of most people; tapestries were more highly valued (and more expensive) when augmented with silk and metal threads. Wool was, however, still useful for covering very large surface areas, as evidenced by the Berkeley Castle hanging (see p. 148).

Much of England's land was devoted to the rearing of sheep and the production of wool, along with the rural culture that revolved around these activities.[2] The process of producing finished cloth from fleece involved different

FIG. 86 Beating and combing wool. Isaac Claesz van Swanenburg (1537–1614), *Het ploten en kammen*, 1594–6, oil on panel. In the foreground the shearers are cutting the wool from sheepskin (though fleece was often shorn from live flocks, too); behind, the fleeces are being beaten, and, to the left, the men are using carders to comb the fibres. Museum De Lakenhal, Leiden.

stages, many of which became specialised professions. *The young man's looking-glass*, a mid-seventeenth-century poem by Richard Watts, lists some of them: the parter (who 'culled' the finer from the coarser wool), dyer, oiler, mixer, carder (who combed the fleece to separate the fibres), spinster (who spun the yarn), weaver, brayer (who scoured the cloth to remove dirt), burler (who picked out knots), fuller (who trampled or beat the cloth to knit the weave more tightly together), rower (who raised the nap of the cloth), shearman (who cut the nap for a smooth finish), and drawer (who mended the holes in the cloth).[3]

The Tudor spinster (or 'spinner' if a man, though traditionally spinning was a woman's preserve) spun by hand, using a spindle, weighted by a 'whorl', and a distaff; an alternative mechanised method involved a great wheel, known as a 'walking wheel', at which she might walk 30 miles a day.[4] Hand-spinning produced the finest yarn. The distaff, a straight stick with prongs at the top, held the carded but unspun wool (fig. 85). The spinster teased out the wool and, using her fingers and the turning spindle (which was weighted down and given impetus in its revolutions by the whorl), she spun a thread of yarn, which she periodically wrapped around the spindle to keep it in order.[5] Spinning too fast created a weak yarn; if the spinning was too slow or irregular, the result was lumpy, thick yarn. The quality of the yarn was defined by its fineness, which was measured by the length of yarn spun from a pound weight of wool.[6] In the year 1550, over 11 million pounds of English wool were spun into yarn, for which there was a demand at home and abroad.[7]

A series of paintings from the mid-1590s, by Isaac Claesz van Swanenburg (1537–1614), illustrates the industrialised process of woollen-cloth production. The paintings are in the collection of the Museum De Lakenhal in Leiden in the Netherlands, a city to which many Flemish refugees fled to escape the religious persecution of Spanish Habsburg rule. Van Swanenburg was mayor of Leiden and clearly felt pride in the industry of his city – the paintings were commissioned to hang in the meeting room of the cloth guild.[8] They show the raw fleece being beaten or 'broken' to remove any remaining dirt and matting (fig. 86). In England the process was called 'willeying', as willow branches were often used to beat the fleece, which was then carded or combed to untangle the fibres. The fleece was spun into yarn, then woven into cloth (fig. 87). The next process,

FIG. 87 Spinning and weaving wool. Isaac Claesz van Swanenburg, *Het spinnen het schere van de ketting, en het weven*, 1594–6, oil on panel. The women spin fleece into yarn with the help of spinning wheels; behind (*left*), a weaver sits at his loom. Museum De Lakenhal, Leiden.

FIG. 88 Fulling and dyeing the wool. Isaac Claesz van Swanenburg, *Het vollen en verven*, 1594–6, oil on panel.
In the foreground the half-naked men are fulling the cloth in large vats. The dyers are at work in the background
(*left*; see fig. 93), and in the distance the cloth is stretched into shape on tenters (wooden frames) to stop it from
warping. In the background on the right, the finished cloth is inspected and measured. Museum De Lakenhal, Leiden.

fulling (fig. 88), involved soaking the cloth in urine (the
ammonia content of which cleaned and whitened it), and
then trampling it by foot or beating it with large hammers
for about six hours to tighten up the weave. After dyeing,
the cloth was hooked up on tenters (wooden frames) to
stretch and smooth the weave. It was then inspected and
measured, to verify its quality and its dimensions for sale
(as can be seen in the top right corner of fig. 88).[9]

LINEN
Linen is made from the long fibres found in hemp, jute
and flax plants. Processing the fibres by hand was time-
consuming, but created a strong, breathable, silky cloth.
Flax was the most popular plant cultivated for linen
during the Tudor period. 'Holland' and 'lawn' were the
names given to the exceptionally fine linen worn by the
nobility and produced by the flax-growing region of

Holland and the French city of Laon. During the Tudor
period, royal linen was almost exclusively made of
Holland. Most people wore and used a much coarser
linen, made from domestically grown flax.

The flax plant was pulled from the root around
midsummer, in June or July, and placed in water for
between ten days and three weeks to break down the
outside of the plant – a process known as 'retting'. It was
then allowed to dry. The flax was beaten, outdoors or in
a large open space as it created a lot of dust; breaking the
plant open revealed long fibres that could then be combed
(fig. 89). The combs used were called 'hackles' and the
process of combing was called 'hackling'. Three-quarters
of the plant was wasted, but the waste material – the 'tow'
– was useful for lighting household fires. Thus prepared,
the long glossy fibres were ready to be spun into linen
yarn and then woven into cloth.[10]

Importantly, linen was easily laundered. It retained its shape, unlike wool, and was robust, unlike silks or embellished garments. It was therefore used for underwear, bed linen, table linen, towels and also for surplices in the royal chapel. As underwear for both men and women, in the form of shirts and shifts, it was the only item of clothing that was regularly washed, and was important in maintaining hygiene at the Tudor court.

SILK

The manufacture of silk, a lustrous, fine, soft and sumptuous fabric, was complicated; the resources required, and the result, justified silk's status as a luxury material. It was one of the most consistently traded commodities throughout the medieval and Tudor period. Historically, most silk originated in eastern Asia and was traded along the silk roads through Asia and into Eastern Europe.[11] Silk production itself moved westward along the trade routes,

with important centres established in the Black Sea region, and reaching Italy in the twelfth century.

Silk was cultivated from the cocoons of the domestic silkmoth, *Bombyx mori*. The silkworm (the larva or caterpillar of the silkmoth) feeds on mulberry leaves, and any region intent on producing silk had to have a suitable climate to maintain both the mulberry plant and the silkworm itself. A whole industry was built on processing the silkworms, partly shown in a series of engravings entitled *Vermis sericus* by the Flemish-born artist Jan van der Straet, also known as Johannes Stradanus (1523–1605). In the 1590s, van der Straet was under the patronage of the Medici in Florence, from where he collaborated with printmakers back in Antwerp, including Philip Galle (1537–1612), who published *Vermis sericus* between 1590 and 1600. Engravings survive in the collection of the British Museum, and the original preparatory drawings in the Royal Collection.[12] The engravings show the cultivation of

FIG. 89 Beating and combing flax. Detail from a tapestry, early 16th century, wool and silk, based on drawings by Bramantino (Bartolomeo Suardi, *c*.1456–1530), woven by Benedetto da Milano. Castello Sforzesco, Milan.

the silkworm. The eggs were spread out on shelves, and maintained at the right – that is, a consistently warm – temperature. 35,000 eggs weighed only an ounce. The hatched silkworm needed to be fed constantly on mulberry leaves (fig. 90).

When the silkworm cocoons itself, it does so by encasing itself in a long, continuous protein fibre (fig. 91). If left, a silkmoth emerges from the cocoon and mates, the female then laying eggs that may, in turn, become part of the silk-producing process. However, most of the cocoons are boiled, or 'cooked', before the moth emerges, so that the silk fibre remains intact and unbroken. The cooking makes extracting the raw silk fibre easier, and one of Stradanus' engravings shows fires being stoked under the heating vats. The long fibre of the cocoon is then unwound or 'reeled out' (fig. 92). It can be used without being spun, but multiple fibres can be spun together to make a stronger, more commercial, thread.[13]

FIG. 90 (ABOVE) Feeding silkworms. Preparatory drawing, pen and ink, with wash and chalk, for an engraving (reversed) in the series *Vermis sericus* by Jan van der Straet (Johannes Stradanus; 1523–1605), published by Philip Galle (n.d. [1590s]). Mulberry leaves are being gathered in large quantities and brought in to feed silkworms laid out on shelving. Royal Collection, RCIN 904764.

FIG. 91 (OPPOSITE, ABOVE) Women examining cocoons. Preparatory drawing, pen and ink, with wash and chalk, for an engraving (reversed) in the series *Vermis sericus* by Jan van der Straet (n.d. [1590s]). The silkworm cocoons itself in a long silk thread which can be 'reeled out' when boiled. Royal Collection, RCIN 904763.

FIG. 92 (OPPOSITE, BELOW) Women winding silk. Preparatory drawing, pen and ink, with wash and chalk, for an engraving (reversed) in the series *Vermis sericus* by Jan van der Straet (n.d. [1590s]). In a vaulted room, women of various ages are reeling silk from the cocoons of the silkworms; in the foreground (*left*), a crouching woman feeds the fire to heat water to 'cook' the cocoons. Royal Collection, RCIN 904766.

In medieval and Tudor England, dyeing domestic woollen cloth was possible with the use of a number of native plants. Hundreds of different hues and shades were possible by adding the right natural ingredients to a cauldron of boiling water on a fire to create a dye-bath (fig. 93). The woollen cloth – mainly dyed by the piece – was pre-treated with a mordant to fix the dye and prevent it from running or fading. Alum is a particularly effective mordant, but cream of tartar (a by-product of wine fermentation) or even tree bark could be used: for example, alder buckthorn bark, in addition to providing a strong yellow colour of its own, is a good fixative. Dyeing became a popular side-industry in areas of large-scale tree felling; in the iron industry, for example, trees were felled for the furnaces, but the bark could usefully be harvested for dyeing.[14]

Added to the dye-bath, vegetable dyes offered a variety of colours. Generally the wool cloth was left in the dye-bath for a few hours or overnight, and then rinsed before drying. However, this method did not provide consistency for large commercial batches, and the range of colours to be had from natural dyes is limited to earthy tones.[15] Many of the same ingredients used in domestic dyeing – including madder, alkanet, broom and woad – were also used for commercial dyeing in Venice, but imported ingredients and chemical compounds were added to enhance the colours, and it was their vivid hues that made Italian fabrics so coveted, and warranted the higher prices that they commanded. A book of rates from 1550 shows that satin made with 'right crimesin' grain was worth 10s. per yard, while 'couterfeite' crimson only commanded 6s. per yard.[16]

The *Plictho de larte de tentori* by Giovanventura Rosetti is a book of recipes and instructions for dyeing cloth, published in Venice in 1548.[17] The book is divided into four parts: the first two parts give recipes for dyeing wool, cotton and linen, as both yarn and cloth; the third part describes recipes for dyeing silk; and the last section deals with leather and furs. The book contains hundreds of recipes and instructions for creating dyes. Medieval and Tudor dyers generally produced dyes from mixtures of the three primary colours of blue, yellow and red. Blues came from woad (which needed fermented urine to activate the colour) and from the indigo plant; yellows from weld, buckthorn berries, alder buckthorn bark, saffron and dyer's broom; reds from a species of insects

FIG. 93 Dyeing wool. Detail from Isaac Claesz van Swanenburg, *Het vollen en verven*, 1594–6, oil on panel. The dye-bath requires constant heating and the cloth must be kept moving. The dyers work with long poles to stir the lengths of cloth in the dye solution. Museum De Lakenhal, Leiden.

called 'kermes' or 'scarlet grains', and from the root of alkanet and madder; dried elderberries yielded shades of purple;[18] and black was produced by the use of iron mordants and tannins extracted from gallnuts, sumac and other similar substances; none of Rosetti's recipes creates black by using the three primary colours. At least a third of the *Plictho*'s recipes were dedicated to creating deep and lasting reds, and thereafter black, both of which were highly sought after, and which Venice had a good reputation for producing. One recipe for scarlet cloth begins with clean water:

> in which half an ounce of rock alum, one ounce of white tartar, and one pound of cloth has been stirred. After boiling this mixture, the cloth is removed, rinsed and dried. Six ounces of grana [kermes] and bran [wheat bran] are mixed in water and the cloth is boiled in it for an hour. The cloth is then placed twice in a

FIG. 94 Cultivating the nopal cactus in Mexico to farm cochineal insects for red dye. From 'Memorial de Don Gonçalo Gomez de Cervantes', 1599, watercolour. The farmer is shown (*above*) hoeing the cactus plants. The tiny insects (*grana cochinilla*) were then transferred to the cactus pads with a fox-hair brush. British Museum, London, Am2006,Drg.210, fol. 198v.

rinse of bran, one pound of tartar, and one pound of alum. Finally it is given a bath in highly diluted arsenic.[19]

Another recipe shows how the basic ingredients of the dye influence the quantities used, with a probable bearing on quality and eventual price too. To dye one pound of silk yarns, 'take four ounces of madder [. . .] of Flanders, and if it were madder of another sort take of it two pounds each for each pound of silk'.[20] Madder of Flanders was evidently highly effective, so that substantially less of it was required to achieve the same results as madder from elsewhere. Typically, silk was dyed in the yarn, requiring, as Rosetti explains, that one should have the 'silk [yarn] in loops' - that is, skeins (see fig. 19).

The basic procedure for all the *Plictho* recipes involves creating a dye-bath in a copper cauldron, which is kept on the heat while the cloth or yarn is stirred through it. These same methods were used in the dyeing process until the end of the nineteenth century, and are still used for batch dyeing even today.[21] Some factors were very much of their time, however, and illuminate a specific moment in the meeting of the Old World with the New. For example, the recipes for red revolve around the use of madder and Armenian and Polish cochineal kermes, which shows that New World reds and the Turkish techniques later known as 'Turkey red' were still not in commercial use in Western Europe.[22] In the 1520s, following the conquest of Mexico, Charles V wrote to Hernán Cortés (1485–1547) asking for a report on the subject of Mexican cochineal dye – the high-quality red dye produced from dried insects. That the emperor himself was requesting this information, illustrates the importance this dye would have in the fortunes of his empire. From the sixteenth century until 1850 cochineal was the most valuable export from the Spanish territory of Mexico, except for silver.[23] Certainly, by the late 1550s Mexican cochineal was replacing kermes and Old World cochineal from Spain, Sicily, Armenia and Poland on the European market.[24] It was of high quality, with a deep and long-lasting colour, and its cost added to its prestige.

Later in the century, in 1599, the preparation of cochineal insects in Mexico was detailed by Gonzalo Gómez de Cervantes, in a pictorial report for the viceroy of New Spain (the American colony of Spain, which encompassed swathes of modern-day North Central America). His report survives in the British Museum. Intricate and full of practical instructions, it consists of seventy-six leaves with thirteen drawings (fig. 94).[25] Cervantes described the cultivation of the prickly pear cactus (nopal), and the transfer of the cochineal eggs onto the pear with a brush made of fox hair (*coa*) . He explained how, when the eggs hatched, the tiny insects found their way to the underside of the cactus pad, where they would be sheltered. Once grown 'to the size of one fat lentil', the insects, or grana, were spooned into a bowl. They could then be killed either by boiling or by heating them in an oven, though Cervantes suggested the easiest way was just to leave them on a mat in the sun for four days.[26] The insect bodies were then ground to a powder, which, when added to water, produced the vibrant red dye.

Within the Tudor court, red was a colour of the royal household and, for Edward VI's coronation, the Great

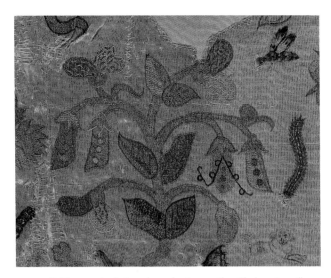

FIG. 95 Golden peas in their pods on the Bacton Altar Cloth, *c.*1600, silk and silver camlet embroidered with silk and metal thread.

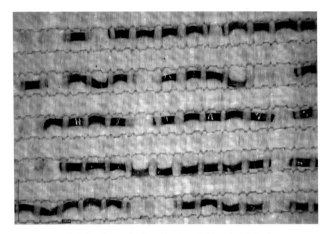

FIG. 96 Detail of the silver strip forming the additional weft in the Bacton Altar Cloth, *c.*1600, silk and silver camlet embroidered with silk and metal thread.

Wardrobe issued crimson velvet of Lucca to the senior nobility and red velvet of Genoa to the officials of the household, while yet more silk satin and red wool were issued for livery to the lower orders.[27]

GOLD AND SILVER

Gold and silver were important raw materials in the production of elite textiles, featuring as thread in embroidery and arras (fig. 95), woven together with silk, or as loops on cloth of tissue.

Creating cloth of gold or silver initially required gold or silver bullion. Goldbeaters would hammer the metal into extremely thin sheets, which were then cut into delicate strips.[28] Typically those thin metal strips were

wound around a silk thread core (*filé*), but they could also be used as flat strips (fig. 96). Gold could be beaten onto an animal membrane (gilt-membrane), leather or even paper, and then cut into strips to wind around a core yarn. This method was cheaper as it used less metal but it was more easily worn off.[29] Drawn wire might also be used.[30] Gold was very fragile to work with, which added to its expense, so silver or silver gilt was often used. Silver gilt was silver that was hammered then plated with a thin layer of gold.[31]

The intersection between the embroiderer and the goldsmith can often be seen in contemporary accounts. In November 1509, Robenet, Henry VII's embroiderer (who continued to serve Henry VIII), was paid for work alongside one 'Harry Holtwheler, goldsmith for the gold work'.[32] Describing Henry VIII's embroidered horse trappers kept at Greenwich, an inventory of 1519 lists 'the arms of Cadwallader on blue velvet, powdered with ostrich feathers of goldsmiths' work' and the harnesses of 'broidery and goldsmiths' work'.[33] Such was the amount of gold and silver contained within the royal textiles that many were bought at the Commonwealth Sale of 1649 by a London goldsmith, John Bolton, who probably burned them to melt down and retrieve their bullion content.[34]

Gold and silver deposits were mined in regions of Europe and Africa, but the metals were in short supply, particularly during the mid- to late fifteenth century.[35] However, the European conquest of the Americas in the first half of the sixteenth century opened up vast deposits of gold and silver for mining and untold wealth of precious artefacts for plunder. Some of Theodor de Bry's engravings (see further p. 23), based on Jacques Le Moyne de Morgues's drawings, depict native people digging for gold and silver in the area that is now Florida,[36] while others show enslaved workers forced to mine for precious metals, revealing the terrible human cost of the so-called Age of Discovery, and the true price of cloth of gold (fig. 97).

TECHNIQUES

WEAVING

Once yarn is spun – be it wool, linen or silk, with or without precious metals – it can be woven. The simplest method is 'plain (tabby) weave', in which the warp threads are held on a loom and the weft thread is passed over and under them to produce cloth (fig. 98). There are, however,

FIG. 97 Enslaved people from Guinea digging for gold and silver in Spanish-held Hispaniola. Engraving by Theodor de Bry after a drawing by Jacques Le Moyne de Morgues, published in volume V (1595) of de Bry's *Great Voyages*. British Library, London, 215.c.15, fol. A2.

many ways in which the threads can be woven, which – depending on the materials, and loom, used – create cloths of different textures and patterns, from fustian to cloth of gold, tabby to figured velvet, and even large-scale tapestries so finely worked that they resemble oil paintings in their colours, shades and detail.

A woodcut depicting the weaver at his loom was created by Jost Amman for *Das Ständebuch* ('The book of trades') by Hans Sachs, published in Frankfurt in 1568 (fig. 99). Amman's woodcut shows the basic features of the shaft loom, the horizontal loom used for weaving wool, linen and silk. Two shafts are suspended from pulleys, attached to a pair of treadles. The warp threads are attached alternately to one shaft and the other in turn. A comb structure called a 'reed' keeps the warp threads

separate and under control. Depressing a treadle sends one shaft up and the other down, raising alternate warps so that the shuttle carrying the weft thread can be passed through the shed (the gap between the threads). The other treadle is then depressed to raise the other set of warps, and so on alternately. This simple loom produced plain-weave cloth and could be operated by a single individual.[37] For more complicated weaves, four shafts or more could be required (fig. 100).[38]

Weaving velvet was highly specialised. Figured textiles are woven on a drawloom, which is operated by two people. The drawloom consists of shafts and treadles, but also a figure harness – a system of cords and pulleys that controls different warp threads to create patterns.[39] During the sixteenth century, Italian weavers created patterned velvet

FIG. 98 (OPPOSITE) A woman weaving at a treadle loom. Pintoricchio (d. 1513), *Penelope at her Loom*, fresco, painted in Palazzo Petrucci, Siena, c.1509. In Homer's *Odyssey*, Penelope, during Odysseus' absence, fends off suitors for her hand until she has finished weaving a shroud; each night she unravels the work she has done during the day. National Gallery, London.

FIG. 99 (RIGHT) 'A weaver at a shaft loom. Jost Amman (1539–1591), 'Der Weber' ('The weaver'), from Hans Sachs, *Das Ständebuch* ('The book of trades') (1568), woodcut. The warp threads are raised and lowered by the activation of the treadles so that the weft passes under and over the warps alternately.

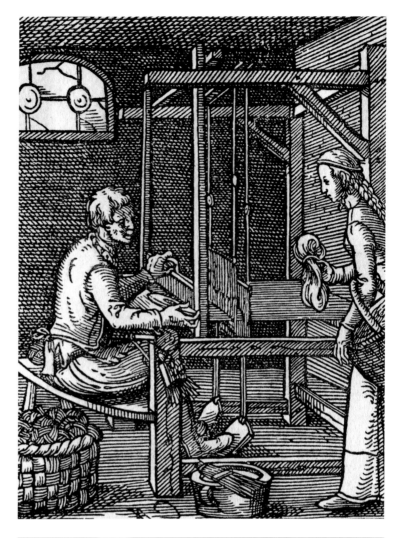

FIG. 100 Venetian silk weaver at the loom. Detail of the signboard of the Guild of Silk Weavers in Venice, 16th century, oil on panel (see fig. 11). Museo Correr, Venice.

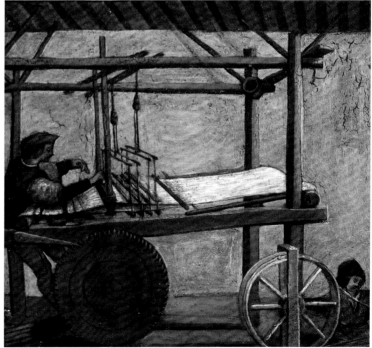

with various levels of pile, and added metallic threads and loops to enhance and enrich the fabric (fig. 101).[40]

Most images of looms show them set up at right angles to windows, so that the light falls across the threads, providing definition.

Cloth of Gold

The 1547 Inventory of Henry VIII's possessions allows us to place a value on the different fabrics at the royal court. The price was naturally dependent on the quality of the dyestuffs and materials, and silk containing gold and silver was the most expensive. Cloth of gold or silver was woven with a metal-thread warp and silk weft.[41] The natural colours of the precious metals could be accentuated by the use of yellow silk (for gold) and white silk (for silver), but silks of different colours were often used, producing fabrics described, for example, as 'crimson cloth of gold'.

The Italian city-states of Florence, Lucca, Milan, Venice and Genoa were well-regarded centres of production for silks woven with gold and silver. Most of the fabrics supplied to the court by the Cavalcanti and Bardi company during the reign of Henry VIII were referred to as 'tissue' or 'cloth of tissue' – velvet or brocatelle incorporating loops of metal thread, with a floral or geometrical motif against a contrasting base of cloth of gold or silver (fig. 102).[42] The finest surviving examples are the Stonyhurst vestments, woven for Henry VII (fig. 103).[43]

Cloth of gold tissue was the most expensive fabric in the inventory, at 53s. 8d. per yard, this one short length equating to eighty-eight days' wages for a skilled tradesman.[44] Green baudekin with venice gold, white damask with silver tinsel, and purple velvet upon velvet paned with cloth of gold all cost 46s. 8d. per yard.[45] During Henry VIII's reign, William (Guglielmo) Corsi (fl. 1530s) provided a tissue of 'cloth of silver of dammaske reysed with venice gold' at more than £4 per yard, and a 'blake cloth of tissewe of damask silver reysed with venis silver' at £7 per yard.[46] The latter equates to a staggering £3,000 per yard in modern money, or the equivalent of almost eight months' work for a skilled tradesman, or indeed the cost of a good horse.[47]

FIG. 101 Polychrome voided satin velvet, with pomegranate seeds in silver gilt, c.1560s, Italy. Voided velvet has a pattern in pile on a non-pile background such as a satin weave. Victoria and Albert Museum, London, 715-1907.

FIG. 102 Cloth of gold tissue, 1500–50, Florence, brocatelle raised with loops of *filé* gold and a ground embellished with silver wire; lower border of plain cloth of silver, with laid and couched silver-gilt *filé*. Victoria and Albert Museum, London, 853b-1892.

FIG. 103 (OPPOSITE) The Stonyhurst chasuble, 1500, Florence, velvet cloth of gold with loops of silver gilt. The embroidered orphrey (cross) is contemporary with the chasuble but is a later addition to the vestment itself. The chasuble was commissioned by Henry VII and taken to the Field of Cloth of Gold by Henry VIII. Stonyhurst College, Lancashire.

Cloth of gold, woven to order and featuring bespoke motifs was exceptionally rare. These sumptuous tissues were usually variations of the Renaissance pomegranate and artichoke design (figs 104 and 105). These bold, stylised patterns featured ogees and curving branches linking the main motif. Pomegranate patterns were fashionable for dress and furnishing textiles during the last quarter of the fifteenth century and into the early sixteenth century. They are prominent in portraiture contemporary with Henry VII's reign, but not long into Henry VIII's reign had become outmoded, certainly for dress. The textiles were incredibly expensive, however, and came to be used in ecclesiastical settings, becoming known as 'churchwork'. Descriptions in the 1547 Inventory attest to the number of pieces of churchwork in the royal collection, and to their scale and beauty. One refers to a 'hanging of white redd and blewe golde

bawdekin paned togethers thupper border being of crymsen and grene cloth of golde Churche worke likewise paned togethers enbrawdered with borders of the kings armes and badges lyned with bockeram conteyning lxviij [68] panes and every pane being in depthe iiij yards quarter [4¼ yards]'.[48]

Carpets

As many as 650 of the 800 carpets listed in the 1547 Inventory may have been knot-pile carpets, and probably well over 600 were made in the Islamic world[49] all of which were hand-knotted. They were made (as traditional carpets still are) with knots of either wool or silk tied around the warps of the foundation. Once a row of knots was completed, a weft strand was beaten down over the row with a comb, and a new row was begun. Often referred to as 'Turkey' carpets in the Tudor period, such

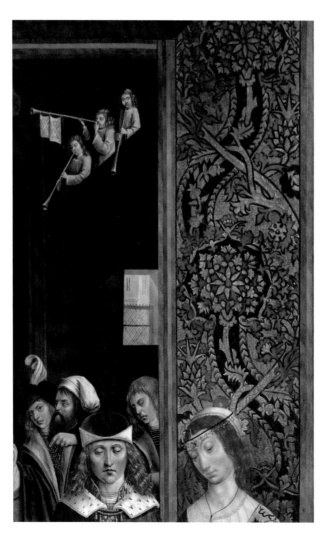

FIG. 104 Velvet cloth of gold with pomegranate pattern, with loops of silver-gilt thread, 1450–1500, Florence. Cleveland Museum of Art, 1973.20.

FIG. 105 Cloth of estate, detail of Master of the Catholic Kings (*fl. c.*1485–1500), *The Marriage at Cana, c.*1495/7, oil on panel (see fig. 61), showing the scrolling pattern popular in the Tudor period. National Gallery of Art, Washington, DC.

pieces were also sometimes called 'Venice' carpets in a simple reference to the city where they were bought and traded. The carpets were made in Asia Minor, Egypt, Persia (Iran), Syria and parts of Islamic Spain, among other places.[50] Some of the smaller carpets in the inventory are unattributed, and may have been individual Islamic prayer rugs.

Different regions produced different designs. Anatolian carpets with contrasting yellow and red patterns are often called 'Lotto' carpets because of their depictions in the paintings of the Italian artist Lorenzo Lotto (c.1480–1556/7) (fig. 106). Hans Holbein often used Turkish carpets in his paintings of the Tudor court, leading to their classification as small- or large-pattern 'Holbein' carpets. Small-pattern Holbein carpets feature arrangements of small knot-like medallions and diamond-shaped strapwork (fig. 107).[51] These are seen in Holbein's

portrait of the Hanseatic merchant Georg Giese (fig. 108), and later in the painting by an unknown artist of the Somerset House Conference of 1608 (see fig. 131). Large-pattern Holbein carpets, which feature designs within large squares, can be seen adorning the top of the cupboard in *The Ambassadors* (see fig. 73), and find surviving comparisons in the Uşak carpets of western Anatolia (fig. 109). In Holbein's paintings, these carpets conveyed the wealth and sophistication of the sitters, showing their ability to acquire and appreciate exotic luxury commodities. More than that, they were arguably seen, in this context, as representing the ideological and cultural triumph of Christianity over the religion of the Ottomans.[52] In a portrait painted at around the time of his accession, the young king Edward VI is shown standing on a Holbein carpet in a pose that directly emulates the stance and stature of his father, Henry VIII (see fig. 33).

FIG. 106 'Lotto' carpet, 16th century, probably Uşak, Turkey, hand-knotted woollen pile on woollen warp and weft. Victoria and Albert Museum, London, T.348-1920.

FIG. 107 Small-pattern 'Holbein' carpet, 15th–16th century, Turkey, hand-knotted wool. Metropolitan Museum of Art, New York, 2009.458.1.

FIG. 108 Hans Holbein the younger (1497/8–1543), portrait of Georg Giese, 1532, oil on panel. Giese was a merchant of the German Steelyard, the main trading base of the Hanseatic League in London in the Tudor period. His work table is covered with a small-pattern 'Holbein' carpet. Gemäldegalerie, Staatliche Museen, Berlin.

FIG. 109 Anatolian carpet, 16th century, hand-knotted wool. The large octagonal medallions resemble those used by Hans Holbein in many of his paintings.

Some of the inventory entries describe tapestry carpets and embroidered carpets, which were not necessarily Eastern hand-knotted rugs. These textiles would have served as décor for tables or cupboards, and would not be under foot. They were fragile, and are described as having linings of canvas or linen. Some of the embroidered motifs are typically English in style, with cutwork Tudor roses on woollen cloth. One was red woollen cloth, embroidered with classical figures encircling the royal motto 'Dieu et mon droit'.[53] Another, of green silk, was embroidered with the king's arms, grotesques, grapes and birds.[54] Another was a 'carpet' of crimson satin, densely embroidered all over in gold and silver, with a central green velvet roundel and borders with embroidered white and red roses.[55] One of the most valuable of all the palace's objects was an embroidered carpet. It had belonged to Henry VIII and is listed in the 1547 Inventory as 7 metres long, of crimson and purple velvet with borders of crimson satin, and embroidered with gold and pearls.[56] It was to be found in the Paradise Chamber at Hampton Court Palace late into Elizabeth's reign; in 1599, Thomas

Platter described it as a 'tapestry' covering a table, 'red and inset with precious stones and pearls'.[57] Another visitor, Baron Waldstein, wrote in 1600 that it was 'a really marvellous thing [...] embroidered all over with pearls' and almost too heavy to lift.[58] It was the most valuable carpet in the royal collection, and was bought for £500 in the Commonwealth Sale by the former royal embroiderer Edmund Harrison, who gave it to Charles II after his restoration to the throne.[59]

An English needlework carpet surviving from around 1600 imitates the style of Anatolian carpets (fig. 110). It features the geometrical motifs typical of Turkey carpets, but here the intersections between the octagons are populated by roses, thistles and heartsease (pansies) derived from herbals and pattern books, such as Jacques Le Moyne de Morgues's *La clef des champs*. At almost 3 metres in length, it is comparable in size to a dining table and to cupboard carpets. It attests to the continuing taste for Eastern carpets to adorn respectable and noble Tudor houses, though now blended with the new fashion for English floral motifs from printed sources.

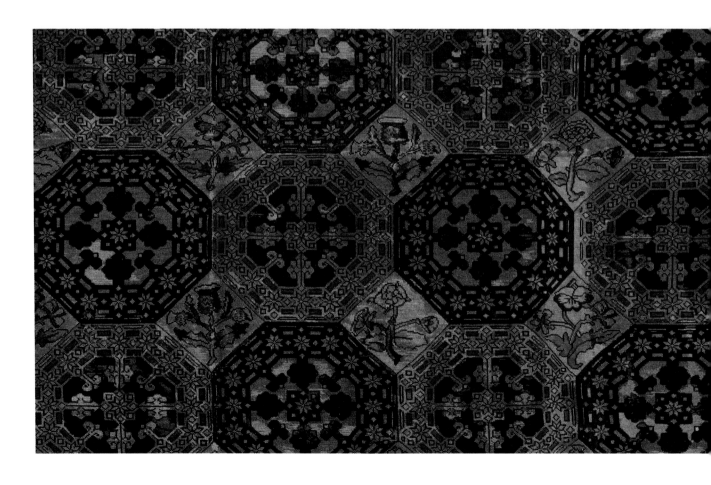

Tapestry

During the late Middle Ages and most of the Tudor period, the best tapestries were sourced from the Low Countries, notably from the cities of Brussels, Arras, Tournai and Antwerp. They were highly prized and very expensive, and were procured by the European royal courts as a primary means of conveying magnificence.

Tapestry was woven on a vertical tapestry loom, known as the *haute lisse*, or high-warp loom (fig. 111).[60] The tapestry weaver sat behind the warp threads, which were suspended vertically overhead. The design was drawn on the warp threads with chalk or charcoal, and the cartoon was hung within view for reference (fig. 112). The weft was not continuous; different colour wefts, kept in order by bobbins, were woven by individual colour block, the weaver building up the picture little by little. The bobbins hung at the back of the tapestry, ready to be picked up and used again when the colour was required. The points of the bobbins, along with a comb, were used to press down on the threads. The tapestry was usually worked sideways across the design, and was wound on rollers in the

FIG. 110 (BELOW, LEFT) Needlework carpet, *c.*1600, England, wool on a linen canvas ground. An English imitation of an Anatolian carpet, with botanical motifs – roses, thistles and pansies. Victoria and Albert Museum, London, T.41-1928.

FIG. 111 (BELOW, RIGHT) *Haute lisse* (high-warp) tapestry loom, 'Tapisserie de haute lisse des Gobelins', copper engraving from Denis Diderot and Jean Le Rond d'Alembert, *Encyclopédie ou Dictionnaire raisonné des sciences, des arts et des métiers*, vol. 9 (1771), plate ix.

FIG. 112 (OVERLEAF, LEFT) Raphael (1483–1520), drawing, or 'cartoon', for the tapestry 'The Miraculous Draft of Fishes', *c.*1515–16, bodycolour over charcoal on paper, mounted on canvas. The full-scale drawing was one of ten commissioned by Pope Leo X as designs for tapestries for the Sistine Chapel. Royal Collection, RCIN 912944.

FIG. 113 (OVERLEAF, RIGHT) Detail of flowers and the hem of a skirt from 'The Virtues Challenge the Vices', early 16th century, Flanders, tapestry, wool and silk. This panel formed part of Cardinal Wolsey's collection. The image is turned through 90 degrees from its correct landscape orientation to show the vertical direction of the warp threads, and the disposition of the design during weaving. Historic Royal Palaces, Hampton Court Palace, 3003478.

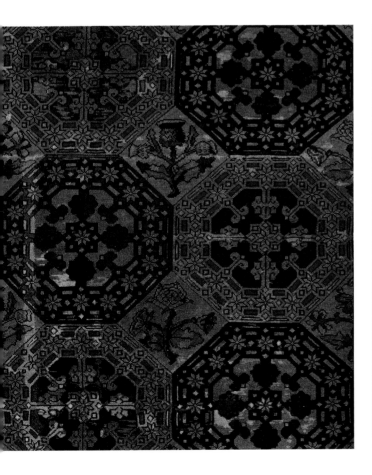

direction of weaving, so the weaver did not see the finished picture until the work was completed (fig. 113). The process was painstaking, often taking years to complete – much like modern tapestry conservation, such as that undertaken at Hampton Court Palace, which is also worked with the aid of two large rollers. Tapestry could also be woven on a horizontal treadle loom called the *basse lisse*, or low-warp loom. With the use of treadles, the weaving was quicker, but more prone to error, and so the products of the *basse lisse* were not viewed with the same respect as those of the *haute lisse*.[61]

Tudor inventories listed tapestry according to their materials.[62] The city of Arras in northern France was once a centre of tapestry weaving, and gave its name to the highest-quality tapestry woven with gold and silver highlights. 'Counterfeit arras' was tapestry woven with silk highlights, and plain 'tapestry' was woven with wool. 'Verdure' was a stylistic term, referring to a design predominantly consisting of foliate, flower or plant motifs.

Arras seems to have been beyond the means of even the senior nobility, and was almost exclusively the preserve of royalty. The inventory of Thomas Howard,

Duke of Norfolk (1443–1524), taken at Framlingham Castle in 1524, lists only 'counterfeit arras'.[63] Later in the century, Bess of Hardwick had only one arras panel in her collection.[64] In contrast, the royal collection of arras was vast, as was the royal tapestry collection in general. Henry VII had inherited several hundred tapestries from his predecessors, some of which dated back to the fourteenth century (fig. 114).[65] In 1547, the inventory of Henry VIII's possessions listed almost 2,500 tapestries, making it the largest tapestry collection in Europe. Only 300 paintings are listed.[66]

Despite there being no evidence of Elizabeth's own procurement of tapestries, a few members of her court are known to have commissioned sets; Bess of Hardwick and Sir Christopher Hatton did so, although their sets were of lower quality in terms of materials and execution than the Henrician royal commissions.[67] Religious persecution by the Catholic Spanish Habsburgs had taken its toll on the great tapestry production centres of the Low Countries. Although tapestry continued to be produced in Flanders and Brabant, tapestry production was also to be found in England, where émigré weavers settled in Norwich, York and London.[68]

FIG. 114 (LEFT) Detached fragment of an armorial tapestry border, 1485–1509?, Netherlands, woven wool, from the collection of Henry VIII. As the Tudor royal arms remained unchanged, it is possible that he inherited this from his father, Henry VII, along with other pieces. Royal Collection, RCIN 1269.

FIG. 115 (BELOW) *The Tapestry Hangings of the House of Lords*, engraving, published by John Pine (1739). It records the Flemish tapestries of the defeat of the Armada, commissioned by Lord Howard of Effingham, designed by Hendrik Cornelisz Vroom (*c.*1562–1640) and woven by Francis Spierincx (1549/51–1630) in the 1590s. British Museum, London, 1861,0518.305-327.

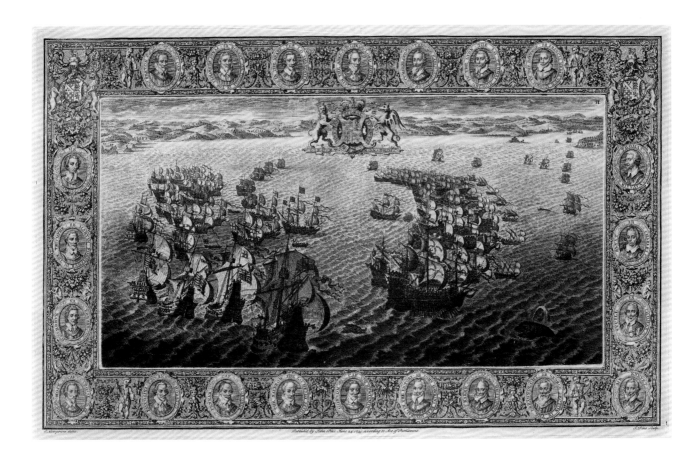

One exceptional set was commissioned by Charles Howard, 2nd Baron Howard of Effingham and 1st Earl of Nottingham (1536–1624), Lord High Admiral of the English navy. He commissioned the Flemish artist Hendrik Cornelisz Vroom (c.1562–1640) to design a set of ten tapestries depicting the defeat of the Spanish Armada in 1588 (see fig. 115). They were woven with gold and silver thread, making them the most expensive tapestries commissioned in England in the late sixteenth century. They were woven in Brussels by Francis Spierincx (1549/51–1630), and following their completion in 1595 they hung in Howard's house where the queen saw them in 1602. Howard sold them to James I in 1616, and they were destroyed in the fire that consumed most of Westminster Palace in 1834.[69]

Napery

Linen was an essential textile of Tudor life, primarily because it was the only one that could be easily washed. It was used for tablecloths, altar cloths, bedsheets and underclothes. As with everything else at court, the finest linen – Holland – was the most fashionable, and costly patterned weaves with embroidered or fringed edging elevated articles made from it above mere functionality.

Margaret Beaufort bequeathed a number of textiles to Christ's College, Cambridge, including a long list of napery. That much of it was used and some of it old shows that textiles were considered too valuable to merely discard, and were still considered worthy gifts, even in a less than pristine state. She bequeathed a 'table clothe diaper', a yard wide and 7 yards long. She also bequeathed seven serving towels, seven washing towels, four old tablecloths (one of 'viii yerdes another of vii yerdes another of vj and another of v yerdes'), a 'towell of diaper containing in length xxvij ells', a tablecloth 'diapre with rosis and portculis containing in length vj ells', and five plain altar cloths.[70] Plain linen altar cloths, sometimes decorated with a border of embroidery or fringing, were commonly placed over more elaborate altar frontals to protect the costlier fabrics from damage (see fig. 57).

Lace

Lace is a qualified inclusion in this section on weaving. Early cutwork needle lace, called *reticella*, was made by pulling the threads from woven linen or cutting a design into it to form a voided pattern that was worked with buttonhole stitch and might have threads thrown across the apertures (as in the linen band in fig. 116, which is further embellished with other embroidery stitches). A later version of *reticella* involved building up rows of buttonhole stitch connected with linking bars of the same stitch. This technique came to be known as *punto in aria*, or 'points in the air' (fig. 117); the latter technique was based on warp and weft directions, and so the results were necessarily geometric. Bobbin lace did not require a needle, but instead involved a type of weaving using bobbins; thread was wound around the bobbin to keep it organised. A drawn pattern was pinned onto a cushion for the lace-maker to follow, with pins stuck vertically through the pattern, around which the thread was twisted and looped to build up the lace; the cushion itself would sit comfortably on the lace-maker's lap (fig. 118). Linen thread was usually used, but gold or silver thread might be used for elite bobbin lace.[71]

The first recorded mention of lace appears in the 1493 inventory of the Sforza family, who ruled Milan at the same time that the Medici presided over Florence.[72] Italy was the home of needle lace, and Venice lace was considered the finest of its type. Federico Vinciolo (*fl.* 1580s), a Venetian lace designer, was under the patronage of Catherine de' Medici (1519–1589), scion of the powerful Florentine family, who married Henry II of France (1519–1559). It has been widely assumed that Catherine was largely responsible for disseminating Italian lace fashions to France. Certainly, while he was in Paris, Vinciolo published a book of lace patterns entitled *Les singuliers et nouveaux pourtaicts pour les ouvrages de lingerie* in 1587, which was reprinted many times thereafter.[73]

From its origins at the end of the fifteenth century, lace developed during the sixteenth century but became popular at the English court only during Elizabeth's reign. It was used for ruffs, but also for handkerchiefs and as trimming for table linen. Lace was invariably made from flax, and the flax-growing regions of Flanders and Holland were, like Italy, exceptionally good at producing lace. Portraiture does not feature lace before the mid-sixteenth century. Before that date the collars and cuffs of shirts and shifts were embellished with embroidery rather than lace. However, following the religious persecution of

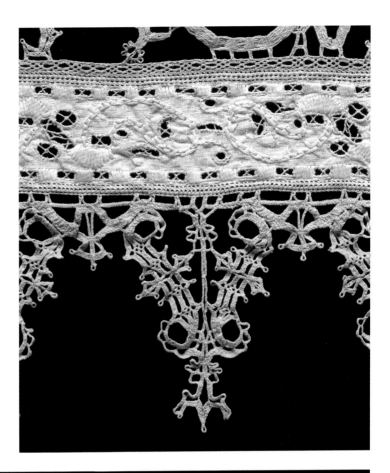

FIG. 116 (RIGHT) Border of a napkin, 1550–1600, Italy, linen embroidered with unbleached linen thread in satin and stem stitches, edged with a band of bobbin lace, worked with unbleached linen thread. Victoria and Albert Museum, London, T.297-1975.

FIG. 117 (BELOW) Needle-lace cover, 1580–1600, Italy, linen. A delicate structure of needle-lace stitches is built up across the spaces in a fine linen ground created by drawing threads. Each of the forty-two squares in the piece has a different design. Victoria and Albert Museum, London, T.166-1959.

Protestants in the Low Countries, refugees arriving in London brought with them many 'luxury' trades, among them glass-making, sugar refining, weaving and lace-making.[74]

The introduction of lace encouraged support industries to thrive, such as the starch industry, which helped to propel lace collars to the extreme dimensions of Elizabethan ruffs. John Stow (1524/5–1605) recorded, in his *Annales* [. . .] *of England*, that the first starcher recorded in London was one Mistress Dinghen van der Plasse, a refugee from Tienen in Brabant, who arrived in 1564 for her 'better safeties'. Stow records that 'this mistris Dinghen was the first that ever taught starching in Englande', and that she instructed English trainees, charging a hefty £4 or £5 for the privilege.[75] But London was evidently some way behind the queen, as another Dutchwoman had become her starcher a couple of years earlier. As Stow wrote:

> in the third yeere of the Raigne of Queene Elizabeth, 1562 [. . .] the Queene had Ruffes made [. . . but] there was none in England could tell how to starch them [. . .] but the Queene made spaciall meanes for some Dutch woman that could starch, and Gwilhams wife was the first starcher the Queen had, and himself was the first Coachman.[76]

Philip Stubbes (c.1555–c.1610), in his pamphlet *The anatomie of abuses* (1583), called starch the 'divell's liquid', describing it as a prop to the devil's own kingdom, 'wherein the divell hath willed them to washe and die their ruffs well, whiche, beeying drie will stande stiff and inflexible about their necks'.[77] The reason for this antipathy was not entirely due to Stubbes's Puritan aversion to fashion in general, which he perceived as excess and frivolity: more particularly, starch was made from grain, such as wheat, which might much better have fed the hungry than clothed the rich. In 1596, a royal proclamation declared that the queen, 'being informed of an abuse greatly tending to make a scarcity of

corn meet to make bread by making of starch within the realm, doth straightly command that no manner of person shall make any starch . . . except such as hath been made by virtue of her majesty's letters patent'.[78]

EMBROIDERY

Medieval English embroidery of the thirteenth and fourteenth centuries was highly prized. Known as *opus anglicanum* (English work), it decorated church vestments and the clothing of royalty.[79] However, by the dawn of the Tudor period it was not as fashionable as it had once been. Some examples of English work can be seen in early Tudor vestments, but the dissolution of the monasteries did away with the last vestiges of ecclesiastical demand for the old style.[80] Imported silks and tapestries were the more fashionable way to convey wealth and status during the reign of Henry VII.[81] Consequently, the clothing of the early Tudor court saw sparing use of embroidery, and embellishments tended to be seen in the form of decorative borders.[82]

There was, however, a revival of English embroidery during the reign of Henry VIII.[83] Some of the more elaborate creations relate to the department of the Stable, and the cloths of the horses beloved by the king for jousting and hunting, particularly in the earlier part of his reign, before his obesity and ulcerated leg kept him from his youthful pastimes. A 1519 inventory of embroidered textiles in the keeping of George Lovekyn, clerk of the Stable (not to be confused with his father, George Lovekyn (1470–1504), tailor to Edward IV and Henry VII), records sumptuous work.[84] A trapper from the king's entry to Tournai on 25 September 1513 was made of 'cloth of white tissue, pendent fashion'. Another was of 'white cloth of tissue, with St. George and a cross of crimson velvet'. Another was made of crimson velvet 'embroidered with a blue heart, and springing out of it branches . . . of cloth of gold . . . powdered with dragons, lions, greyhounds and unicorns.'[85] Other heraldic devices included Tudor roses, the arms of England and France, portcullises, the arms of Ireland, and pomegranates. Heraldry was clearly a useful identifier on the tournament field, but alongside these devices there are motifs of the chivalric romances that Henry enjoyed emulating: one of his trappers was of 'purple velvet and rich cloth of tissue, with a white and red rose, and H and K, fringed with silver

FIG. 118 *Making bobbin lace. Detail of an illustration from Gervasius Fabricius, 'Album amicorum', 1603–37 (see fig. 50). One of the ladies works at a cushion on a wooden stand in front of her; she uses bobbins to weave a lace trim or border of triangles, guided by a pattern pinned in place on the cushion. British Library, London, Add. MS 17025, fol. 50.*

and green silk', and another was of 'cloth of gold and purple velvet paned, with red and white velvet roses and H and K' and 'true loves hearts with H and K'.[86] Later inventories show that the king's embroiderer, William Ibgrave, provided a number of H and K motifs, which suggests that these were cutwork.[87]

Cutwork, which we now know as appliqué, was a decorative technique used for textiles for tournaments, tents and revels, involving motifs cut from fabric and attached using embroidery. It imitated the elaborate patterns and scrolling motifs of court dress and furnishings, but writ large. It made a statement at a distance, and was also more quickly achieved than intricate embroidery at that scale. This can be seen in the descriptions in Lovekyn's inventory: one trapper had

> one half black velvet, embroidered with cut work of blue tynsyn, fringed with flat gold of damask, lined

with black satin; the other half white velvet, with cut work of cloth of silver, and lined with cloth of silver, fringed with flat gold of damask, with a border containing 143½ letters and 25 ciphers.[88]

At Berkeley Castle, Gloucestershire, the main staircase is lined with a striking red cloth decorated with scrolling black cutwork.[89] Family tradition maintains that the cloth once formed the panels of a tent from the Field of Cloth of Gold, perhaps arriving into family ownership via Sir Maurice Berkeley (1467–1523), who acted as a commissioner at the Field of Cloth of Gold and was also lieutenant of the castle at Calais, 'which was of great profit unto him in regard to the fees and allowances belonging to those offices'.[90] Whether or not the cloth was present at the great event of 1520, the scale of it supports the use of cutwork for undertakings of large proportions.

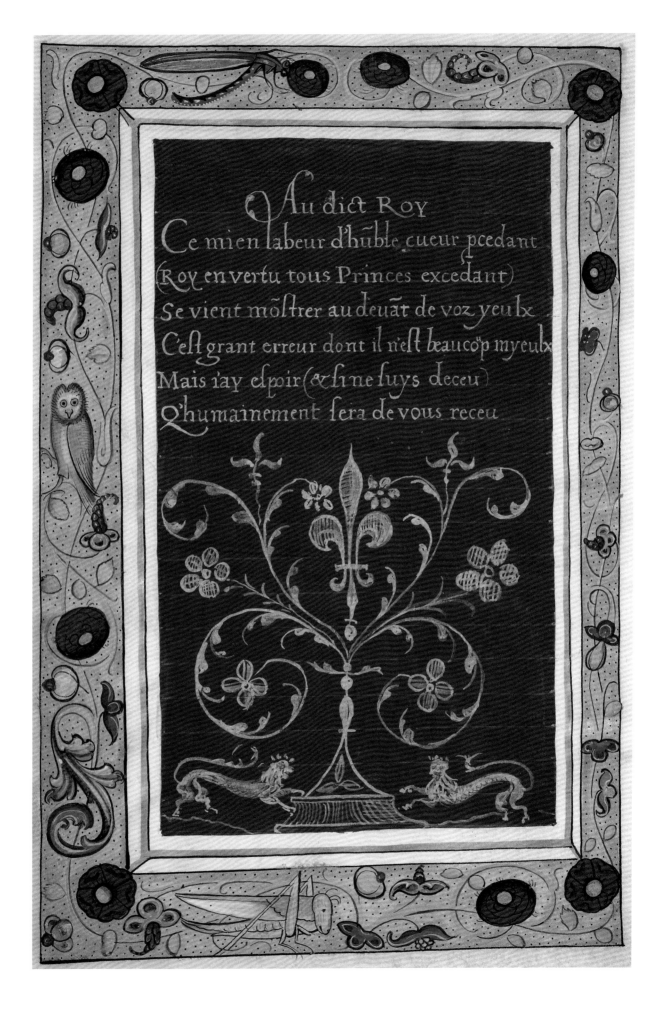

Au dict ROY
Ce mien labeur d'hũble cueur pcedant
(Roy en vertu tous Princes excedant)
Se vient mõstrer au deuãt de voz yeulx
C'est grant erreur dont il n'est beaucõp myeulx
Mais i'ay espoir (& si ne suys deceu)
Q'humainement sera de vous receu

Imported embroidery techniques were more coveted than traditional English work, and new styles were emerging on the continent. One such technique was *or nué* ('shaded gold'), first documented at the French royal court in the late fourteenth century, in which laid gold threads were embroidered with coloured silks to provide shading, light and a more naturalistic image.[91] The technique of working interlacing moresque patterns with couched metal threads on satins and velvets had similarly spread from the continent, specifically from Italy in the 1490s (figs 119 and 120).[92] 'Moresque' derived from 'moorish', meaning 'in the style of the moors' (Arab people); it was also known as 'arabesque' (figs 121, 122 and 124). It became highly popular during the reign of Henry VIII, and can be seen in abundance in the portrait of himself with his family (see fig. 5). The intricate scrolling and interlacing designs were popularly disseminated to goldsmiths and embroiderers in *Morysse and damashin renewed and encreased very profitable for goldsmythes and embroderars* (1548) by Thomas Geminus (1510–1562), which offered 'moresque' and 'damascene' patterns. Similarly, grotesque style (fig. 123) was highly fashionable at the French court and, consequently, at the English one (see p. 90). The 1547 Inventory details a number of items, such as bed hangings, with typically 'grotesque' motifs such as 'antique heddes' and 'putti'.[93] One of Henry VIII's embroiderers, named as

John de Paris, had settled in London from France, and perhaps he and others – such as 'John de Molyn', listed as a 'stranger' in the 1514 royal accounts – were employed to bring these new and coveted techniques from France and the Low Countries.[94]

Many embroidered furnishings, including cloths of estate, bed hangings, chairs and cushions were recorded in the 1547 Inventory. Many of the embroideries listed, particularly those on larger items such as bed furnishings, would have been padded out to give a three-dimensional character to the motifs; the padding or wadding was covered over with cutwork and couched with silk and metal thread (see fig. 122).[95]

Embroidery patterns were drawn on paper. The lines were then pricked with holes, and a powder pounced through to mark the design on the fabric below. Chalk or charcoal might be used, so that the indicative lines could be brushed away at the end. For some fabrics, however, chalk might not suffice. The Bacton Altar Cloth motifs are embroidered within inked lines. The drawing of the design directly onto the fabric might be a virtuoso demonstration of the skill of the professional embroiderer who worked the cloth – a show of confidence in his abilities. Or, more likely, it may have been to do with the colour and quality of the fabric: chalk would not show, and charcoal would have stained the white ribbed silk.[96] The fabric was tacked into a wooden frame, as shown in fig. 125. The embroiderer worked at a specially constructed table, set near a large window for light. The table had horizontal struts or arms at either side to support the frame, allowing the embroiderer to work a large panel with ease. An amateur embroiderer, such as a gentle- or noblewoman, worked with a smaller frame (see fig. 50). A lady might work slips on a small frame, embroidering individual motifs before cutting them out and applying them onto another fabric.

It is highly likely that court artists designed patterns for the embroiderer. Holbein is known to have contributed designs for various forms of decorative art, from jewellery to gold cups and table fountains, so it is not beyond the realms of possibility that he may have sketched some patterns to be translated into embroidery.[97] Other artists probably provided patterns too. Gerard Horenbout (d. 1540/41) was a Flemish painter and draughtsman, active in the city of Ghent, where he painted miniatures, tapestries, altarpieces and portraits (fig. 126).

FIG. 123 (ABOVE) Detail of a tester, c.1550, school of Fontainebleau, France, satin cutwork on silk satin embroidered in silk thread (see fig. 68). The grotesque style seen here was inspired by classical art and was a fashionable aesthetic at the royal courts of Europe. Victoria and Albert Museum, London, T.405-1980.

FIG. 124 (OPPOSITE) Antonis Mor (d. 1576?), portrait of Mary I, 1554, oil on panel. Mary sits on a red velvet chair of estate, which is fringed and embroidered with gold and silver thread in an arabesque design. Her skirt is a rich silver cloth of tissue. Museo del Prado, Madrid.

Susanna Horenbout (c.1503–c.1554), his daughter, learned her father's craft. Her work was admired by the artist Albrecht Dürer (1471–1528), who bought one of her illuminations, of which he wrote, 'it is a great wonder that a woman should be able to do such work'.[98] Henry VIII brought the Horenbout family to his court to create portrait miniatures and to record his achievements and activities in illuminated manuscripts (see fig. 57).[99] Susanna became the first recorded female artist in England, active in the 1520s to the 1540s. Her name was anglicised to Hornebolt and she was named as a 'gentlewoman' of the court, favoured by the king and by Anne of Cleves and Katherine Parr. She made a good marriage, to John Parker, who served as a yeoman of the robes and purchased textiles from the Cavalcanti and other merchants.[100] No surviving work can be directly attributed to Susanna, though a number of illuminations and paintings potentially show her hand.[101] Given her skills and her role as a gentlewoman of the Privy Chamber, it is highly likely that she produced embroidery designs for the various queens and their ladies.[102]

While the court may have utilised the skills of the resident artists and draughtsmen, other factors influenced the design of embroidery during the Tudor period. From the late fifteenth century onwards, the development of the printing press had a revolutionary effect on learning and the dissemination of information. In addition to religious treatises, domestic and secular books began to be printed.[103] As we have seen, the fashionable moresque designs were widely disseminated via the printed pages of Thomas Geminus' *Morysse and damashin*, as they were in Remy de Gormont's *Le livre de moresque* (1546). In addition, herbals, which started out as an exercise in scientific and medical categorisation, became fashionable embroidery

FIG. 125 An embroiderer at his frame. Jost Amman (1539–1591), 'Der Seidensticker' ('The silk embroiderer'), from Hans Sachs, *Das Ständebuch* ('The book of trades') (1568), woodcut. The silk is stretched on a frame supported at either end on struts extending from the work table.

FIG. 126 Workshop of Gerard Horenbout, *The Visitation*, c.1500, Flanders, tempera and gold leaf on parchment. Motifs such as the exquisite flowers and insects seen here inspired domestic embroidery. J. Paul Getty Museum, MS Ludwig IX 17, fol. 16.

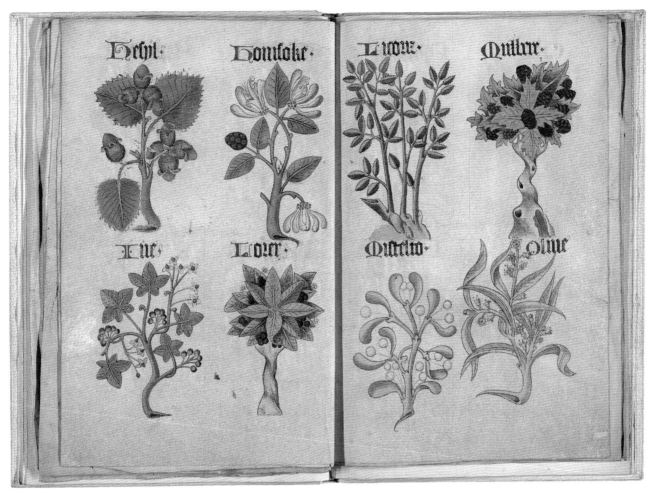

FIG. 127 An opening from the Helmingham herbal and bestiary, *c*.1500, pen and ink and watercolour on parchment. These pages show hazel, honeysuckle, ivy, laurel, liquorice, mulberry, mistletoe and olive. Yale Center for British Art, Paul Mellon Collection, New Haven, C 2014 4, fols 11v–12r.

pattern books. Indeed, the term 'slip' for canvas squares of embroidered flowers was taken from the gardener's word for a cutting.[104] English herbals and other works of natural history, long established in manuscript (figs 127 and 128), were first printed in the 1520s, and their influence can be seen in stylised single flowers used in designs of the reign of Henry VIII, such as the heartsease (pansy) on the Princess Elizabeth's embroidery for her stepmother (see fig. 38), and in insects and animals in many embroideries. Their popularity was particularly evident in the later Elizabethan period, especially after the publication of Le Moyne's *La clef des champs* (1586), whose purpose – as the dedication reads – was to serve those wishing to 'prepare themselves for the arts of painting or engraving [. . .] and others for embroidery [. . .] and also for all kinds of needlework' (see figs 44 and 45).

Aristocratic ladies were both patrons and purchasers of these publications. The evidence of this can be found in collections of domestic embroidery in numerous museums, which show how gentlewomen interpreted the patterns published in the pages of books by embroidering and arranging slips, and thereby configured the natural world in miniature in their work, and populated it with motifs of flora, fauna and wildlife (figs 129 and 130).

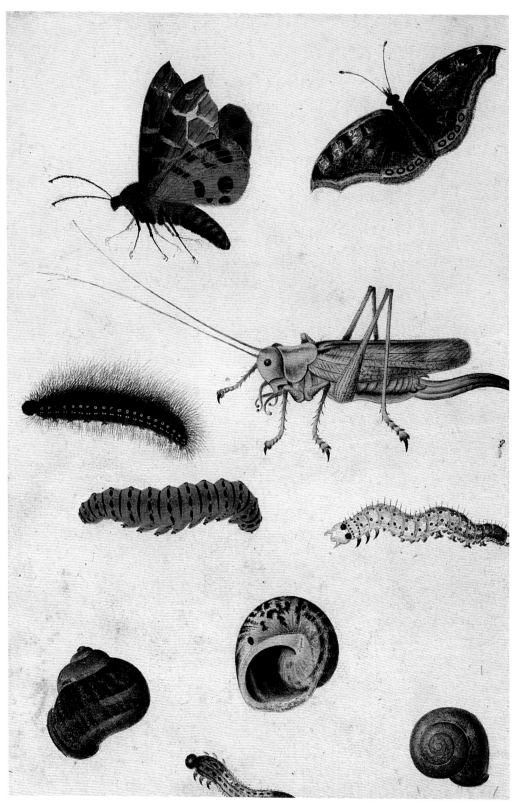

FIG. 128 Jacques Le Moyne de Morgues (*c*.1533–1588), studies of insects and shells, 1585, watercolour, from an album on which Le Moyne based stylised woodcuts published in *La clef des champs* (1586). British Museum, London, 1962,0714.1.2.

FIG. 129 Embroidery pattern, 1600–25, England, linen canvas with drawings of animal motifs; the butterfly is taken from Le Moyne's watercolour drawing (see fig. 128). Victoria and Albert Museum, London, T.88-1925.

FIG. 130 Cushion cover, *c.*1600, silk velvet with applied linen needlework slips embroidered in silk and metal threads. Victoria and Albert Museum, London, T.80-1946.

6 EPILOGUE

In 1603, Elizabeth I – last of the Tudors – died at Richmond Palace. One year later, in the summer of 1604, a peace conference was held at Somerset House, London, between England and Spain. A treaty, signed on 16 August, brought an end to almost twenty years of war between the two countries, which had included the attempted invasion of England by the Spanish Armada in 1588. A painting commemorates the treaty (fig. 131). The Spanish Habsburg delegation (including representatives from the Spanish Netherlands) sits on the left, headed by Louis Verreyken (1552–1621), the *audiencier* of Brussels, and the English, led by Robert Cecil, on the right.[1] Spain agreed to recognise Protestant rule in England under King James I, and England ended its support for Protestant rebels in the Spanish Netherlands.

Laid out on the table between them was a Turkish carpet – a 'small-pattern Holbein' carpet made in Anatolia. Carpets of this kind were ubiquitous items of luxury furnishing, and such a fine example as this may well have

FIG. 131 Unknown artist, *The Somerset House Conference*, 1604, oil on canvas. National Portrait Gallery, London.

come from the stores of the Great Wardrobe, perhaps originally acquired by Cardinal Wolsey or Henry VIII. However, displayed thus between the two powers, it spoke of much more than exotic décor or simple wealth. Here it was arguably an assertion of British reach and power. It spoke of Elizabethan associations with the Ottoman Empire, and served as a reminder to the Spanish that England was no longer an isolated island.[2] It was certainly not as it had been when Henry VII seized the throne in the late fifteenth century and sought – perhaps rather desperately – to establish an alliance with Spain through the marriage of his son to Katherine of Aragon.[3] The Armada had been defeated. England was a rising global power.

Behind the Spanish delegation hangs a tapestry. Its subject, literally speaking, is an armoured soldier kneeling to a crowned king – a reminder, perhaps, of the threat of warfare and eventual martial submission if diplomacy should fail. It very probably, however, depicts the biblical scene of King David handing Uriah the Hittite the sealed message that is his own death sentence – a recognised symbol of deceit or betrayal to sixteenth-century eyes.[4] We know that Henry VIII owned a set of tapestries depicting King David and Uriah the Hittite, which he purchased in 1520 from the Italian merchant Giovanni Cavalcanti, and took to the Field of Cloth of Gold that same year.[5] When the Venetian ambassador saw the set displayed at a tournament at Greenwich in May 1527, he described the tapestries as 'the richest in England'.[6] Another set of David tapestries was delivered to Henry in 1528, by the merchant Richard Gresham (see p. 46). The representation of the tapestry as the backdrop to the conference may have been artistic licence, but it is not beyond the realms of possibility that it was in the room and was, indeed, one of Henry's tapestries, chosen specifically to draw parallels with biblical history and to comment upon contemporary events. There was precedent for this: tapestries were selected from the royal collection for important and state occasions, and while in 1604 it might have been a case of choosing the most expensive or most venerable tapestry to make a statement of wealth and power, the adornment of the council chamber was also an opportunity for political statement.[7] The cartouches to either side of the window, behind the delegates, bear the date 1560. It has been suggested that the year might refer to the Ottoman victory over the fleet of the Holy League – a direct snub to the Spanish, reinforcing the message of the central Ottoman carpet.[8]

This painting gives us the opportunity to reflect on different aspects of the subject of this book. Of course, there is much that it does not show: the chivalric and heraldic motifs of the tiltyards and tents, especially of the early Tudor period, were a world away from the more subtle aesthetics of 1604; nor can we see the exquisite embroidery commissioned or rendered by noble and royal women, copied from herbals and printed pattern books. However, here are red velvet chairs of estate, with embroidery and gold fringing. Here is the might and magnificence of Henry VIII, embodied by his tapestry collection – 'the richest in England'– supplied by merchants like Cavalcanti and Gresham, who amassed fortunes and power in the process. Here is the figurative purpose of tapestries, conveying meaning and narratives to those who saw them. Here are the Turkey carpets that adorned the court and Holbein's portraits, representing luxury and trade and England's new global outlook. Here is Robert Cecil, patron of Richard Hakluyt, being passed a private note by his neighbour in an echo of the codes and secret symbols of the late Elizabethan reign. Here is the story of Antwerp and the Low Countries, and the persecution that changed the nature of textile manufacture and trade with England, encouraging new exploration and the first glimpses of British Empire. Ultimately, here are textiles, taking centre stage to convey more than the sum of their parts. They symbolise status, magnificence and political meaning (fig. 132). The dawn of the Stuart age was replete with the power and the legacy of Tudor textiles.

FIG. 132 The Tudor rose, detail from the Bacton Altar Cloth, c.1600, silk and silver camlet embroidered with silk and metal thread.

Glossary

aglet A decorative metal tag at the end of a tie or lace used to fasten a garment.

alkanet (alchenna, archenda) A perennial herb, *Anchusa (Alkanna) tinctoria*, and the red to purple dye produced from its roots.

alum An astringent mineral salt (potassium aluminium sulphate), used as the principal *mordant in the dyeing process; alum was often referred to as 'lume' after the Italian phrase *dare la lume*, 'to give light' or 'to illuminate'. The word 'alum' was also applied to other compounds that resembled it: *lume de fezza*, 'alum of lees', the burnt sediment of white wine; *lume catine*, 'soda ash'; and *lume de rocha*, 'tree alum'.

antique (antick) *See* *grotesque.

arabesque *See* *moresque.

arras A *tapestry woven with gold and/or silver thread to create highlights; it was named for the town in Flanders pre-eminent in the production of fine tapestries in the late Middle Ages; *see also* *counterfeit arras.

baudekin (baldekyn, baudekyn, bawdekin, etc.; from It. *baldacchini*: Italian lampas silks with a twill or satin ground) (1) Monochrome or polychrome figured silk, often woven with gold or silver threads, used for ecclesiastical and ceremonial purposes. (2) A canopy of state for an altar or throne.

bay (bays, bayes) A napped woollen fabric. Sixteenth-century bays was of a finer texture than modern 'baize'.

braccio An Italian unit of measurement for silk, approximately 60 cm.

Brazil (Braxilio, Brasil) A hardwood tree, *Caesalpinia echinata*, found in the Americas; its bark yields a weak red dye that can be enhanced by combining it with other dyes.

broadcloth A high-quality woollen cloth; it was an important English product and export in the fifteenth and sixteenth centuries.

brocading A weave effect achieved by a supplementary weft, inserted only where required to form a pattern.

brocatelle (from It. *broccatello*) A lampas silk with a thick linen ground weft.

broom (dyer's broom) A deciduous flowering shrub, *Genista tinctoria*, the flowers of which yield a yellow dye.

buckthorn (Persian berries) A small tree, *Rhamnus cathartica*, that bears purple-black fruit; the unripe berries produce a yellow-green dye.

caffa A silk, often satin or damask, imported from Caffa, a Genoese possession on the Black Sea.

cambric Originally a fine white linen, named for the town of Cambrai in the Low Countries; since the eighteenth century cambric has been made from cotton.

camlet (chamblet, chamblette) A warp-faced tabby (*see* *tabby weave), with a pronounced fine weft rib; made variously of silk, of silk with gold or silver, or of wool.

carders Hand-held paddles set with multiple metal teeth, used to comb, separate and untangle raw wool fibres so that they can be spun. They were used in pairs, one in each hand, brushed back and forth against each other with the wool between them.

carding The process of preparing wool fibres for spinning, using *carders.

cartoon A sketch or drawing at full size to be used as the design for a tapestry.

celure The roof canopy of a cloth of estate or a bed hanging; *see also* *tester.

chalice veil A cloth placed over the cup used for wine at the Mass.

chasuble A sleeveless outer vestment worn by a cleric.

churchwork Rich Renaissance textiles, usually silk velvets, featuring large ogival pomegranate designs. These designs reached the height of popularity in the mid- to late fifteenth century, but had fallen from fashion for dress by 1540, and were relegated to ecclesiastical functions thereafter – hence the term 'churchwork'.

cipher The personal badge or arms of a member of the royal family or nobility.

cloth of estate A canopy placed over a chair of estate or a throne, consisting of a celure and tester, and often featuring the royal arms.

cloth of gold A silk fabric woven with a weft of metal thread. Cloth of gold was often woven with yellow silk, cloth of silver with white; however, other colours, such as crimson or purple, were also used.

cloth of silver *See* *cloth of gold.

clove A unit of weight for wool, 7 lb.

cochineal The red dye (carminic acid) obtained from the crushed bodies of the cochineal insect, and the insect itself (*Dactylopius coccus*, native to south America; and *Margarodidae*, native to eastern Europe).

cope A long, full cloak, worn as a liturgical vestment; it was usually semi-circular and fastened across the chest.

cotton In the Tudor period, a fine woollen cloth produced by a process called 'cottoning', which raised the nap of the fabric. Cotton made from the cotton plant was not in common use in England until the eighteenth century, though its raw fibres were sometimes used as a stuffing or as a weft for fabrics such as fustian.

couching An embroidery technique in which decorative thread on the surface of the fabric is secured by a different thread – the couching thread.

counterfeit arras A *tapestry woven with silk highlights instead of gold or silver highlights (*see* *arras). Although counterfeit arras was less expensive than tapestry woven with metal thread, it was still costly, and was of higher status than tapestry woven with wool alone.

counterpane (counterpoint) A quilted coverlet or blanket.

coverlet A bed covering; a blanket.

coverpain (coverpane) A square of fine linen used to cover bread on the dining table.

cutwork Motifs cut from fabric and applied to a ground with embroidery; they might be padded and couched for a three-dimensional effect. Cutwork was often used for large-scale embroidery, such as textiles for tournaments, or tents. The term 'appliqué' was not used.

damask A figured textile based on satin weave, whose pattern is formed by contrasting shiny (warp-faced) areas with duller (weft-faced) ones.

distaff A tool used in the spinning process, consisting of a stick with fork-like prongs at the top to hold unspun fibres of wool or flax. The spinster (or 'spinner' if male) held the distaff at her left side, or propped up between her knees or at her waist. The maternal line of the family was traditionally known as 'the distaff side'.

dyed in the wool Fleece that is dyed before carding and spinning, which provides yarn of a uniform colour; the phrase became proverbial, meaning thoroughly steeped in, or 'out-and-out'.

ell (elne, nell) A unit of measurement for lengths of cloth, originating as the length of a man's arm from the elbow to the tip of the middle finger. The English ell was 45 inches, a Flemish ell 27 inches, and a French ell 54 inches. In England, linen was sold by the English ell, but tapestry and arras were sold by the Flemish ell.

ell-stick (ellwand) A stick cut to a standardised measurement of an ell.

embroidery Fine decorative stitching in silk, cotton, gold, silver or other thread. During the Tudor period, 'embroidery' was a precise term that did not include stitched linen or canvas (to which the term 'needlework' was applied), but did include *cutwork.

floss The rough silk fibres that surround a silkworm's cocoon.

frieze A coarse, tabby woollen cloth with a raised nap on one side; it was used for coats and cloaks because of its warmth.

frizado (friseadowe) A woollen cloth with a napped surface on one side, similar to frieze but of higher quality.

fulling The process of finishing a cloth after weaving, to make the fibres mesh together. This can be done by stamping on the cloth for many hours, or can be mechanised using large fulling hammers.

fustian (bustian) A brushed cloth made of mixed linen or wool and cotton. It was used for linings, bedding and pillowcases, and also for the livery of members of the royal household.

gilt A thin covering of gold leaf applied to a ground: 'gilt-membrane' is gold hammered onto a ground of animal membrane; similar terms indicate gold leaf applied to other materials – 'gilt leather' and 'gilt paper', for example. Silver gilt is silver onto which thinly hammered gold ('gold leaf') is soldered (usually with a material containing copper).

grain (grana) *See* *kermes.

grosgrain (grograne, grograve) A form of *camlet with a more prominent rib.

grotesque (from It. *grotto*) A style of decoration featuring masks, figures and mythological creatures, entwined with scrolls of foliate tendrils. Originating in the classical aesthetic of ancient Rome, it was revived in the Renaissance period, and was sometimes referred to as 'antique' or 'antick'.

ground weave The foundation weave for figured fabrics, such as lampas, into which supplementary yarns are woven to create a pattern.

Holland A very fine linen fabric, produced in the flax-growing region of the province of Holland in the Netherlands. It was used for bedsheets and underwear (shirts, shifts, nightshirts and nightcaps). Royal linen in the Tudor period was almost always made from Holland.

indigo A rich blue dye produced from the leaves of the Asiatic plant *Indigofera tinctoria.*

kermes (grain) A species of scale insect, *Kermes vermilio Planchon*, and the vibrant red dye produced from the dried bodies of this species.

kersey A coarse, ribbed woollen cloth with a short nap. It may have originated in the village of Kersey, Suffolk, a centre of cloth production.

knot pile The pile of a traditional type of carpet, made by hand: lengths of wool or silk are knotted around the warp threads of the foundation (made of wool or flax), the cut ends of the knotted material forming the pile.

lac (laccha, shellac) A red resinous substance secreted by the scale insect *Coccus lacca*, which feeds on the sap of certain trees, including the fig and the banyan. It is ground to produce a red dye.

lace A decorative openwork fabric used for borders, trims and inserts; it was usually made with linen threads but sometimes with gold, silver or silk threads. There are different types of lace-making: needle lace is made using a needle and thread, cutwork is made by removing threads from woven linen fabric, and bobbin lace is made by interlacing linen threads attached to bobbins and following a pattern pinned to a pillow.

lampas A luxury figured silk, in which the pattern is formed by one or more supplementary wefts.

lawn A very fine linen, originally from Laon in France.

linen A fine fabric made from the long fibres of hemp, jute or flax. It was used for shirts, shifts and other undergarments, bedding, towels and napery. Linen yarn was also mixed with other yarns in some fabrics, such as fustian. The word is also used collectively to refer to garments and other articles made of linen – as, for example, in the terms 'bed linen' and 'table linen'.

livery In the Tudor period, a uniform worn by servants or officials of the royal household, often distinguished by colour and the wearing of a badge. Different members of the royal family were represented by different colours.

madder A herbaceous plant, *Rubia tinctorum* (also known as *Robbia roza*), and the orange to red dye produced from its root.

mercer One who deals in *mercery.

mercery The trading of silk, linen, piece-goods (including worsted cloth for gowns or blankets), small dress accessories and bedding. Trading in wool did not qualify as mercery (though worsted – a woollen cloth – was an exception to this rule).

Merchant Adventurers The Company of Merchant Adventurers of London was established in the early fifteenth century. Its members' main business was the export of cloth, especially undyed *broadcloth.

millefleurs A design consisting of many small flowers and plants on a green background. A millefleurs tapestry might be covered entirely with such motifs, or they might provide the foundation or background for other elements, such as coats of arms.

mordant A base treatment applied to yarn or fabric before dyeing, so that it will absorb and hold dyes.

moresque (arabesque) Moorish patterns, featuring scrolling tendrils within geometric forms. In the Middle Ages and Tudor period, 'moor' was a catch-all term for Arab or Islamic people.

nail A unit of measurement for cloth, usually a sixteenth of a yard, 2¼ inches.

nap The raised fibres of a woven cloth; napping is the process whereby fibres are raised or teased to create a soft, fuzzy surface to the fabric.

needlework In sixteenth-century parlance, specifically a ground of linen or canvas entirely worked over with stitches – a technique often used for furnishings, including cushions, chair covers, table carpets and wall hangings, in addition to smaller items, such as floral or botanical slips.

orphrey A decorative band on an ecclesiastical vestment, such as a cope or chasuble; often embroidered, orphrey bands can adorn the edge of a cope, the centre back of a chasuble or the front of a chasuble in the shape of a cross.

paned Of cloth, having two fabrics of different or contrasting colours placed next to each other.

piece-goods Cut lengths of cloth, produced and sold by standard dimensions or pieces, such as sheets or handkerchiefs.

pillowbere A pillow cover, usually of linen.

plain weave *See* *tabby.

plied threads Multiple threads, usually of different colours, threaded into a single needle.

pricking (pouncing) A technique used by embroiderers to mark the outline of a design onto fabric. Small holes are punched in a paper pattern, which is placed over the ground fabric; charcoal or chalk is then dusted through the holes to mark the design in dotted lines.

rayne (reynes) A fine plain-weave linen, originally from Rennes in Brittany or Reims in north-eastern France.

rush Any member of a family of flowering plants (Juncaceae) that superficially resemble tall grass, but have evergreen leaves containing a white spongy pith. When dried, rushes can be plaited to create an insulating and durable matting for floors. *See also* *sweet rush.

sarcenet A soft silk in tabby or twill weave, often used as a lining material during the sixteenth century. The name is derived from 'saracen cloth', a saracen being an Arab or Muslim.

satin of Bruges A half-silk fabric, made with a silk warp with a wool or linen weft, making a cheaper fabric than pure satin.

satin weave A glossy fabric, in which the weave produces an uninterrupted smooth, lustrous surface and a contrasting dull back.

saye (say) A woollen cloth, originally woven in the west and south-west of England; it was sometimes woven with a silk warp.

scarlet (skarlet, skarlettes) (1) Fine red woollen cloth, typically from the Low Countries, used for dress at the courts of the late Middle Ages, but relegated to bed furnishings during the sixteenth century. (2) A blanket made of red woollen or kersey cloth.

serge A durable twilled woollen fabric.

shaft The part of the loom that moves alternate warp threads up and down to create a shed through which the weft can pass.

skein A length of thread or yarn loosely coiled and knotted to keep it tidy.

slips Motifs embroidered onto small pieces of canvas and then cut out and applied to another fabric. In the sixteenth century, the motifs were often floral or botanical. The technique allowed ladies to work with small frames on their laps, and the slips could be re-applied and re-used as required. The name was derived from the term for plant cuttings taken by gardeners.

sperver (sparver) A bed canopy.

spindle A tool used in the spinning process, consisting of a round stick used in combination with a *whorl to spin raw fibre into yarn.

Staple (i) A town or city whose merchants have the exclusive right to produce, trade or export certain goods, especially wool. English wool exports were concentrated in one town (called the Staple) to facilitate the collection of export duties; from the fourteenth century, Calais was the Staple, from 1558, it was Bruges. *See also* *Staplers.

staple (ii) The length of the fibres in shorn wool. Short staple was around 2 inches, while long staple could be 5 or 6 inches long.

Staplers (Merchants Staplers) The Company of the Merchants of the Staple was an English company that controlled the export of English raw wool from the late thirteenth century to the end of the sixteenth century.

strapwork A kind of ornament, popular in the fifteenth and sixteenth centuries, consisting of narrow ribbon-like forms (hence 'strap') folded and interlaced to form a geometrical design.

stuff A catch-all term for woven textiles, often used to describe *worsted wools.

sweet rush (sweet flag) A species of flowering plant, *Acorus calamus*, with strap-shaped leaves that were strewn on floors for cleanliness and insulation.

tabby weave The simplest method of weaving, in which the weft thread passes over and under the individual warp threads. Tabby (UK) is also known as plain weave (US).

taffeta A compactly woven tabby silk.

tannin An astringent substance extracted from the galls (or gallnuts) commonly found on oak trees. Tannins were used with iron mordants in the dyeing process to change brown colours to fast black dyes.

tapestry A textile woven in *tapestry weave. Tapestries were usually large-scale wall hangings featuring biblical or mythical scenes, heraldry, or plants and flowers, but tapestry weave could also be used for smaller items such as carpets or cushions. The Tudor court recognised a hierarchy of what are now referred to as 'tapestries': *arras, woven with gold and/or silver highlights; *counterfeit arras, woven with silk highlights; tapestry, woven with wool alone; and *verdure, a stylistic (rather than a technical) description, referring to imagery of scrolling leaves and plants. *See also* *millefleurs.

tapestry weave A weft-faced plain weave, in which the warp threads are completely covered by the weft; the weft is not continuous but is built up with blocks of colour to execute the design.

tenter A long rectangular frame used to stretch newly fulled fabric (*see* *fulling) to prevent it puckering; the fabric was secured to the tenter with *tenterhooks.

tenterhook A small hook used to attach fabric to a *tenter; hundreds of tenterhooks were positioned around the tenter frame to hold the fabric taut. The word gave rise to the expression 'to be on tenterhooks' – that is, to be in a state of suspense, anxiety or impatience.

tester The vertical hanging of a cloth of estate, behind the chair of estate or throne; *see also* *celure. The term was also used for the vertical hanging at the head of a bed.

thread A length of tightly twisted strands of yarn, of flax, cotton, wool, silk or other fibre, used in sewing, weaving, embroidery, etc. *See also* *warp, *weft.

tick A fabric case filled with feathers or other material to form a mattress, quilt or pillow.

tissue (cloth of tissue) A rich cloth of *velvet or *brocatelle, having a raised floral or geometrical pattern against a contrasting ground of *cloth of gold or silver, and incorporating gold or silver loops.

trapper A cloth covering put over a horse, often decorative and/or featuring the livery or heraldic colours of its rider.

twill weave A weave that creates fine diagonal lines or ridges on the surface of the textile.

valance A width of fabric attached to the edge of a *cloth of estate, a bed hanging or other textile so that it hangs vertically and hides the frame or support of the structure.

velvet A closely woven silk fabric with a dense raised pile.

venice gold Thread with a yellow silk core wrapped in a fine strip of silver gilt, imported from Venice. Large quantities were recorded in the royal wardrobes.

verdigris (Grecian green; from Anglo-Norman *vert de Grece*) A greenish blue mineral substance, derived from copper, used to produce a green dye.

verdure (from Fr. *vert*: 'green') A *tapestry with a design predominantly of foliate, flower or plant motifs, sometimes with small animals and birds.

warp The lengthways threads of woven fabric.

weft The widthways threads of woven fabric. The weft threads are passed over and under the *warp threads.

weld (dyer's mignonette) A Mediterranean biennial plant (*Reseda luteola*), called *herba gualda* in the Middle Ages, and the yellow dye produced from it.

whorl (spindle whorl) A small spherical weight, with a hole in the middle, attached to the *spindle to give it momentum in spinning.

woad A flowering plant, *Isatis tinctoria*, commonly grown in Britain, and the blue dye produced from its leaves.

woolfell Unshorn animal skin; the skin of a sheep with the fleece still on it.

worsted A yarn spun from the combed long-staple fibres of wool (*see* *staple (ii)), and the fabric woven from it; true worsteds were not fulled.

yarn Spun fibres used to weave or knit textiles.

Notes

ACKNOWLEDGEMENTS

1. Hayward 2004; Hayward 2009; Hayward 2012; Hayward 2016; Hayward and Kramer 2007.
2. Starkey (ed.) and Ward (transcr.) 2012; Hayward and Ward 2012.
3. Monnas 2008; Monnas 2012b.
4. Arnold 1980; Arnold 1988.
5. Alford 2017; Brotton 2016; Das 2011; Das 2017; Jardine 1996; Jardine and Brotton 2000.

INTRODUCTION

1. Richardson 2013.
2. *LP* III 869.
3. Sylvius 1991, pp. 71, 83.
4. Based on accounts from 'The King's Book of Payments, 1509', *LP* II, pp. 1441–4; TNA Currency Converter, equates £117 to 3,900 days' wages for a skilled tradesman.
5. Lennard 2006, p. 4.
6. Nichols 1823, p. 48.
7. Published by Yale University Press in association with Historic Royal Palaces; Lynn 2017.
8. Rosetti 1969, p. 186.
9. I am indebted to my colleague Charles Farris for bringing this image to my attention.
10. Sylvius 1991, p. 73.
11. Edmund Spenser, *The Faerie Queene* (1590), Book 3, Canto XI, stanza xxviii.
12. Morgan 2017, p. 107.
13. 'Revels: Miscellaneous 1519', *LP* III, p. 1559.
14. For Richard Gibson see chapter 4, p. 106, 108; see also Bindoff 1982.

1 THE GLOBAL STORY

1. Lipson 1965, p. 87; Postan 1973, p. 342.
2. The term was a common way of referring to wool from around the middle of the fourteenth century; Postan 1973, p. 342.
3. The Woolsack was the seat of the Lord Chancellor from the 1360s until 2006, when the role was changed as a result of the Constitutional Reform Act 2005, and separated from the function of Lord Speaker of the House of Lords; *Companion to the Standing Orders and Guide to the Proceedings of the House of Lords*, 25th edn (London: HMSO, 2010).
4. Accounts of Carmarthen and the Lordship of Kidwelly, TNA, DL 29/574–7, with detailed coverage of the late medieval manorial fulling industry; see also Jack 1981, pp. 87, 93–4. My thanks to the staff of Amgueddfa Wlân Cymru (National Wool Museum, Wales) for information on the fulling industry in Wales.
5. Five of the 'great twelve' city livery companies of London – that is, the highest-ranking companies as ordained by the Court of Aldermen in 1515, based on their economic power – were related to the textiles industry; Hazlitt 1892.
6. Berger 1992, p. 95.
7. The importance of duties paid can be gleaned from records of the resources the crown invested to collect them; for example, *LP* I 885.
8. Berger 1992, p. 95.
9. Coleman 1969, p. 422; see also Carus-Wilson 1952, p. 646; Power and Postan 1933, p. 43.
10. Anon., 'England's Commercial Policy', in Thomas Wright, ed., *Political Poems and Songs Relating to English History* (London: HMSO, 1861), p. 282; see also Bland, Brown and Tawney 1914, p. 187.
11. Alford 2017, p. xii; Ash 2002.
12. Roover 1999, p. 346–55; see also Wehle 1953.
13. Heard and Whitaker 2013, pp. 28–9.
14. Roover 1999, p. 357.
15. 'The Intercursus Magnus', in Pollard 1914, p. 291.
16. Fisher 1996, p. 589; Alford 2017, p. xiii.
17. Alford 2017, p. xiii.
18. Macpherson 1805, pp. 692–3; the sum of £3.5 million is as calculated by TNA Currency Converter.
19. 'The King's Book of Payments, 1509', *LP* II, pp. 1441–4; see also *LP* II 4148. Portinari himself fell from grace with the Medici because of his bad investments while at the Bruges branch of the Medici bank: it was he who tried to establish the alum cartel whose failure caused the Medici retreat from Bruges.
20. Gottfried von Strassburg and A. T. Hatto, trans., *Tristan [. . .] with the Surviving Fragments of the Tristan of Thomas*, Penguin Classics (Harmondsworth: Penguin, 1960), p. 346.
21. Lloyd 1982, p. 3; Sutton 2016, p. 3.
22. Ibid.
23. Phipps 2010, p. 29; Sutton 2016, pp. 3–4.
24. Brotton 2016, p. 41.
25. Phipps 2010, p. 30.
26. Sutton 2016, pp. 3–4.
27. Wubs-Mrozewicz and Jenks 2012, p. 50.
28. Lynn 2017, p. 20.
29. Crowfoot, Pritchard and Staniland 1992, p. 89.
30. Hayward 2007, p. 75; see also Lynn 2017, p. 19; Ross 1997, p. 261.
31. Monnas 2012a, p. 283.
32. Hale 2005, p. 8.
33. Bruscoli 2007, pp. 167–76; see also Miskimin 1978, p. 147; Singer 1948.
34. Lynn 2017, p. 20; McCabe 2015, p. 23.
35. For example, Domenico Ghirlandaio

(1449–1494), *Madonna and Child Enthroned with Saints*, c.1483, Galleria degli Uffizi, Florence; Domenico di Bartolo (c.1400–c.1447), *The Marriage of the Foundlings*, c.1440–42, Spedale di Santa Maria della Scala, Siena; Carlo Crivelli (c.1430/5–c.1494), *Annunciation with St Emidius*, 1486, SS. Annunziata, Ascoli, now in the National Gallery, London; and Hans Memling (c.1430–1494), *St John Altarpiece*, 1479, Sintjanshospitaal, now in the Memling Museum, Bruges.

36. Stabel 2012, p. 92.
37. Pinner and Denny 1986, p. 32.
38. Sicca 2002, p. 166.
39. Emery 2000, pp. 49–50.
40. For example, *LP* I 969, 1262; see also Bratchel 2016, p. 11.
41. *LP* I 1262. £1,400 would equate to almost £1 million in today's money, as calculated by TNA Currency Converter.
42. *LP* I 1315.
43. *LP* I 1311.
44. *LP* I 1504.
45. Sicca 2002, pp. 178–9.
46. Ibid., p. 170.
47. Monnas 2012a, p. 244.
48. *LP* III 1021.
49. Thomson 1993, p. 154.
50. Burgon 1839, pp. 360–62.
51. Sir Thomas Gresham to Sir Thomas Parry, 24 June 1560, in Burgon 1839, p. 362.
52. *LP* XIX/i 410, 448, 988.
53. *LP* XIX/i 725.
54. *LP* XIX/i 458.
55. *Calendar of the Patent Rolls [. . .] Edward VI.* vol. III: *1549–1551*, pp. 208–9.
56. Blockmans and Prevenier 1999, p. 174–205.
57. Ibid.
58. Whitelock 2009, p. 288.
59. Finlay 1981, p. 67.
60. Unwin 1963, p. 246.
61. 'Scotland and the Flemish People', University of St Andrews project, https://flemish.wp.st-andrews.ac.uk/2014/02/07/flemish-religious-emigration-in-the-16th17th-centuries-2/ (accessed 5 October 2018).
62. Levey 1998, pp. 24–5.
63. Wyld 2012 credits the work of Sophie Schneebalg-Perelman on routine retouching with paint at Flemish tapestry centres; see Schneebalg-Perelman 1961; see also Levey 1998, pp. 24–5; Vanwelden 1999, p. 49–75
64. Kerridge 1985, pp. 80–81.
65. Turner 2002.
66. TNA, PRO, C 5/49, fols 317–19; *Calendar of the Patent Rolls: Elizabeth I*, vol. IV: *1566–1569*, 2573.

67. Turner 2012; see also Kerridge 1985, p. 80.
68. Kemp 1898, p. 48.
69. It was made for Robert Dudley, Earl of Leicester, Queen Elizabeth's long-term favourite.
70. For example, Le Moyne 1586 (see p. 22).
71. Coleman 1969, p. 427.
72. I am indebted to Dr Stephanie Makins of Enjoy Norwich for sharing this information with me; personal communication, November 2018.
73. Coleman 1969, p. 427.
74. I am indebted to the National Trust team at the Guildhall of Corpus Christi, Lavenham, Suffolk; personal communication, December 2018.
75. Fisher 1940; Clay 1984, pp. 113–14.
76. Brotton 2016, pp. 39–40.
77. Haynes 1740, p. 409.
78. Alford 2017, p. xv; see also *LP* X 25.
79. 'Cecil Papers: April 1576', *Calendar of the Cecil Papers in Hatfield House*, vol. II: *1572–1582*, 376.
80. Ash 2002, p. 7.
81. Ibid., p. 8.
82. Phipps 2010, p. 27.
83. Ash 2002, p. 10.
84. *Calendar of the Patent Rolls: Philip & Mary*, vol II: *1554–1555*, p. 57.
85. Tittler 1991, pp. 49–50.
86. *Calendar of the Patent Rolls: Philip & Mary*, vol II: *1554–1555*, pp. 56–9.
87. *Calendar of State Papers, Domestic: Elizabeth I, Addenda, 1566–1579*, no. 44, p. 23.
88. Alford 2017.
89. Hakluyt 1809, pp. 486–7.
90. Ibid.
91. Ash 2002, p. 14.
92. Alford 2017, p. 152–4; Brotton 2016, p. 226–7; Das 2011.
93. Baskett et al. 2007, p. 240.
94. Armitage 1990, p. 304. It is likely that Le Moyne only just escaped with his life, so his drawings and watercolours are probably based on later reconstructions.
95. Laudonnière 1587, fol. 1v.
96. Rosenwald Collection, Library of Congress Rare Book and Special Collections Division, Washington, DC, G159.B7; see also Armitage 1990, p. 304; Groesen 2008.
97. Groesen 2008, p. 202.
98. Carey and Jowitt 2012, pp. 61, 95–6.
99. Broudy 1979, p. 140.
100. Phipps 2010, p. 31.
101. Brunello 1973, p. 183.
102. Rosetti 1969, p. xi.
103. The first edition is sometimes cited with a publication date of 1540; however, Borghetty

and Edelstein have conclusively argued that '1540' was a printing error, and that the date of the first print run was 1548; Rosetti 1969.
104. Ibid., p. 89.
105. Brunello 1973, p. 183.
106. Rosetti 1969, pp. 136, 94.
107. Ibid., p. xviii.
108. Phipps 2010, p. 32.
109. As revealed by HRP conservation analysis, Hampton Court Palace, 2018.
110. 'Friseadowe' or 'frizado' was woollen cloth with a raised nap on one side, commonly – and probably in this context – imported from the Netherlands; see Kerridge 1985, pp. 91–3.
111. Nichols 1823, p. 449; see also Stafford 1581.

2 POWER AND LIGHT

1. Lynn 2017, p. 65.
2. Sneyd 1847, p. 46.
3. Ibid.
4. Gunn and Janse 2006.
5. Hayward 2005, p. 6.
6. Jones and Underwood 1992, p. 76.
7. The vestments that survive were rescued by the Jesuits from destruction by Protestants, at an unknown date; how they came into the hands of the Jesuits is likewise unknown. They had been smuggled out of the country to the Jesuit College at Saint-Omer by 1609, well before the outbreak of the Civil War, which precipitated the destruction of the rest of the set.
8. 'Payment Book, October 1499 to October 1502', TNA, E101/415/3, fol. 19. This sum would equate to almost £200,000 in modern money or almost 10,000 days wages for a skilled tradesman in 1500, as calculated by TNA Currency Converter.
9. Monnas 1989, p. 346.
10. Astle 1775, p. 37.
11. Jan Graffius, curator, Stonyhurst College, personal communication, June 2018.
12. When the Jesuit order was suppressed in France in the eighteenth century, the surviving vestments were brought back to England and taken to Stonyhurst College, Lancashire, which succeeded the Jesuit college at Saint-Omer. Jan Graffius, curator, Stonyhurst College, personal communication, June 2018.
13. MacGregor 1989, p. 334.
14. As calculated by TNA Currency Converter.
15. 1547 Inventory, no. 9762; cited in Monnas 2012a, p. 285.
16. Campbell 2012, p. 9.

17. Ibid., pp. 49, 51.
18. Goodman and Gillespie 1999, p. 10.
19. BNF, Département des Manuscrits, 138. The manuscript has been digitised and is available online at https://gallica.bnf.fr/ark:/12148/btv1b90589090 (accessed 18 January 2018). Another copy is Abbaye de Saint-Bertin, Saint-Omer, MS 723.
20. Campbell 2012, p. 12.
21. McKendrick 1987, pp. 521–4.
22. Kipling 1981, p. 137–42.
23. Ibid.
24. Campbell 2002, p. 19.
25. 'Records of the Keeper of the Privy Seal', TNA, PSO 2/3; see Campbell 1877, pp. 280–81.
26. McKendrick 1991, p. 57.
27. V&A catalogue record, E.2224-1924; see also McKendrick 1991, p. 60.
28. Kipling 1977, p. 61.
29. BL, Harley MS 1419, fol. 217r; see Kipling 1981, pp. 142–4.
30. Thomas Campbell suggests that the depiction in the lost piece was 'probably of [the wedding of] Henry himself to Elizabeth of York'; Campbell 2012, p. 15. Kipling suggests that the purported marriage piece is not lost but is identifiable with the surviving 'Betrothal of Prince Arthur' at Founders' Tower, Magdalen College, Oxford – a Brussels tapestry of c.1500, probably from the workshop of Pieter van Aelst of Enghien's workshop; Kipling 1981, p. 142.
31. Kipling 1981, p. 142.
32. The textiles were recorded as part of the 1547 Inventory, after Henry VIII's death, though they were inherited from his father; Monnas 2012a, p. 276.
33. Campbell 2007, pp. 92–3.
34. Ibid.; see also Campbell 2012, pp. 17, 56.
35. Campbell 2007, pp. 92–3.
36. BL, Harley MS 642, fols 206–225 (originally fols 198–217), in Nichols 1790, p. 126. David Starkey suggests that these ordinances are an antiquarian composite of instructions on household articles of 31 December 1493 and provisions in the earlier Ryalle Book; see Starkey 1999, pp. 107–33.
37. Campbell 2007, pp. 92–3; see also Campbell 2012, p. 17.
38. Jardine and Brotton 2000, p. 70.
39. Scott 1898, p. 365.
40. Jones and Underwood 1992, pp. 71–4.
41. 'Spain: July 1498, 21–31', Calendar of State Papers, Spain, vol. I: 1485–1509, no. 210, pp. 167–80.
42. Jones and Underwood 1992, p. 153.
43. Ibid., p. 189.

44. Scott 1898, p. 356.
45. Anglo 1997; a counter position is offered in Gunn and Janse 2006, p. 142.
46. Hall 1809, p. 508.
47. Ibid., pp. 507–8.
48. 'The King's Book of Payments, 1509', LP II, pp. 1441–4. In 1509, £1 would have been equivalent to a month's wages for a skilled craftsman, as calculated by TNA Currency Converter.
49. Hall 1809, pp. 507–8.
50. Ibid.
51. Richardson 2013, p. 8.
52. Cavendish 1708, pp. 87–8.
53. Giustinian 1854, p. 47, cited in Hayward 2007, p. 226.
54. Richardson 2013, p. 64.
55. King 1994.
56. Calendar of State Papers Relating to English Affairs in the Archives of Venice, vol. IV: 1527–1533, pp. 56–66.
57. Russell 1969, p. 30
58. Richardson 2013, pp. 42–3; see also Glenn Richardson, 'Temporary Magnificence, Permanent Peace? The Meaning of the Field of Cloth of Gold', unpublished paper delivered at 'Temporary Magnificence: The Ephemerality of Early Modern Courts', AHRC / Hampton Court Palace conference, 27 October 2018.
59. LP III 869.
60. Sylvius 1991, pp. 79, 83.
61. Richardson 2013, p. 68.
62. Hall 1809, p. 608.
63. Sylvius 1991, p. 71.
64. LP III 869.
65. I am indebted to Alden Gregory, curator, HRP, who devised and led the Historic Royal Palaces' 'Portable Palaces' research project (2018, funded by AHRC), for sharing this research with me.
66. Hayward 2012b, pp. 119–20. The Ewery was the department of the royal household where ewers and towels and other linen were stored.
67. LP I, Appendix, 'Commissions of the Peace and Miscellaneous', 25.
68. Giustinian 1854, p. 192.
69. Hall 1809, pp. 722–3. That it was Holbein who painted the cloths is deduced from the accounts of the festivities, TNA, SP 2/C, calendared in LP IV 2375–3506; see Foister 2001.
70. 1547 Inventory, no. 9191.
71. Nichols 1855, p. 23.
72. 1547 Inventory, no. 8988.
73. Ibid., no. 9207.
74. 'The Household Book of Sir Anthony Denny, Keeper of the Palace at Westminster, 34

Henry VIII – 2 Edward VI', TNA, E315/160, fol. 7v.
75. Campbell 2012, p. 9.
76. 1547 Inventory, nos 11959–12051.
77. Olson 2013, p. 49.
78. LP III 1021.
79. 'Justice Disarmed by Mercy', Royal Collection Trust, RCIN 1046, on display at Hampton Court Palace; for Wolsey's inventory of January 1530 see BL, Harley MS 599, calendared in LP IV 6184.
80. BL Harley MS 599, calendared in LP IV 6184.
81. Ibid.; see also Campbell 2004.
82. BL Harley MS 599, calendared in LP IV 6184; Campbell 2012, pp. 21–2.
83. 'The Triumphs of Petrarch', Royal Collection Trust catalogue record, RCIN 1270; BL, Harley MS 599, calendared in LP IV 6184.
84. John Skelton, Collyn Clout, Book II, lines 936–81, in Dyce 1843, pp. 347–9.
85. Giustinian 1854, p. 314. A ducat is worth about £100 in today's money.
86. BL, Harley MS 599, calendared in LP IV 6184.
87. Cavendish 1708, p. 142.
88. 'Treasurer of the Chamber's Accounts', TNA, E101/420/11, fol. 5v, calendared in Lists and Analysis of State Papers, Foreign Series: July 1593 – December 1594, p. 304.
89. For example, see LP IV/ii 3233, 3419; see also Doran and Durston 2003, p. 62.
90. Campbell 2007, pp. 92–3; see also Campbell 2012, p. 31.
91. Royal Collection Trust catalogue record, RCIN 1255; see also Campbell 2007, p. 207.
92. Campbell 2007, p. 207.
93. Royal Collection Trust catalogue record, RCIN 1046.
94. Ibid.
95. Chatsworth Archives, Hardwick MS 7, fols 18r, 21v, 28v.
96. Royal Collection Trust catalogue record, RCIN 1046.
97. 1547 Inventory, no. 15204; see also Campbell 2012, p. 54.
98. 1547 Inventory, nos 15267–15279.
99. Monnas 2012a, p. 48.
100. The occasion depicted in the lost mural is slightly doubtful. According to Dale Hoak, the image shows a grand procession to Westminster Palace on 19 February 1547, before Edward's coronation on the following day; 'Edward VI (1537–1553)', ODNB (accessed 2 June 2019).
101. 'State Papers Domestic, Edward VI, Letters and Papers Jan–Apr 1549', TNA, SP 10/6, calendared in Calendar of State Papers, Domestic: Edward VI, 1547–1553, no. 204, pp. 94–5.

102. Westfall 2001, p. 271.
103. Feuillerat 1914, p. *59*.
104. Nichols 1850, p. 167.
105. *Calendar of State Papers Relating to English Affairs in the Archives of Venice*, vol. V: *1534–1554*, no. 898, p. 511.
106. Nichols 1850, p. 152.
107. See the Fundación Carlos de Amberes, Patrimonio Nacional y Groupo Enciclo, research and digitisation project 'Tapices Flamencos en España', http://tapestries.flandesenhispania.org (accessed 29 September 2018); see also Vega and Carretero 1986, pp. 73–92.
108. Calvert 1912, p. 32.
109. *LP* IX 596.
110. Ibid.
111. Whitelock 2009, p. 301.
112. Campbell 2007, p. 350.
113. Chatsworth Archives, Hardwick MS 7, fols 18r, 21v, 28v.
114. Royal Collection Trust catalogue records, RCIN 28120–28123.
115. See *LP* XVIII.
116. Howard 1987; see also Maurice Howard, 'Monarchs and Courts on the Move: Ephemeral Buildings in Sixteenth-Century Europe', unpublished paper delivered at 'Temporary Magnificence: The Ephemerality of Early Modern Courts', AHRC / Hampton Court Palace conference, 27 October 2018
117. Williams 1937, p. 199.
118. Campbell 2007, p. 352; Thurley 2003, pp. 87, 102.
119. Williams 1937, pp. 202–3.
120. Millar 1972, p. 166.
121. Lynn 2018.
122. Williams 2006.
123. Edmund Spenser, *The Faerie Queene* (1590), Book 3, Canto I, stanza xxxiv.
124. Jefferson B. Fletcher, 'The Painter of the Poets', *Studies in Philology*, vol. 14 (1917), pp. 153–66, cited in Hard 1930, p. 182.
125. Brill 1971, pp. 20–22.
126. Furnivall 1877, p. 238. The veracity of William Harrison's statement is questionable, given that even the greatest nobles counted only one or two gold-woven tapestries in their collections.
127. Parker 2010.
128. Madden 1831, p. 150.
129. Ibid., pp. 97, 139, 143, 145, 149, 150, 155, 171.
130. Ibid., p. 50.
131. *Calendar of Letters, Despatches, and State Papers Relating to the Negotiations between England and Spain*, vol. IV, pt ii: *Henry VIII, 1531–1533*, p. 582.
132. See Jones and Stallybrass 2000, pp. 145, 158.

133. Parker 2010, pp. 73–5.
134. BL, Royal MS 7 D X; see also Davenport 1899, ch. 2.
135. Letter from Sir Nicholas Throckmorton to Queen Elizabeth, 19 July 1567, BL, Cotton MS Caligula C I, fol. 18, calendared in *Calendar of the State Papers Relating to Scotland and Mary, Queen of Scots, 1547–1603*, vol. II, p. 355.
136. Haynes 1740, p. 510.
137. Durant 1978, p. 73; see also Ellis 1996, p. 291.
138. Ellis 1996, p. 281.
139. The details of these hangings are found in the acrimonious letters sent in 1586 by Bess to her husband after their marriage deteriorated, justifying and criticising the cost of the hangings; 'Cecil Papers: August 1586', *Calendar of the Cecil Papers in Hatfield House*, vol. III: *1583–1589*, pp. 158–61.
140. Ellis 1996, pp. 280–81.
141. Detail of the Marian hanging, worked by Mary, Queen of Scots, and Elizabeth Talbot, Countess of Shrewsbury, 1570–85, V&A, T.29-1955.
142. Fumerton 1986, p. 97.
143. Reputedly the speech given by Elizabeth at Tilbury in 1588, awaiting the Spanish invasion force of the Armada; there is some debate about the veracity of the transcript, for which see Montrose 2006, p. 148.
144. Vallaro 2018, pp. 113–18.
145. Sir Philip Sidney, *The Defence of Poesy*; see also Hamilton 1977, p. 42.
146. Francesco Petrarch was a classical scholar, considered by many as the 'Father of Humanism'. He created pseudonyms for friends and for idealised or allegorical figures in his works; see Ascoli and Falkeid 2015, p. 27. For more on Elizabeth's nicknames for courtiers see Lynn 2017, p. 90.
147. Stewart 1930, p. 94.
148. Frye 2010, p. 78.
149. Strong 1973, p. 73.
150. Fumerton 1986, p. 60.
151. Hilliard 1992, p. 43.
152. Fumerton 1986, p. 68; see also Norman 1911–12, p. 54.
153. Haldane 1976, pp. 60–61, 65.
154. Whitney 1586, 'To the Reader', p. ii.
155. Ibid., frontispiece.
156. Lynn 2017, pp. 90–100.
157. Arnold 1988, pp. 300–01.
158. Le Moyne 1586. Only three recorded copies of the book survive: BL, C.70.aa.14; Rachel Lambert Mellon Collection, Oak Spring Garden Library, Upperville, Va., 32 (3) 7; and BM, 1952,0522.1.1.
159. Paul Hulton believed that Lady Mary Sidney (née Dudley; 1530/35–1586), mother

of Philip and Mary, was Le Moyne's 'Madame de Sidney'; Hulton 1962.
160. Nicholas Hilliard's portrait is inscribed 'The Lady Mary Sydney Countess of Pembroke', *c.*1590, watercolour on vellum, NPG 5994. In BL, Add. MS 12503, fol. 151, she refers to herself as 'the sister of Sir Philip Sidney'.
161. Hannay 2002, p. 26.
162. Trans. J. W. Joliffe; quoted in Hulton 1977, pp. 186–7.
163. BL, C.70.aa.14.
164. For the notes in Anne Fitzwilliam's hand, instructing her household servants Mrs Fisher and Mrs Leyell to draw up the slips, see V&A, T.54-1972.
165. Anne Fitzwilliam (née Sidney) was the sister of Sir Henry Sidney (1529–1586). Henry married Lady Mary Dudley, sister of Robert Dudley, Earl of Leicester. Among their children were Sir Philip Sidney and Mary Sidney (later Mary Herbert, Countess of Pembroke).
166. Levey 1998.
167. Hardwick Hall, Derbyshire (National Trust), F/398, T/192, T/155, F/513, F/362.
168. The following paragraphs on the Bacton Altar Cloth are based on the author's research for Lynn 2018. The article includes a comprehensive history and provenance of the cloth, including a discussion of previous academic identifications of the cloth as a kirtle, such as Janet Arnold's; see Arnold 1988.
169. Hooper 1915.
170. I am indebted to Clare Browne for her contributions to the study of the Bacton Altar Cloth, May 2017.
171. I am indebted to Cynthia Jackson for her thoughts on the insect embroidery on the Bacton Altar Cloth.
172. I am indebted to Anna Lavelle for identifying the de Bruyn motifs and bringing them to my attention; examples can be found in the British Museum, London (see, among others, 'Winged Birds and Creatures', 1594, BM, Gg,4G.16) and the Rijksmuseum, Amsterdam (see 'Drie beren' ('Three bears'), 1594, RP-P-1897-A-19558).
173. Richardson 2007.
174. Levey 1998, p. 13.
175. For more on this see Lynn 2018. Parry's heirs did not retain Blanche's prominence at court, and her affection for the small village of Bacton is recorded in a costly effigy (which she intended to serve as her tomb, though in the end she was buried at Westminster), a generous gift of alms, and an annual bequest of £14 that is still being paid to this day.

176. Arnold 1980, p. 14.

177. Ibid.

178. Goldring et al. 2014, pp. 484–91.

179. Kolkovich 2009, p. 290; Kolkovich 2016, pp. 298–303.

180. *Speeches Delivered to her Maiestie this Last Progresse, at the Right Honorable the Lady Russels, at Bissam, the Right Honourable the Lorde Chandos at Sudely, at the Right Honoroable the Lorde Norris, at Ricorte* (Oxford: Joseph Barnes, 1592); digitised by Early English Books Online and available at http://name.umdl.umich.edu/A21246.0001.001 (accessed 24 December 2018).

181. Kolkovich 2009, p. 313; see also Leahy 2005, pp. 143–50.

182. The Stowe Inventory is BL, Stowe MS 557, and TNA, LR2/121; the documents are transcribed and edited in Arnold 1988.

183. Arnold 1988, item 41, p. 258; item 20, p. 262; item 59, p. 267; item 88, p. 270; item 37, p. 274.

184. 21 September 1593; TNA, LC 5/36.

185. Golding et al. 2014, p. 101.

186. Arnold 1988, items 5, 6, p. 252.

187. Ibid., items 7, 8, p. 252.

3 PRIVATE SPACES

1. Mitchell 2012, p. 201.

2. Ives 1995, pp. 16–21.

3. Frye 2010, p. 78.

4. BL, Add. MS 71009, fol. 21v, cited in Hayward 2004, p. 4; see also Kisby 2003.

5. Thurley 2003, p. 50

6. 'Ordinances of Eltham, January 1526', TNA, SP 2/B, fols 219, 220, in Nichols 1790, p. 156.

7. Borman 2016; Falkus 1974; Starkey 1977; Starkey 1987.

8. Ives 1995, p. 13.

9. Hayward 2005, p. 5.

10. BL, Add. MS 71009, fol. 14r–v, cited in Hayward 2005, p. 4; see also Kisby 2003.

11. BL, Add. MS 71009, fol. 21v.

12. TNA, E101/417/3, 84, calendared in *LP* I 394.2.

13. Campbell 2012, p. 56.

14. 1547 Inventory, no. 9216.

15. Nichols 1855, p. 27.

16. Hayward 2005, p. 5.

17. BL, Harley MS 599, calendared in *LP* IV 6184.

18. Thurley 2003, p. 87.

19. Ibid.

20. Williams 1937, p. 203.

21. Groos 1981, p. 151.

22. Mitchell 2012, p. 188.

23. Ibid., p. 204.

24. 'Regulations to be observed by Gentleman Ushers upon the various feasts and festivals during the year', in 'A volume illustrative of the duties of a Gentleman of the Royal Household (given 1 Feb. 1648 to — by Mr. Cheslym)', BL, Sloane MS 1494, fols 17–85 (at fol. 63), cited in Mitchell 2012, pp. 203–4.

25. Round 1903, p. 280; see 'A Breviate touching the Order and Government of a Nobleman's house', 1605, ed. Joseph Banks, *Archaeologia*, vol. 13 (1800), pp. 315–89.

26. Borman 2016, p. 304.

27. Mitchell 1997; Mitchell 2012, p. 218.

28. A napkin almost identical with that in fig. 61 was made in Kortrijk; see Abegg-Stiftung, Riggisbert, 4534a, based on the engraving of 1559 by the Netherlander Frans Huys (1522–1562).

29. See Hayward 2005.

30. Morgan 2017, pp. 85, 111.

31. Penelope Eames, cited in Hayward 2005.

32. Nichols 1855, p. 27.

33. Hayward 2005, p. 1.

34. 1547 Inventory, no. 11432.

35. BL, Harley MS 642, fols 206–225 (originally fols 198–217), in Nichols 1790, pp. 122–5. Household ordinances were a set of detailed instructions for the government and organisation of the royal household.

36. Nichols 1790, p. 122.

37. Ibid., p. 125.

38. Levey 1998, p. 30; Monnas 2012a, p. 282.

39. Nicolas 1830, pp. 82–3.

40. Borman 2016, p. 31.

41. Nichols 1790, p. 125.

42. Hayward 2007, p. 198.

43. Nichols 1790, p. 125.

44. 1547 Inventory, no. 12162.

45. Ibid.

46. Levey 2012, p. 147.

47. 1547 Inventory, no. 9219.

48. BL, Harley MS 599, calendared in *LP* IV 6184.

49. This set was the subject of significant research by the V&A's curator Donald King and recorded in the museum's catalogue records; King 1981. For the art-historical reading of the grotesque, see Morel 1997.

50. Hume 1896, p. 263; for Elizabeth's preparations for 'Monsieur's' arrival see *Calendar of State Papers, Foreign: Elizabeth*, vol. XV: *January 1581 – April 1582*, no. 369; and *Calendar of the Cecil Papers in Hatfield House*, vol. II: *1572–1582*.

51. 1547 Inventory, no. 9035.

52. Levey 2012, p. 149.

53. *Calendar of State Papers Relating to English Affairs in the Archives of Venice*: vol. IV: *1527–1533*, no. 822, pp. 355–68.

54. Hentzner 1757, pp. 40–41.

55. 'Account Book of Sir Ralph Sadler, keeper of the Great Wardrobe, April 1543–1545', TNA, E101/423/10, fol. 74.

56. Campbell 2007, p. 166.

57. Campbell 2012, p. 57.

58. Campbell 2007, p. 207.

59. 1547 Inventory nos 12881, 9208; see also Levey 2012, p. 147.

60. Frick Collection, New York, and National Portrait Gallery, London (two versions).

61. Frick Collection, New York.

62. BL, Harley MS 599, calendared in *LP* IV 6184.

63. BM, G,3.178, 1548, engraving. The engraving is after Holbein, signed with the initials 'I.f.', for the engraver Jacob (or Jakob) Faber. The image occurs on fol. 263v of the 1548 version of Halle's *The union of the two noble and illustre fameiles of Lancastre & Yorke*, for which see Dodgson 1938, p. 9. It also appears in a 1550 edition in a private collection (sold at auction in April 2016, New York), with the modified motto 'God Save the Kyng'.

64. King 2012, p. 131–42.

65. About seventy-five carpets were listed at each of Greenwich and Westminster, with others distributed around other palaces.

66. Sicca 2002, p. 194.

67. Levey 2012, p. 148.

68. Ibid.; 1547 Inventory, no. 12762.

69. Madden 1831, pp. 50, 97, 139, 143, 145, 149, 150, 155, 171.

70. BL, Harley MS 599, calendared in *LP* IV 6184.

71. Levey 1998, p. 30.

72. 1547 Inventory, nos 10505, 11910, 11917, 11129; see also Lynn 2017, p. 73.

73. 1547 Inventory, nos 1424, 2411, 2427, 2556, 2561, 2612, 3186, 10425, 10433, 10454.

74. Ibid., nos 10414, 10535, 11374.

75. Ibid., nos 11073, 11092.

76. The idea that Henry fathered other illegitimate children whom he did not acknowledge has inspired popular historical fiction, particularly respecting Mary Boleyn's children, Catherine (c.1524–1569) and Henry Carey (1526–1596), who may have been Henry's offspring. Henry himself acknowledged only Henry Fitzroy.

4 THE GREAT WARDROBE

1. Hayward 2007, p. 265.

2. Arnold 1988, p. 163.

3. Ibid., p. 165. Westminster Palace was the main royal residence until 1512, when much of it burned down. In 1536 the king

confiscated Wolsey's nearby residence, York Place, later renamed Whitehall, and effectively merged it with the adjoining ancient palace, renaming it the King's Palace at Westminster. References to the palaces of Whitehall and Westminster are synonymous, particularly in the Elizabethan period.

4. Hentzner 1757, p. 20.
5. Monnas 2012a, p. 235.
6. As calculated by TNA Currency Converter.
7. Stabel 2006.
8. 'Gibson, Richard, of London and New Romney, Kent', in Bindoff 1982; see also regular entries in *LP*, vols I–VII.
9. 'Officers of the Revels and Tents', Streitberger 1994, pp. 430–32.
10. Hayward 2012b, p. 112.
11. Research undertaken by Cinzia Maria Sicca into the records of the Cavalcanti and Bardi company has provided significant new information on the business of the company and Tudor trading practices; see Sicca 2002.
12. Sicca 2007, p. 97.
13. Ibid., p. 102.
14. Nicolas 1827: for Parker see pp. 16, 83, 254, 269, 271, 279, 282; for Gresham see pp. 7, 116, 261; for Lock see pp. 14, 45, 74, 78, 87, 128, 144, 163, 261, 276; see also Sicca 2007, footnote 81, p. 102.
15. *LP* III 2214 (20).
16. Ibid.
17. Sicca 2007, p. 98.
18. As established by Cinzia Maria Sicca's research in the Archivio di Stato, Florence, fondo Venturi Ginori Lisci; see Sicca 2007, p. 98.
19. *Calendar of State Papers and Manuscripts, Venice*, vol. III: *1520–1526*, nos 13, 35, 133, pp. 4, 10, 92.
20. *LP* XIII/ii 1185.
21. *LP* IV 6748 (13).
22. *LP* III 1153; see also Jefferson 2009, p. 1014.
23. *LP* IV 6184.
24. Hanham 1985, p. 427.
25. 'Cromwell's Remembrances', *LP* VI 1382.
26. 'The King's Book of Payments by John Heron, Treasurer of the Chamber, April 1509–April 1518', TNA, E36/215, fol. 533, calendared in 'The King's Book of Payments, 1517', *LP* II, p. 1476. For the conclusion that the king was involved see Campbell 2012, pp. 21, 36.
27. As calculated by TNA Currency Converter; the modern-day equivalent is £780,000.
28. 'Revels: Miscellaneous', *LP* III, p. 1550.
29. TNA, SP 1/29, fols 192r–193v, calendared in 'Revels: Miscellaneous 1519', *LP* III/ii 1548.
30. Ibid.

31. *LP* IV 6184.
32. An act of attainder deprived someone held guilty of treason or a felony of their estate and extinguished their right to inherit or transmit property by descent; an attainder was passed by parliament and took effect without trial.
33. Campbell 2012, p. 37.
34. Cromwell's 'goods' were distributed to 'Davy Vyncent, Mr. Cyssyll, Brystowe, Mr. Baynton, Mr. Henege; Cotton, Mr. Henege's man; John Gate and my lord of Sussex; the "robes of the Garter of crimson and purple velvet" remain at Hampton Court by the King's command'; *LP* XV 917.
35. Although Heylyn's work was published more than a hundred years after the fact, the results of which he spoke may well still have been within living memory; Heylyn 1661, p. 134.
36. Stuart 1874, p. 14.
37. Warrant of 3 April 1588, BL, Egerton MS 2806, fol. 227; see Lynn 2017, p. 97.
38. Arnold 1988, p. 93.
39. Goldring et al. 2014, pp. 238–51; p. 248 for Parry's gift.
40. Williams 1937, p. 203.
41. 'Exchequer Accounts', *LP* I 417 (4).
42. Burke 1852, p. 140.
43. *LP* XIII/ii 1201.
44. She is referred to as 'Mrs Vaughanne, silkwoman' in *LP* X 914. For Stephen Vaughan's intercessions on her behalf to Thomas Cromwell, see Hayward 2007, p. 328.
45. Dale 1933, pp. 138–45; Lynn 2017, p. 149.
46. Hewetson was a Merchant Taylor; see 'The 1541 Orphans' Book', Lang 1993, no. 441, pp. 298–315. Lock (Lok) is referred to numerous times in the records and accounts of court; for example, see *LP* X 914.
47. *LP* IV 3469.
48. Warley 2005, p. 47.
49. Mitchell 2012, p. 197.
50. Nichols 1790, p. 235.
51. The officers of the Green Cloth were the clerks of accounts, and the clerk or clerks comptroller, responsible for the financial administration of the royal household under the lord steward. They were so named after the green cloth that was placed on the table around which they conducted business. See the administrative and background descriptions and entries for 'Records of the Lord Steward, the Board of Green Cloth and other officers of the Royal Household', TNA, LS, though a fire of 1698 destroyed most records.
52. Nichols 1790, p. 215.
53. Ibid.

54. Ibid., p. 236.
55. *LP* XII/i 450.
56. *LP* XIV/i 1145.
57. *LP* IV 6184.
58. Kipling 1981, pp. 137–42.
59. Ibid.; see also Hayward 2006, p. 13.
60. *LP* III 5243 (20).
61. 'The King's Book of Payments, 1517', *LP* II, p. 1476, where van Aelst is called Peter van Enghien; see also Campbell 2007, p. 213.
62. 'Cecil Papers: September 1578', *Calendar of the Cecil Papers in Hatfield House*, vol. II: *1572–1582*, no. 566, pp. 199–208.
63. Arnold 1988, p. 232.
64. Ibid., p. 231.
65. 1547 Inventory, no. 9034.
66. TNA, LC5/49, fol. 314, cited in Arnold 1988, p. 234.
67. Campbell 1877, pp. 25–6.
68. Ibid.
69. Ibid., p. 25.
70. Nicolas 1830, p. 140.
71. BL, Add. MS 71009, fol. 17, cited in Kisby 2003, p. 25.
72. Ibid.
73. Cavendish 1708, p. 87.
74. Ibid.
75. *LP* III/i 804. Sir Henry Wyatt (*c*.1460–1537) was one of the longest-serving Tudor courtiers, under both Henry VII and Henry VIII.
76. Nichols 1823, p. 168.
77. J. Paul Getty Museum, Los Angeles, MS Ludwig I 15.
78. Maurice Howard, 'Monarchs and Courts on the Move: Ephemeral Buildings in Sixteenth-Century Europe', unpublished paper delivered at 'Temporary Magnificence: The Ephemerality of Early Modern Courts', AHRC / Hampton Court Palace conference, 27 October 2018.
79. Jackson 1896, pp. 26–8.
80. Thurley 2003, p. 86.
81. Adams 1995, p. 194.
82. Ibid., p. 183.
83. Ibid., p. 145.
84. Rye 1865, p. 13.
85. BL, Harley MS 599, calendared in *LP* IV 6184.
86. 'Mr Althams' was Mark Hall in Essex, belonging to James Altham (1529–1583), alderman and sheriff of London. For the account of Wingfield's preparations see Colthorpe and Bateman 1977, p. 28.
87. Cawarden's appointment was backdated, so is often given as 1544; *LP* XX/i 465 (27); Hayward 2012b, p. 110.
88. Hayward 2004, p. 97.
89. *LP* XXI/i 1464.

90. *Calendar of State Papers, Domestic: Elizabeth*, vol. V: *1598–1601*, no. 94, p. 315.

5 TUDOR TEXTILES

1. Scarlet came to be used for bed furnishings instead of for dress; Monnas 2012a, p. 282.
2. I am indebted to Amgueddfa Wlân Cymru (National Wool Museum, Wales), Llandysul, for much of the information in the following section.
3. Richard Watts, *The young man's looking-glass, Or, A summary discourse between the ant and the grashopper* (London, 1641), pp. 42–4; see also *Victoria County History: Somerset*, vol. II, ed. William Page (London: Constable, 1911), pp. 411ff.
4. Muldrew 2012, p. 520. I am indebted to the Weald and Downland Museum, West Sussex, for information on the walking wheel; the museum owns a reconstruction.
5. My first job at a museum was to demonstrate spinning for York Archaeological Trust, whose Coppergate excavation site (now the Jorvik Viking Centre) had yielded 230 spindle whorls dating from the eight to the tenth centuries. That I never mastered spinning, despite my best efforts and much practice, leaves me in admiration of the skill of the spinster.
6. Muldrew 2012, p. 503.
7. Ibid., p. 512.
8. Museum De Lakenhal, Leiden, catalogue records S 420–422.
9. I am indebted to Museum De Lakenhal, Amgueddfa Wlân Cymru, the Weald and Downland Museum and the Guildhall of Corpus Christi in Lavenham for information on the production of woollen cloth.
10. I am indebted to the living-history teams at the Monreagh Heritage Centre, County Donegal, and the Weald and Downland Museum for information on the production of linen cloth.
11. Sutton 2016, pp. 3–4.
12. BM, F,1.164; BM, F,1.166–168; see also BM, 1948,0410.4.210–215.
13. Burnham 1980, p. 124.
14. King 2005, pp. 1–9.
15. I am indebted to the Weald and Downland Museum for information on dyeing.
16. Monnas 2012a, p. 251.
17. Rosetti 1969.
18. Ibid., p. xiv.
19. Ibid., p. 236.
20. Ibid., p. 151.
21. Edelstein 1966, p. 396.
22. Brunello 1973, p. 188.
23. Marichal 2006, p. 76.
24. Phipps 2010, p. 26.
25. 'Gomez de Cervantes' Memorial and the Anonymous Pictorial Manuscript "Memorial de Don Gonçalo Gomez de Cervantes del modo de vivir que tienen los indos, y del beneficio de las minas de la plata, y de la cochinella")', late sixteenth century, Mexico, BM, Add. MS 13964, inv. no. Am2006,Drg.210.
26. Phipps 2010, p. 14.
27. Monnas 2012a, p. 280.
28. I am indebted to Tessitura Luigi Bevilacqua, Venice, Italy, for information on this process.
29. Anna Karatzini, 'Metal Threads: The Historical Development', unpublished conference paper delivered at 'Traditional Textile Craft: An Intangible Cultural Heritage?', Jordan Museum, Amman, 24–7 March 2014, https://conferences.saxo.ku.dk/traditionaltextilecraft (accessed 25 September 2018).
30. Monnas 2012a, p. 259.
31. Hawthorne and Smith 1979, p. 156, cited in Karatzini, 'Metal Threads: The Historical Development' (see note 30).
32. *LP* I 239.
33. TNA, SP 1/29, fols 192r–193v, calendared in *LP* III, p. 1548.
34. MacGregor 1989, p. 334.
35. Blanchard 2005, esp. pp. 1063–88.
36. Theodore de Bry, reputedly after Jacques Le Moyne de Morgues, Theodor de Bry, *Der ander Theyl [. . .] so die Frantzosen in Floridam* (Frankfurt, 1603); see British Library, G.6625.(2).
37. I am indebted to Amgueddfa Wlân Cymru, Esgair Moel Woollen Mill at St Fagans (Amgueddfa Cymru / National Wool Museum, Wales) and the Weald and Downland Museum for information on weaving.
38. Mitchell 2012, p. 191.
39. With thanks to Lisa Monnas for her assistance with the definitions and processes of looms.
40. Phipps 2010, p. 32.
41. Sicca 2007, p. 97.
42. See Monnas 1998.
43. Tatton-Brown and Mortimer 2003, p. 71.
44. As calculated by TNA Currency Converter. Monnas 2012a, p. 238.
45. Ibid.
46. Guglielmo Corsi is mentioned in the 'Cromwell Papers', *LP* VI 1701; see Monnas 2012a, p. 278.
47. As calculated by TNA Currency Converter.
48. 1547 Inventory, no. 9193.
49. King 2012, p. 142.
50. King 2012.
51. Erdmann 1970, p. 53.
52. Stabel 2012, p. 101.
53. 1547 Inventory, no. 12145.
54. Ibid., no. 13034.
55. Ibid., no. 9925.
56. Ibid., no. 12137.
57. Williams 1937, p. 203.
58. Groos 1981, p. 151
59. King 2012, p. 132.
60. Broudy 1979, p. 60.
61. Ibid.
62. For example, see 1547 Inventory, nos 9260–9295.
63. Ridgard 1985, p. 129.
64. Wyld 2012.
65. See p. 30.
66. Campbell 2012, p. 9.
67. Wyld 2012.
68. Kerridge 1985, p. 80.
69. I am indebted to the curators at the Palace of Westminster, London, for their time in introducing me to these tapestries, as depicted in the reproduction paintings, 2010, in the Princes Chamber of the House of Lords. The tapestries cost £1,582 in the 1590s, the equivalent of eighty-seven years' wages for a skilled craftsman at the time, as calculated by TNA Currency Converter.
70. Scott 1898, p. 366.
71. Ploeg 2014; see Sophie Ploeg's contemporary interpretations of historic lace and her informative blogs at www.sophieploeg.com/blog/historyofearlylace/, 16 June 2017 (accessed 26 March 2019).
72. 'Istrumento di divisione tra le sorelle Angela ed Ippolita Sforza Visconti di Milano, 12 Settembre 1493'; see Palliser 1865, p. 55.
73. Federico Vinciolo, *Les singuliers et nouveaux pourtraicts et ouvrages de lingerie* (Paris, 1587); other books on the subject had been published in Venice, see Matio Pagano *La gloria e l'honore de ponti tagliati et ponti in aere* (Venice, 1554).
74. Luu 2005, p. 115.
75. Stow 1614, p. 869; see also Korda 2011, p. 226; Luu 2005, p. 117. £5 is worth over £1,000 in today's money, as calculated by TNA Currency Converter.
76. Stow 1615, pp. 867–8.
77. Stubbes 1877–9, p. 52.
78. Cited in Jones and Stallybrass 2000, p. 69.
79. The Victoria and Albert Museum cares for a large number of surviving examples of *opus anglicanum*, notably ecclesiastical vestments; a particularly fine example is the

Butler Bowdon Cope, 1330–50, V&A, T.36-1955. See also a surcoat belonging to Edward the Black Prince (dated before 1376) in the collection of Canterbury Cathedral.

80. See the Thornton Chasuble, 1510–33, V&A, 697-1902; and the Fishmongers' Pall, 1512–*c.*1538, Worshipful Company of Fishmongers, London.

81. Levey 2012, p. 159.

82. Lynn 2017, p. 35.

83. Levey 2012, p. 159.

84. TNA, Prob. 11/14/69; see also Ransome 1964, p. 239.

85. TNA, SP 1/29, fols. 192r–193v, calendared in 'Revels 1519', *LP* III, p. 1548.

86. Ibid.

87. 'Account book of Andrew, Lord Windesore, keeper of the Great Wardrobe, 25 and 26 Hen. VIII, April 1533 – April 1535', TNA, E101/421/16, fol. 6v.

88. 'Revels 1519', *LP* III, p. 1549.

89. I am indebted to Charles Farris for sharing his research about the Berkeley hanging.

90. Smyth 1883, p. 205.

91. Lisa Monnas, 'The Making of Medieval Embroidery' in Brown 2016, pp. 7–23, esp. p. 19.

92. Levey 2012, p. 175.

93. 1547 Inventory, no. 1493 ('worke grotestan'; in this case a basin, the description of which makes this direct reference to 'grotesque'); in addition, nos 13034, 12124 ('antique heads'), 12167 ('antique boys and women') and 13607 ('antique imagery') might be read as examples of the grotesque style.

94. 'The King's Book of Payments, 1514', *LP* II, p. 1464; see also Rimer, Richardson and Cooper 2009, p. 90.

95. In addition to objects within the collection at the V&A (for example, 37-1903, T.74-1972, T.82-1978), this technique is also evident in a number of ceremonial textiles within HRP's Royal Ceremonial Dress Collection.

96. I am indebted to Dr Susan Kay-Williams for sharing her thoughts with me on various aspects of the Bacton Altar Cloth.

97. Hans Holbein the younger, design for jewellery, 1536–7, BM, SL,5308.117; design for a gold cup, 1536–7, Ashmolean Museum, University of Oxford, WA 1863.424.

98. Campbell and Foister 1986, p. 725.

99. Paget 1959; Campbell and Foister 1986.

100. Nicolas 1827, pp. 16, 83, 254, 269, 271, 279, 282.

101. Kren and McKendrick 2003, pp. 432–4.

102. Frye 2010, p. 78.

103. Eisenstein 1979, pp. 3, 134, 428–9.

104. I am indebted to the Gardens Team at Hampton Court Palace for botanical information; see also Levey 2012, p. 179.

6 EPILOGUE

1. Strong 1969, pp. 351–3.

2. Maclean 2007, p. 38; see also Gerald Maclean, 'Ottoman Things in Early Modern England', unpublished conference paper delivered at the third annual conference of the 'Text and Event in Early Modern Europe' programme 'Contemplating Early Modernities: Concept, Content & Context', Freie Universität, Berlin, 30 October – 1 November 2014, for more on which, see Brotton 2016.

3. Penn 2011, pp. 41–2.

4. Campbell 2008, p. 111.

5. Campbell 2012, p. 20.

6. *Calendar of State Papers Relating to English Affairs in the Archives of Venice*, vol. IV: *1527–1533*, 105.

7. Campbell 2008, p. 111.

8. Hearn 2004; Maclean 2007, p. 38.

Bibliography

PRIMARY SOURCES

Selected Letters and Papers, Foreign and Domestic of Henry VIII (LP)

J. S. Brewer, J. Gairdner and R. H. Brodie, eds, *Letters and Papers, Foreign and Domestic, of the Reign of Henry VIII*, 23 vols. in 38 (London: HMSO, 1862–1932; repr. 1965) [volumes cited in the notes are listed below; references consist of the abbreviation *LP*, followed by volume, part (where relevant) and item numbers, unless otherwise indicated]

LP, vol. I: *1509–1514*, ed. J. S. Brewer (London: HMSO, 1920)

LP, vol. II: *1515–1518*, ed. J. S. Brewer (London: HMSO, 1864)

LP, vol. III: *1519–1523*, ed. J. S. Brewer (London: HMSO, 1867)

LP, vol. IV: *1524–1530*, ed. J. S. Brewer (London: HMSO, 1875)

LP, vol. V: *1531–1532*, ed. James Gairdner (London: HMSO, 1880)

LP, vol. VI: *1533*, ed. James Gairdner (London: HMSO, 1882)

LP, vol. VII: *1534*, ed. James Gairdner (London: HMSO, 1883)

LP, vol. IX: *August–December 1535*, ed. James Gairdner (London: HMSO, 1886)

LP, vol. X: *January–June 1536*, ed. James Gairdner (London: HMSO, 1887)

LP, vol. XII, pt i: *January–May 1537*, ed. James Gairdner (London: HMSO, 1890)

LP, vol. XII, pt ii: *June–December 1537*, ed. James Gairdner (London: HMSO, 1891)

LP, vol. XIII, pt i: *January–July 1538*, ed. James Gairdner (London: HMSO, 1892)

LP, vol. XIII, pt ii: *August–December 1538*, ed. James Gairdner (London: HMSO, 1893)

LP, vol. XIV, pt i: *January–July 1539*, ed. James Gairdner and R. H. Brodie (London: HMSO, 1894)

LP, vol. XIV, pt ii: *August–December 1539*, ed. James Gairdner and R. H. Brodie (London: HMSO, 1895)

LP, vol. XV: *1540*, ed. James Gairdner and R. H. Brodie (London: HMSO, 1896)

LP, vol. XIX, pt i: *January–July 1544*, ed. James Gairdner and R. H. Brodie (London: HMSO, 1903)

LP, vol. XIX, pt ii: *August–December 1544*, ed. James Gairdner and R. H. Brodie (London: HMSO, 1905)

LP, vol. XX, pt i, *January–July 1545*, ed. James Gairdner and R. H. Brodie (London: HMSO, 1905)

LP, vol. XXI, pt i, *January–August 1546*, ed. James Gairdner and R. H. Brodie (London: HMSO, 1908)

Selected Calendared Papers

Calendar of State Papers, Spain, vol. I: *1485–1509*, ed. G. A. Bergenroth (London: HMSO, 1862)

Calendar of State Papers and Manuscripts, Venice, vol. III: *1520–1526*, ed. Rawdon Lubbock Brown (London: 1896)

Calendar of State Papers Relating to English Affairs in the Archives of Venice, vol. IV: *1527–1533*, ed. Rawdon Brown (London: HMSO, 1871)

Calendar of Letters, Despatches, and State Papers Relating to the Negotiations between England and Spain, Preserved in the Archives at Simancas and Elsewhere, vol. IV, pt ii: *Henry VIII, 1531–1533*, ed. Pascual de Gayangos (London: HMSO, 1882; repr. 1969)

Calendar of State Papers Relating to English Affairs in the Archives of Venice, vol. V: *1534–1554*, ed. Rawdon Brown (London: HMSO, 1873)

Calendar of State Papers, Domestic: Edward VI, 1547–1553, ed. C. S. Knighton (London: HMSO, 1992)

Calendar of State Papers, Domestic: Edward VI, Mary and Elizabeth, 1547–1580, ed. Robert Lemon (London: HMSO, 1856)

Calendar of the State Papers Relating to Scotland and Mary, Queen of Scots, 1547–1603, vol. II, ed. Joseph Bain (Edinburgh: General Register Office, 1900)

Calendar of the Patent Rolls Preserved in the Public Record Office: Edward VI, vol. III: *1549–1551* (London: HMSO, 1925)

Calendar of the Patent Rolls Preserved in the Public Record Office: Philip & Mary, vol. II: *1554–1555* (London: HMSO, 1936)

Calendar of the Patent Rolls Preserved in the Public Record Office: Elizabeth I, vol. IV: *1566–1569* (London: HMSO, 1964)

Calendar of State Papers, Domestic: Elizabeth I, Addenda, 1566–1579, ed. Mary Anne Everett Green (London: HMSO, 1871)

Calendar of State Papers, Foreign: Elizabeth, vol. XV: *January 1581 – April 1582*, ed. Arthur John Butler (London: HMSO, 1907)

Lists and Analysis of State Papers, Foreign: July 1593 – December 1594, ed. J. S. Brewer, R. H. Brodie and J. Gairdner (London: HMSO, 1965)

Calendar of State Papers, Domestic: Elizabeth, vol. V: *1598–1601*, ed. Mary Anne Everett Green (London: HMSO 1869)

Calendar of the Cecil Papers in Hatfield House, vol. II: *1572–1582* (London: HMSO, 1888)

Calendar of the Cecil Papers in Hatfield House, vol. III: *1583–1589* (London: HMSO, 1889)

Secondary Sources

ADAMS 1995

Simon Adams, ed., *Household Accounts and Disbursement Books of Robert Dudley, Earl of Leicester, 1558–1561, 1584–1586*, Camden Society, 5th ser., vol. VI (Cambridge: Cambridge University Press, 1995)

ALFORD 2017

Stephen Alford, *London's Triumph: Merchant Adventurers and the Tudor City* (London: Allen Lane, 2017)

ANGLO 1997

Sydney Anglo, *Spectacle, Pageantry, and Early Tudor Policy* (Oxford: Clarendon Press, 1997)

ARMITAGE 1990

David Armitage, 'The Procession Portrait of Queen Elizabeth I: A Note on a Tradition', *Journal of the Warburg and Courtauld Institutes*, vol. 53 (1990), pp. 301–7

ARNOLD 1980

Janet Arnold, *'Lost from Her Majesties Back': Items of Clothing and Jewels Lost or Given Away by Queen Elizabeth I between 1561–1585, Entered in One of the Day Books*, Costume Society Extra Series, vol. 7 (London: Costume Society, 1980)

ARNOLD 1988

Janet Arnold, *Queen Elizabeth's Wardrobe Unlock'd: The Inventories of the Wardrobe of Robes Prepared in July 1600* (Leeds: Maney, 1988)

ASCOLI AND FALKEID 2015

Albert Russell Ascoli and Unn Falkeid, eds, *The Cambridge Companion to Petrarch* (Cambridge: Cambridge University Press, 2015)

ASH 2002

Eric H. Ash, '"A Note and a Caveat for the Merchant": Mercantile Advisors in Elizabethan England', *Sixteenth Century Journal*, vol. 33 (2002), pp. 1–31

ASTLE 1775

Thomas Astle, ed., *The Will of King Henry VII* (London: T. Payne and B. White, 1775)

BASKETT ET AL. 2007

John Baskett, et al., *Paul Mellon's Legacy: A Passion for British Art. Masterpieces from the Yale Center for British Art* (New Haven and London: Yale University Press, 2007)

BEEM 2011

Charles Beem, ed., *The Foreign Relations of Elizabeth I* (Basingstoke: Palgrave Macmillan, 2011)

BERGER 1992

Ronald M. Berger, *Most Necessary Luxuries: The Mercers' Company of Coventry, 1550–1680* (University Park: Pennsylvania State University Press, 1992)

BINDOFF 1982

S. T. Bindoff, ed., *The History of Parliament: The House of Commons, 1509–1558* (London: Secker & Warburg for History of Parliament Trust, 1982)

BLANCHARD 2005

Ian Blanchard, *Mining, Metallurgy, and Minting in the Middle Ages*, vol. III: *Continuing Afro-European Supremacy, 1250–1450* (Stuttgart: Franz Steiner Verlag, 2005)

BLAND, BROWN AND TAWNEY 1914

A. E. Bland, P. A. Brown, and R. H. Tawney, eds, *English Economic History: Select Documents* (London: G. Bell and Sons, 1914)

BLOCKMANS AND PREVENIER 1999

Wim Blockmans and Walter Prevenier, *The Promised Lands: The Low Countries under Burgundian Rule, 1369–1530*, trans. Elizabeth Fackelman, ed. Edward Peters (Philadelphia: University of Pennsylvania Press, 1999)

BORMAN 2016

Tracy Borman, *The Private Lives of the Tudors* (London: Hodder & Stoughton, 2016)

BRATCHEL 2016

M. E. Bratchel, 'Italian Merchant Organization and Business Relationships in Early Tudor London', in Subrahmanyan 2016, pp. 1–28

BRILL 1971

Lesley W. Brill, 'Chastity as Ideal Sexuality in the Third Book of The Faerie Queene', *Studies in English Literature, 1500–1900*, vol. 11 (1971), pp. 15–26

BROTTON 2016

Jerry Brotton, *This Orient Isle: Elizabethan England and the Islamic World* (London: Allen Lane, 2016)

BROUDY 1979

Eric Broudy, *The Book of Looms: A History of the Handloom from Ancient Time to the Present* (Hanover and London: University Press of New England, 1979)

BROWNE 2016

Clare Browne et al., *Opus Anglicanum* (New Haven and London: Yale University Press/Victoria and Albert Museum, 2016)

BRUNELLO 1973

Franco Brunello, *The Art of Dyeing in the History of Mankind*, trans. Bernard Hickey (Vicenza: Neri Pozza, 1973)

BRUSCOLI 2007

Franceso Guidi Bruscoli, *Papal Banking in Renaissance Rome: Benvenuto Olivieri and Paul III, 1534–1549*, trans. Nicola Hargreaves (Aldershot: Ashgate Publishing, 2007)

BRY 1590-1634

Theodore de Bry, *The Great and Small Voyages* (Frankfurt and Oppenheim, 1590–1634)

BURGON 1839

John William Burgon, ed., *The Life and Times of Sir Thomas Gresham, Compiled Chiefly from his Correspondence Preserved in Her Majesty's State-Paper Office*, vol. II (London: Robert Jennings, 1839)

BURKE 1852

J. Bernard Burke, *A Genealogical and Heraldic Dictionary of the Landed Gentry of Great Britain and Ireland*, vol. I (London: Colburn and Co., 1852)

BURNHAM 1980

Dorothy Burnham, *Warp and Weft: A Textile Terminology* (Toronto: Royal Ontario Museum, 1980)

CALVERT 1912

Albert F. Calvert, *The Spanish Royal Tapestries* (London: John Lane, n.d. [1912])

CAMPBELL 1877

William Campbell, ed., *Materials for a History of the Reign of Henry VII*, vol. II (London: Longman & Co. et al., 1877)

CAMPBELL 2002

Thomas Campbell, *Tapestry in the Renaissance: Art and Magnificence* (New Haven and London: Yale University Press, 2002)

CAMPBELL 2004

Thomas Campbell, 'New Evidence on "Triumphs of Petrarch" Tapestries in the Early Sixteenth Century. Part 1: The French Court', *Burlington Magazine*, vol. 146 (2004), pp. 376–85

CAMPBELL 2007

Thomas Campbell, *Henry VIII and the Art of Majesty: Tapestries at the Tudor Court* (New Haven and London: Yale University Press, 2007)

CAMPBELL 2008

Thomas Campbell, ed., *Tapestry in the Baroque: Threads of Splendor* (New Haven and London: Yale University Press, 2008)

CAMPBELL 2012

Thomas Campbell, 'The Art and Splendour of Henry VIII's Tapestry Collection', in Hayward and Ward 2012, pp. 9–65

CAMPBELL AND FOISTER 1986

Lorne Campbell and Susan Foister, 'Gerard, Lucas and Susanna Horenbout', *Burlington Magazine*, vol. 128 (1986), pp. 719–27

CAREY AND JOWITT 2012

Daniel Carey and Claire Jowitt, eds, *Richard Hakluyt and Travel Writing in Early Modern Europe*, Hakluyt Society Extra Series, vol. 47 (Farnham: Ashgate Publishing, 2012)

CARUS-WILSON 1952

E. M. Carus-Wilson, 'The Woollen Industry', in Edward Miller, Cynthia Postan and M. M. Postan, eds, *The Cambridge Economic History of Europe*, vol. II: *Trade and Industry in the Middle Ages* (Cambridge: Cambridge University Press, 1952), pp. 613–90

CAVENDISH 1708

William [*recte* George] Cavendish, *Memoirs of the Life of Cardinal Woolsey*, 2nd edn (London: B. Bragg, 1708)

CLAY 1984

C. G. A. Clay, *Economic Expansion and Social Change: England, 1500–1700*, vol. II (Cambridge: Cambridge University Press, 1984)

COLEMAN 1969

D. C. Coleman, 'An Innovation and its Diffusion: The "New Draperies"', *Economic History Review*, vol. 22 (1969), pp. 417–29

COLTHORPE AND BATEMAN 1977

Marion Colthorpe and Linley Herbert Bateman, *Queen Elizabeth I and Harlow* (Harlow: Harlow Development Corporation, 1977)

CROWFOOT, PRITCHARD AND STANILAND 1992

Elisabeth Crowfoot, Frances Pritchard and Kay Staniland, *Textiles and Clothing, c.1150–c.1450*, Medieval Finds from Excavations in London, vol. 4 (London: HMSO, 1992)

DALE 1933

Marian K. Dale, 'The London Silkwomen of the Fifteenth Century', *Economic History Review*, vol. 4 (1933), pp. 324–35

DAS 2011

Nandini Das, 'Elizabeth and India', in Beem 2011, pp. 201–20

DAS 2017

Nandini Das, ed., *Hakluyt's Principall Navigations, Voyages, Traffikes, and Discoveries of the English Nation, 1598–1600*, vol. VI: *Elizabethan Levant Trade and South Asia* (Oxford: Oxford University Press, 2017)

DAVENPORT 1899

Cyril Davenport, *English Embroidered Bookbindings* (London: Kegan Paul, Trench, Trübner and Co., 1899)

DAVIES AND GALLOWAY 2012

Matthew Davies and James A. Galloway, eds, *London and Beyond: Essays in Honour of Derek Keene* (London: University of London, School of Advanced Study, 2012)

DODGSON 1938–9

Campbell Dodgson, 'Woodcuts Designed by Holbein for English Printers', *Volume of the Walpole Society*, vol. 27 (1938–9), pp. 1–11

DORAN AND DURSTON 2003

Susan Doran and Christopher Durston, *Princes, Pastors, and People: The Church and Religion in England, 1500–1700*, 2nd edn (Abingdon and New York: Routledge, 2003)

DURANT 1978

David N. Durant, *Bess of Hardwick: Portrait of an Elizabethan Dynasty* (New York: Atheneum, 1978)

DYCE 1843

Alexander Dyce, ed., *The Poetical Works of John Skelton*, vol. I (London: Thomas Rodd, 1843)

EDELSTEIN 1966

Sidney M. Edelstein, 'Dyeing Fabrics in Sixteenth-Century Venice', *Technology and Culture*, vol. 7 (1966), pp. 395–7

EISENSTEIN 1979

Elizabeth L. Eisenstein, *The Printing Press as an Agent of Change: Communications and Cultural Transformations in Early-Modern Europe*, 2 vols. (Cambridge: Cambridge University Press, 1979)

ELLIS 1996

Margaret Ellis, 'The Hardwick Wall Hangings: An Unusual Collaboration in English Sixteenth-Century Embroidery', *Renaissance Studies*, vol. 10 (1996), pp. 280–300

EMERY 2000

Anthony Emery, *Greater Medieval Houses of England and Wales, 1300–1500*, vol. II: *East Anglia, Central England and Wales* (Cambridge: Cambridge University Press, 2000)

ERDMANN 1970

Kurt Erdmann, *Seven Hundred Years of Oriental Carpets*, ed. Hanna Erdmann, trans. May H. Beattie and Hildegard Herzog (Berkeley and Los Angeles: University of California Press, 1970)

FALKUS 1974

Christopher Falkus, ed., *The Private Lives of the Tudor Monarchs* (London: Folio Society, 1974)

FEUILLERAT 1914

Albert Feuillerat, ed., *Documents Relating to the Revels at Court in the Time of King Edward VI. and Queen Mary: The Loseley Manuscripts* (Louvain: A. Uystpruyst, 1914; repr. 1968)

FINLAY 1981

Roger Finlay, *Population and Metropolis: The Demography of London, 1580–1650* (Cambridge: Cambridge University Press, 1981)

FISHER 1940

F. J. Fisher, 'Commercial Trends and Policy in Sixteenth-Century England', *Economic History Review*, vol. 10 (1940), pp. 95–117

FISHER 1996

John R. Fisher, 'Casa de Contratación', in *Encyclopedia of Latin American History and Culture*, vol. I (New York: Charles Scribner's Sons, 1996), pp. 589–90

FOISTER 2001

Susan Foister, 'Holbein's Paintings on Canvas: The Greenwich Festivities of 1527', in Mark Roskill and John Oliver Hand, eds, *Hans Holbein: Paintings, Prints and Reception*, Studies in the History of Art, vol. 60 (Washington, DC: National Gallery of Art, 2001), pp. 108–23

FRYE 2010

Susan Frye, *Pens and Needles: Women's Textualities in Early Modern England* (Philadelphia: University of Pennsylvania Press, 2010)

FUMERTON 1986

Patricia Fumerton, '"Secret" Arts: Elizabethan Miniatures and Sonnets', *Representations*, no. 15 (1986), pp. 57–97

FURNIVALL 1877

Frederick J. Furnivall, ed., *Harrison's Description of England in Shakespeare's Youth*, vol. I (London: Trübner, 1877)

GIUSTINIAN 1854

Sebastian Giustinian, *Four Years at the Court of Henry VIII: Selection of Dispatches Written by the Venetian Ambassador . . . and Addressed to the Signory of Venice, January 12th 1515, to July 26th 1519*, vol. I, trans. Rawdon Brown (London: Smith, Elder & Co., 1854)

GOLDRING ET AL. 2014

Elizabeth Goldring, Faith Eales, Elizabeth Clarke and Jayne Elisabeth Archer, eds, *John Nichols's The Progresses and Public Processions of Queen Elizabeth I*, vol. I (Oxford: Oxford University Press, 2014)

GOODMAN AND GILLESPIE 1999

Anthony Goodman and James L. Gillespie, eds, *Richard II: The Art of Kingship* (Oxford: Clarendon Press, 1999)

GROESEN 2008

Michiel van Groesen, *The Representations of the Overseas World in the De Bry Collection of Voyages, 1590–1634* (Leiden: Brill, 2008)

GROOS 1981

G. W. Groos, trans. and ed., *The Diary of Baron Waldstein: A Traveller in Elizabethan England* (London: Thames & Hudson, 1981)

GUNN AND JANSE 2006

Steven Gunn and Antheun Janse, eds, *The Court as a Stage: England and the Low Countries in the Later Middle Ages* (Woodbridge: Boydell Press, 2006)

HAKLUYT 1809

Richard Hakluyt, *Hakluyt's Collection of the Early Voyages, Travels and Discoveries of the English Nation*, vol. I (London: R. H. Evans, 1809)

HALDANE 1976

Robert Aylmer Haldane, *The Hidden World* (London: Hale, 1976)

HALE 2005

John Hale, *England and the Italian Renaissance*, 4th edn (Hoboken, NJ: Wiley-Blackwell, 2005)

HALL 1548

Edward Hall, *The union of the two noble and illustre famelies of Lancastre & Yorke* (London: Richard Grafton, 1548)

HALL 1809

Edward Hall, *Hall's Chronicle: Containing the history of England, during the reign of Henry the Fourth, and the succeeding monarchs, to the end of the reign of Henry the Eighth, in which are particularly described the manners and customs of those periods. Carefully collated with the editions of 1548 and 1550* (London: J. Johnson et al., 1809)

HAMILTON 1977

A. C. Hamilton, *Sir Philip Sidney: A Study of his Life and Work* (Cambridge: Cambridge University Press, 1977)

HANHAM 1985

Alison Hanham, *The Celys and their World: An English Merchant Family of the Fifteenth Century* (Cambridge: Cambridge University Press, 1985)

HANNAY 2002

Margaret P. Hannay, 'The Countess of Pembroke's Agency in Print and Scribal Culture', in Justice and Tinker 2002, pp. 17–49

HARD 1930

Frederick Hard, 'Spenser's "Clothes of Arras and of Toure"', *Studies in Philology*, vol. 27 (1930), pp. 162–85

HAWTHORNE AND SMITH 1979

J. G. Hawthorne and C. S. Smith, *Theophilus: On Divers Arts* (New York: Dover Publications, 1979)

HAYNES 1740

Samuel Haynes, ed., *A collection of State papers relating to the affairs in the reigns of King Henry Viii, King Edward VI, Queen Mary, and Queen Elizabeth, from the year 1542 to 1570. Transcribed from original letters . . . left by William Cecil Lord Burghley* (London: William Bowyer, 1740)

HAYWARD 2004

Maria Hayward, *The 1542 Inventory of Whitehall: The Palace and its Keeper* (London: Illuminata Publishers for the Society of Antiquaries of London, 2004)

HAYWARD 2005

Maria Hayward, 'Symbols of Majesty: Cloths of Estate at the Court of Henry VIII', *Furniture History*, vol. 41 (2005), pp. 1–11

HAYWARD 2006

Maria Hayward, 'Fit for a King? Maintaining the Early Tudor Tapestry Collection', in Frances Lennard and Maria Hayward, eds, *Tapestry Conservation: Principles and Practice* (Oxford: Butterworth-Heinemann, 2006), pp. 13–19

HAYWARD 2007

Maria Hayward, *Dress at the Court of King Henry VIII* (Leeds: Maney, 2007)

HAYWARD 2009

Maria Hayward, *Rich Apparel: Clothing and the Law in Henry VIII's England* (Farnham: Ashgate Publishing, 2009)

HAYWARD 2012A

Maria Hayward, *The Great Wardrobe Accounts of Henry VII and Henry VIII* (London: London Record Society, 2012)

HAYWARD 2012B

Maria Hayward, 'Temporary Magnificence: The Offices of the Tents and Revels in the 1547 Inventory', in Hayward and Ward 2012, pp. 101–44

HAYWARD 2016
Maria Hayward, 'In the Eye of the Beholder: "Seeing" Textiles in the Early Modern Interior', *Textile History*, vol. 47 (2016), pp. 27–42

HAYWARD AND KRAMER 2007
Maria Hayward and Elizabeth Kramer, eds, *Textiles and Text: Re-establishing the Links between Archival and Object-Based Research* (London: Archetype Publications, 2007)

HAYWARD AND WARD 2012
Maria Hayward and Philip Ward, eds, *The Inventory of King Henry VIII*, vol. II: *Textiles and Dress* (London: Harvey Miller Publishers for the Society of Antiquaries of London, 2012)

HAZLITT 1892
W. Carew Hazlitt, *The Livery Companies of the City of London* (London: S. Sonnenschein & Company, 1892)

HEARD AND WHITAKER 2013
Kate Heard and Lucy Whitaker, *The Northern Renaissance: Dürer to Holbein* (London: Royal Collection Publications, 2013)

HEARN 2004
Karen Hearn, *Talking Peace 1604: The Somerset House Conference Paintings* (London: Somerset House, 2004)

HENTZNER 1757
Paul Hentzner, *A Journey into England in the Year MDXCVIII* (London: Strawberry Hill Press, 1757; repr. 1807)

HERMAN 1994
Peter C. Herman, ed., *Rethinking the Henrician Era: Essays on Early Tudor Texts and Contexts* (Urbana and Chicago: University of Illinois Press, 1994)

HEYLYN 1661
Peter Heylyn, *Ecclesia restaurata; or The history of the reformation of the Church of England* (London: H. Twyford, T. Dring, J. Place, W. Palmer, 1661)

HILLIARD 1992
Nicholas Hilliard, *A Treatise concerning the Arte of Limning*, ed. R. K. R. Thornton and T. G. S. Cain (Ashington: Mid Northumberland Arts Group in association with Carcanet Press, 1992)

HOOPER 1915
Wilfred Hooper, 'The Tudor Sumptuary Laws', *English Historical Review*, vol. 30 (1915), pp. 433–49

HORSTMANN 1887
Carl Horstmann, ed., *The Life of Saint Werburge of Chester by Henry Bradshaw, English A.D. 1513, printed by Pynson A.D. 1521*, Early English Text Society, vol. 88 (London: Trübner, 1887)

HOWARD 1987
Maurice Howard, *The Early Tudor Country House: Architecture and Politics, 1490–1550* (London: George Philip, 1987)

HULTON 1962
Paul Hulton, 'An Album of Plant Drawings by Jacques Le Moyne de Morgues', *British Museum Quarterly*, vol. 26, nos 1–2 (1962), pp. 37–9

HULTON 1977
Paul Hulton, *The Work of Jacques Le Moyne de Morgues: A Huguenot Artist in France, Florida and England*, vol. I (London: British Museum Publications, 1977)

HUME 1896
Martin A. S. Hume, *The Courtships of Queen Elizabeth: The History of the Various Negotiations for her Marriage* (New York: Macmillan; London: T. Fisher Unwin, 1896)

IVES 1995
Eric Ives, 'Henry VIII: The Political Perspective', in MacCulloch 1995, pp. 13–34

JACK 1981
R. I. Jack, 'Fulling-Mills in Wales and the March before 1547', *Archaeologia Cambrensis*, vol. 130 (1981), pp. 70–127

JACKSON 1896
Catherine Charlotte, Lady Jackson, *The Court of France in the Sixteenth Century, 1514–1559*, vol. II (Boston: Joseph Knight, 1896)

JARDINE 1996
Lisa Jardine, *Worldly Goods: A New History of the Renaissance* (London: Macmillan, 1996)

JARDINE AND BROTTON 2000
Lisa Jardine and Jerry Brotton, *Global Interests: Renaissance Art Between East and West* (Ithaca, NY: Cornell University Press, 2000)

JEFFERSON 2009
Lisa Jefferson, *The Medieval Account Books of the Mercers of London: An Edition and Translation*, vol. I (Farnham, and Burlington, Vt: Ashgate Publishing, 2009)

JONES AND STALLYBRASS 2000
Ann Rosalind Jones and Peter Stallybrass, *Renaissance Clothing and the Materials of Memory* (Cambridge: Cambridge University Press, 2000)

JONES AND UNDERWOOD 1992
Michael K. Jones and Malcolm G. Underwood, *The King's Mother: Lady Margaret Beaufort, Countess of Richmond and Derby* (Cambridge: Cambridge University Press, 1992)

JUSTICE AND TINKER 2002
George L. Justice and Nathan Tinker, eds, *Women's Writing and the Circulation of Ideas: Manuscript Publication in England, 1550–1800* (Cambridge: Cambridge University Press, 2002)

KEMP 1898
Thomas Kemp, ed., *The Black Book of Warwick* (Warwick: Henry T. Cooke and Son, 1898)

KERRIDGE 1985
Eric Kerridge, *Textile Manufactures in Early Modern England* (Manchester: Manchester University Press, 1985)

KING 1981
Donald King, 'A Set of Embroideries', in Alvar González-Palacios, ed., *Objects for a Wunderkammer*, exh. cat., P. & D. Colnaghi (London: P. & D. Colnaghi, 1981)

KING 1994
John N. King, 'Henry VIII as David: The King's Image and Reformation Politics', in Herman 1994, pp. 78–92

KING 2005
P. W. King, 'The Production and Consumption of Bar Iron in Early Modern England and Wales', *Economic History Review*, vol. 58 (2005), pp. 1–33

KING 2012
Donald King, 'From the Exotic to the Mundane: Carpets and Coverings for Tables, Cupboards, Window Seats and Floors', in Hayward and Ward 2012, pp. 131–43

KIPLING 1977
Gordon Kipling, *The Triumph of Honour: Burgundian Origins of the Elizabethan Renaissance* (Leiden: Leiden University Press, 1977)

KIPLING 1981
Gordon Kipling, 'Henry VII and the Origins of Tudor Patronage', in Lytle and Orgel 1981, pp. 117–64

KISBY 2003
Fiona Kisby, 'Religious Ceremonial at the Tudor Court: Extracts from Royal Household Regulations', in Ian W. Archer et al., eds, *Religion, Politics, and Society in Sixteenth-Century England*, Camden Society, 5th ser., vol. 22 (Cambridge: Cambridge University Press, 2003), pp. 1–34

KOLKOVICH 2009
Elizabeth Zeman Kolkovich, 'Lady Russell, Elizabeth I, and Female Political Alliances through Performance', *English Literary Renaissance*, vol. 39 (2009), pp. 290–314

KOLKOVICH 2016
Elizabeth Zeman Kolkovich, *The Elizabethan Country House Entertainment: Print, Performance and Gender* (Cambridge: Cambridge University Press, 2016)

KORDA 2011
Natasha Korda, 'Accessorizing the Stage: Alien Women's Work and the Fabric of Early Modern Material Culture', in Mirabella 2011, pp. 223–32

KREN AND MCKENDRICK 2003
Thomas Kren and Scot McKendrick, *Illuminating the Renaissance: The Triumph of Flemish Manuscript Painting in Europe*, exh. cat., J. Paul Getty Museum, Los Angeles, and Royal Academy of Arts, London (Los Angeles: J. Paul Getty Museum, 2003)

LANG 1993
R. G. Lang, ed., *Two Tudor Subsidy Assessment Rolls for the City of London, 1541 and 1582* (London: London Record Society, 1993)

LAUDONNIÈRE 1587
René de Laudonnière, *A notable historie containing four voyages made by certayne French captaynes unto Florida* [. . .] *newly translated out of French into English by R.H.*, trans. Richard Hakluyt (London: Thomas Dawson, 1587)

LEAHY 2005
William Leahy, *Elizabethan Triumphal Processions* (Aldershot: Ashgate Publishing, 2005)

LE MOYNE 1586
Jacques Le Moyne de Morgues, *La clef des champs* (Blackfriars: [T. Vautrollier] for Jacques Le Moyne de Morgues, 1586)

LENNARD 2006
Frances Lennard, 'The Art of Tapestry Conservation', in Frances Lennard and Maria Hayward, eds, *Tapestry Conservation: Principles and Practice* (Oxford: Butterworth-Heinemann, 2006), pp. 3–12

LEVEY 1998
Santina Levey, *An Elizabethan Inheritance: The Hardwick Hall Textiles* (London: National Trust, 1998)

LEVEY 2012
Santina Levey, 'The Art of the Broderers', in Hayward and Ward 2012, pp. 145–85

LEWIS 1977
Ioan Lewis, ed., *Symbols and Sentiments: Cross-Cultural Studies in Symbolism* (London, New York and San Francisco: Academic Press, 1977)

LIPSCOMB 2009
Suzannah Lipscomb, *1536: The Year that Changed Henry VIII* (Oxford: Lion, 2009)

LIPSON 1965
Ephraim Lipson, *The History of the Woollen and Worsted Industries* (London: Franck Cass & Co., 1965)

LLOYD 1982
T. H. Lloyd, *Alien Merchants in England during the High Middle Ages* (Brighton: Harvester Press, 1982)

LUU 2005
Lien Bich Luu, *Immigrants and the Industries of London, 1500–1700* (Farnham: Ashgate, 2005)

LYNN 2017
Eleri Lynn, *Tudor Fashion* (New Haven and London: Yale University Press in association with Historic Royal Palaces, 2017)

LYNN 2018
Eleri Lynn, 'The Bacton Altar Cloth: Elizabeth I's "Long-lost Skirt"?', *Costume*, vol. 52 (2018), pp. 3–25

LYTLE AND ORGEL 1981
Guy Fitch Lytle and Stephen Orgel, eds, *Patronage in the Renaissance* (Princeton: Princeton University Press, 1981)

MCCABE 2015
Ina Baghdiantz McCabe, *A History of Global Consumption: 1500–1800* (Abingdon and New York: Routledge, 2015)

MACCULLOCH 1995
Diarmaid MacCulloch, ed., *The Reign of Henry VIII: Politics, Policy and Piety* (Basingstoke: Palgrave, 1995)

MACGREGOR 1989
Arthur MacGregor, ed., *The Late King's Goods: Collections, Possessions and Patronage of Charles I in the Light of the Commonwealth Sale Inventories* (London and Oxford: A. McAlpine in association with Oxford University Press, 1989)

MCKENDRICK 1987
Scot McKendrick, 'Edward IV: An English Royal Collector of Netherlandish Tapestry', *Burlington Magazine*, vol. 129 (1987), pp. 521–4

MCKENDRICK 1991
Scot McKendrick, 'The Great History of Troy: A Reassessment of the Development of a Secular Theme in Late Medieval Art', *Journal of the Warburg and Courtauld Institutes*, vol. 54 (1991), pp. 43–82

MACLEAN 2007
Gerald Maclean, *Looking East: English Writing and the Ottoman Empire before 1800* (Basingstoke: Palgrave Macmillan, 2007)

MACPHERSON 1805
David Macpherson, *Annals of Commerce, Manufactures Fisheries and Navigation*, vol. I (London: Nichols and Son, 1805)

MADDEN 1831
Frederick Madden, ed., *The Privy Purse Expenses of the Princess Mary . . . afterwards Queen Mary* (London: William Pickering, 1831)

MARICHAL 2006

Carlos Marichal, 'Mexican Cochineal and the European Demand for American Dyes, 1550–1850', in Steven Topik, Carlos Marichal and Zephyr Frank, eds, *From Silver to Cocaine: Latin American Commodity Chains and the Building of the World Economy, 1500–2000* (Durham, NC, and London: Duke University Press, 2006

MEÛTER ET AL. 1999

Ingrid de Meûter et al., *Les tapisseries d'Audenarde* (Tielt: Lannoo, 1999)

MILLAR 1972

Oliver Millar, ed., *The Inventories and Valuations of the King's Goods, 1649–1651*, Walpole Society, vol. 43 (Glasgow: Walpole Society, 1972)

MIRABELLA 2011

Bella Mirabella, ed., *Ornamentalism: The Art of Renaissance Accessories* (Ann Arbor: University of Michigan Press, 2011)

MISKIMIN 1978

Harry A. Miskimin, *The Economy of Later Renaissance Europe, 1460–1600* (Cambridge: Cambridge University Press, 1978)

MITCHELL 1997

David Mitchell, 'Table Linen Associated with Queen Elizabeth's Visit to Gresham's Exchange', in Ann Saunders, ed., *The Royal Exchange* (London: Topographical Society, 1997), pp. 50–56

MITCHELL 2012

David Mitchell, 'Napery for Tables and Linens for Beds', in Hayward and Ward 2012, pp. 187–233

MONNAS 1989

Lisa Monnas, 'New Documents for the Vestments of Henry VII at Stonyhurst College', *Burlington Magazine*, vol. 131 (1989), pp. 345–9

MONNAS 1998

Lisa Monnas, 'Tissues in England during the Fifteenth and Sixteenth Centuries', *Bulletin du CIETA*, vol. 75 (1998), pp. 62–80

MONNAS 2008

Lisa Monnas, *Merchants, Princes and Painters: Silk Fabrics in Italian and Northern Paintings, 1300–1550* (New Haven and London: Yale University Press, 2008)

MONNAS 2012A

Lisa Monnas, 'Plentie and Abundaunce': Henry VIII's Valuable Store of Textiles', in Hayward and Ward 2012, pp. 235–94

MONNAS 2012B

Lisa Monnas, *Renaissance Velvets* (London: Victoria and Albert Museum, 2012)

MONTINI AND PLESCIA 2018

Donatella Montini and Iolanda Plescia, eds, *Elizabeth I in Writing: Language, Power and Representation in Early Modern England* (New York: Palgrave Macmillan, 2018)

MONTROSE 2006

Louis Montrose, *The Subject of Elizabeth: Authority, Gender, and Representation* (Chicago and London: University of Chicago Press, 2006)

MOREL 1997

Philippe Morel, *Les Grotesques* (Paris: Flammarion, 1997)

MORGAN 2017

Hollie L. S. Morgan, *Beds and Chambers in Late Medieval England: Reading, Representations and Realities* (Woodbridge: York Medieval Press, 2017)

MULDREW 2012

Craig Muldrew, '"Th'ancient Distaff" and "Whirling Spindle": Measuring the Contribution of Spinning to Household Earnings and the National Economy in England, 1550–1770', *Economic History Review*, vol. 65 (2012), pp. 498–526

NICHOLS 1790

John Nichols, ed., *A collection of ordinances and regulations for the government of the Royal household . . . From King Edward III. to King William and Queen Mary* (London: John Nichols for the Society of Antiquaries, 1790)

NICHOLS 1823

John Nichols, ed., *The Progresses and Public Processions of Queen Elizabeth*, vol. I (London: John Nichols and Son, printers to the Society of Antiquaries, 1823)

NICHOLS 1850

John Gough Nichols, ed., *The Chronicle of Queen Jane and of Two Years of Queen Mary*, Camden Society, old ser., vol. 48 (London: Camden Society, 1850)

NICHOLS 1855

John Gough Nichols, ed., 'View of the Wardrobe Stuff of Katharine of Aragon', *Camden Miscellany* 3, no. 61 (1855), pp. 23–41

NICOLAS 1827

N. H. Nicolas, ed., *The Privy Purse Expences of King Henry the Eighth from November MDXXIX, to December MDXXXII* (London: William Pickering, 1827)

NICOLAS 1830

N. H. Nicolas, ed., *Privy Purse Expenses of Elizabeth of York; Wardrobe Accounts of Edward the Fourth* (London: William Pickering, 1830)

NORMAN 1911-12

Philip Norman, ed., 'Nicholas Hilliard's Treatise Concerning "The Arte of Limning"', *Walpole Society*, vol. 1 (1911–12), pp. 1–54

OLSON 2013

Rebecca Olson, *Arras Hanging: The Textile that Determined Early Modern Literature and Drama* (Newark: University of Delaware Press, 2013)

PAGET 1959

Hugh Paget, 'Gerard and Lucas Hornebolt in England', *Burlington Magazine*, vol. 101 (1959), pp. 396–402

PALLISER 1865

Bury Palliser, *History of Lace* (London: Sampson Low, Son & Marston, 1865)

PARKER 2010

Rozsika Parker, *The Subversive Stitch: Embroidery and the Making of the Feminine* (London and New York: I. B. Tauris, 2010)

PENN 2011

Thomas Penn, *Winter King: The Dawn of Tudor England* (London: Allen Lane, 2011)

PHIPPS 2010

Elena Phipps, 'Cochineal Red: The Art History of a Color', *Metropolitan Museum of Art Bulletin*, vol. 67, no. 3 (2010), pp. 4–48

PINNER AND DENNY 1986

Robert Pinner and Walter B. Denny, eds, *Oriental Carpet & Textile Studies*, vol. II: *Carpets of the Mediterranean Countries, 1400–1600* (London: Hali Magazine, 1986)

PLOEG 2014
Sophie Ploeg, *The Lace Trail. Fabric and Lace in Early 17th Century Portraiture: An Interpretation in Paint* (San Francisco: Blurb Books, 2014)

POLLARD 1914
A. F. Pollard, ed., *The Reign of Henry VII from Contemporary Sources*, University of London Historical Series, no. 1 (London: Longmans, Green and Co., 1914)

POSTAN 1973
Michael Moïssey Postan, *Medieval Trade and Finance* (Cambridge: Cambridge University Press, 1973)

POWER AND POSTAN 1933
Eileen Power and Michael Moïssey Postan, *Studies in English Trade in the 15th Century* (London: G. Routledge and Sons, 1933)

RANSOME 1964
David Ransome, 'Artisan Dynasties in London and Westminster in the Sixteenth Century', *Guildhall Miscellany*, vol. 2/6 (1964), pp. 236–47

RICHARDSON 2007
Ruth E. Richardson, *Mistress Blanche: Queen Elizabeth I's Confidante* (Eardisley, Herefordshire: Logaston Press, 2007; rev. edn 2018)

RICHARDSON 2013
Glenn Richardson, *The Field of Cloth of Gold* (New Haven and London, Yale University Press, 2003)

RIDGARD 1985
John Ridgard, ed., 'Inventory, Framlingham Castle, 28th May 1524', in John Ridgard, ed., *Medieval Framlingham: Select Documents, 1270–1524*, Suffolk Record Society, vol. 27 (Woodbridge: Boydell Press for the Suffolk Records Society, 1985), pp. 129–69

RIMER, RICHARDSON AND COOPER 2009
Graeme Rimer, Thom Richardson and J. P. D. Cooper, eds, *Henry VIII: Arms and the Man, 1509–2009*, exh. cat., Tower of London (London: Royal Armouries and Historic Royal Palaces, 2009)

ROOVER 1999
Raymond de Roover, *The Rise and Decline of the Medici Bank, 1397–1494* (Washington, DC: Beard Books, 1999)

ROSETTI 1969
Giovanventura Rosetti, *The Plictho: Instructions in the Art of the Dyers, which Teaches the Dyeing of Woolen Cloths, Linens, Cottons, and Silk by the Great Art as well as by the Common, Translation of the First Edition of 1548*, trans. Hector C. Borghetty and Sidney M. Edelstein (Cambridge, Mass.: Massachusetts Institute of Technology Press, 1969)

ROSS 1997
Charles Derek Ross, *Edward IV* (New Haven and London: Yale University Press, 1997)

ROUND 1903
J. H. Round, 'The King's Pantler', *Archaeological Journal*, vol. 60 (1903), pp. 268–83

RUSSELL 1969
Joycelyne G. Russell, *The Field of Cloth of Gold: Men and Manners in 1520* (London: Routledge & Kegan Paul, 1969)

RYE 1865
William Brenchley Rye, *England as Seen by Foreigners in the Days of Elizabeth and James the First* (London: John Russell Smith, 1865)

SCHNEEBALG-PERELMAN 1961
Sophie Schneebalg-Perelman, '"Le retouchage" dans la tapisserie bruxelloise ou les origines de l'édit impérial de 1544', *Annales de la Société Royale d'Archéologie de Bruxelles*, vol. 50 (1961), pp. 191–210

SCOTT 1898
R. F. Scott, 'On a List (Preserved in the Treasury of St John's College) of the Plate, Books and Vestments Bequeathed by the Lady Margaret to Christ's College)', *Proceedings of the Cambridge Antiquarian Society*, no. 39 (vol. 9, no. 3) (1898), pp. 349–67

SICCA 2002
Cinzia M. Sicca, 'Consumption and Trade of Art between Italy and England in the First Half of the Sixteenth Century: The London House of the Bardi and Cavalcanti Company', *Renaissance Studies*, vol. 16 (2002), pp. 163–201

SICCA 2007
Cinzia M. Sicca, 'Fashioning the Tudor Court', in Hayward and Kramer 2007, pp. 93–104

SINGER 1948
Charles Singer, *The Early Chemical Industry* (London: Folio Society, 1948)

SMYTH 1883
John Smyth, *The Berkeley Manuscripts: The Lives of the Berkeleys*, ed. John Maclean, vol. II (Gloucester: J. Bellows, 1883)

SNEYD 1847
Charlotte Augusta Sneyd, trans., *A Relation, or rather A True Account of the Island of England . . . about the Year 1500*, Camden Society, old ser., vol. 37 (London: J. B. Nichols and Son for Camden Society, 1847)

STABEL 2006
Peter Stabel, 'For Mutual Benefit? Court and City in the Burgundian Low Countries', in Gunn and Janse 2006, pp. 101–17.

STABEL 2012
Peter Stabel, 'A Taste for the Orient? Cosmopolitan Demand for "Exotic" Durable Consumables in Late Medieval Bruges', in Davies and Galloway 2012, pp. 87–102

STAFFORD 1581
William Stafford, *A compendious or briefe examination of certayne ordinary complaints, of divers of our country men in these our dayes* (London: Thomas Marshe, 1581)

STARKEY 1977
David Starkey, 'Representation through Intimacy: A Study in the Symbolism of Monarchy and Court Office in Early Modern England', in Lewis 1977, pp. 42–78

STARKEY 1987
David Starkey, 'Intimacy and Innovation: The Rise of the Privy Chamber, 1485–1547', in Starkey et al. 1987, pp. 71–118

STARKEY 1999
David Starkey, 'Henry VI's Old Blue Gown: The English Court under the Lancastrians and Yorkists', *Court Historian*, vol. 4 (1999), pp. 1–28

STARKEY ET AL. 1987
David Starkey et al., *The English Court from the Wars of the Roses to the Civil War* (London: Longman 1987)

STARKEY AND WARD 1998

David Starkey, ed., and Philip Ward, transcr., *The Inventory of King Henry VIII: Society of Antiquaries MS 129 and British Library MS Harley 1419*, vol. I: *The Transcript*, with an index by Alasdair Hawkyard (London: Harvey Miller Publishers for the Society of Antiquaries of London, 1998)

STEWART 1930

Francis Stewart, ed., *Memoirs of Sir James Melville of Halhill, 1535–1617* (New York: E. P. Dutton and Company, 1930)

STOW 1615

John Stow, *The annales, or a generall chronicle of England, begun first by maister John Stow* (London: Thomas Adams, 1615)

STREITBERGER 1994

W. R. Streitberger, *Court Revels, 1485–1559* (Toronto: University of Toronto Press, 1994)

STRONG 1969

Roy C. Strong, *Tudor and Jacobean Portraits*, vol. I (London: HMSO, 1969)

STRONG 1973

Roy Strong, *Splendour at Court: Renaissance Spectacle and Illusion* (London: Weidenfeld and Nicolson, 1973)

STUART 1874

John Stuart, *A Lost Chapter in the History of Mary Queen of Scots Recovered: Notices of James, Earl of Bothwell, and Lady Jane Gordon, and of the Dispensation for their Marriage* (Edinburgh: Edmonston and Douglas, 1874)

STUBBES 1877–9

Philip Stubbes, *Anatomy of the Abuses in England in Shakespeare's Youth*, A.D. 1583, pt i, ed. Frederick J. Furnivall, New Shakespeare Society Publications, 6th ser., vols 4, 6 (London: Trübner & Co., 1877–9) [orig. pubd as *The anatomie of abuses*, pt 1 (London: Richard Jones, 1583)]

SUBRAHMANYAN 2016

Sanjay Subrahmanyan, ed., *Merchant Networks in the Early Modern World, 1450–1800* (Abingdon and New York: Routledge, 2016) [first pubd 1996]

SUTTON 2016

Anne F. Sutton, *The Mercery of London: Trade, Goods and People, 1130–1578* (Abingdon and New York: Routledge, 2016) [first pubd 2005]

SYLVIUS 1991

Jacobus Sylvius (Jacques Dubois), 'Francisci francorum regis et Henrici anglorum colloquium', trans. and ed. Jean Dupèbe and Stephen Bamforth, *Renaissance Studies*, vol. 5, nos. 1–2 (1991), pp. ii–237

TATTON-BROWN AND MORTIMER 2003

Tim Tatton-Brown and Richard Mortimer, eds, *Westminster Abbey: The Lady Chapel of Henry VII* (Woodbridge: Boydell Press, 2003)

THOMSON 1993

David Thomson, *Renaissance Architecture: Critics, Patrons, Luxury* (Manchester: Manchester University Press, 1993)

THURLEY 2003

Simon Thurley, *Hampton Court Palace* (New Haven and London: Yale University Press, 2003)

TITTLER 1991

Robert Tittler, *The Reign of Mary I*, 2nd edn (London and New York: Longman, 1991)

TURNER 2002

Hilary L. Turner, 'Finding the Sheldon Weavers: Richard Hyckes and the Barcheston Tapestry Works Reconsidered', *Textile History*, vol. 33 (2002), pp. 137–61

TURNER 2012

Hilary L. Turner, 'Working Arras and Arras Workers: Conservation in the Great Wardrobe under Elizabeth I', *Textile History*, vol. 43 (2012), pp. 43–60

UNWIN 1963

George Unwin, *The Gilds and Companies of London*, 4th edn (London: Frank Cass, 1963)

VALLARO 2018

Cristina Vallaro, 'Elizabeth I as Poet: Some Notes on "On Monsieur's Departure" and John Dowland's "Now, O now, I needs must part"', in Montini and Plescia 2018, pp. 109–26

VANWELDEN 1999

Martine Vanwelden, 'Fascination de la politique, 1544–1585', in Meûter et al. 1999, pp. 49–75

VEGA AND CARRETERO 1986

Paulina Junquera de Vega and Concha Herrero Carretero, *Catálogo de tapices del Patrimonio Nacional*, vol. I: *Siglo XVI* (Madrid: Editorial Patrimonio Nacional, 1986)

WARLEY 2005

Christopher Warley, *Sonnet Sequences and Social Distinction in Renaissance England* (Cambridge: Cambridge University Press, 2005)

WEHLE 1953

Harry B. Wehle, 'Maria Portinari', *Metropolitan Museum of Art Bulletin*, vol. 11 (1953), pp. 129–31

WESTFALL 2001–2

Suzanne Westfall, 'The Boy who would be King: Court Revels of King Edward VI, 1547–1553', *Comparative Drama*, vol. 35 (2001–2), pp. 271–90

WHITELOCK 2009

Anna Whitelock, *Mary Tudor: England's First Queen* (London: Bloomsbury, 2009)

WHITNEY 1586

Geffrey Whitney, *A choice of emblemes, and other devises* (Leiden: Plantyn, 1586)

WILLIAMS 1937

Clare Williams, ed., *Thomas Platter's Travels in England, 1599* (London: Jonathan Cape, 1937)

WILLIAMS 2006

Deanne Williams, 'Dido, Queen of England', *ELH*, vol. 73 (2006), pp. 31–59

WUBS-MROZEWICZ AND JENKS 2012

Justyna Wubs-Mrozewicz and Stuart Jenks, eds, *The Hanse in Medieval and Early Modern Europe* (Leiden: Brill, 2012)

WYLD 2012

Helen Wyld, 'The Gideon Tapestries at Hardwick Hall', *West 86th: A Journal of Decorative Arts, Design History, and Material Culture*, vol. 19 (2012), pp. 231–54

Index

Page numbers in *italic* refer to the illustrations

Aberdeen, Bishop of 108
Abraham (tapestries) x, 48–9, *48–9*
Aelst, Pieter Coecke van 48, *48*
Aelst, Pieter van 33, 48, 107, 110
Aeneas 46–8, *47*, 56, 57, 93
Africa 9
Agas, Ralph, map of London *104*
aglet 164
al-Andalus 12
Albert, Prince Consort 55
Alembert, Jean Le Rond d', *Encyclopédie 139*
Alençon, Francis, Duke of 60, 90
Alençon, Jean, Duke of 90
Aleppo 12
Alexander the Great 35
alkanet 126, 164
altar cloths 35, 77, 108, 144
    see also Bacton Altar Cloth
alum 2, 9, 12, 126, 164
Americas 23, 26, 127, 128
Amman, Jost: 'An embroiderer at his frame' 152,
    154
    'A weaver at a shaft loom' 129, *131*
Anatolian carpets 135, *137*, 138, 161
Anet, Château d' *114–15*
Anglo-French Treaty (1514) *1*
Anne of Cleves 88, *88–9*, 154
Annebault, Claude d' 113
Antwerp 9, 11, 13, 15, 17, 18, 20, 123, 139, 162
appliqué 148
Arnold, Janet 67
Arras 31, 139, 142
arras 15, 31, 35, 38, 39, 43–6, 142, 164
Arthur, Prince 30, 31
Asia 13, 123
Asia Minor 135
Aviz dynasty 35

Baconsthorpe, Norfolk 15

Bacton Altar Cloth *Frontispiece*, x, 23, *24–5*, 26,
    64–7, *66*, 71, 90, *128*, 152, *163*
Baltic states 9
banks 11–12
Barbarossa, Khayr ad-Din 54
Barbary 26
Bardi, Pierfrancesco de' 15, 106, 132
baudekin 49, 88, 132, 164
bay 164
Baynard's Castle 30, 77, 83, 105
Beaufort, Margaret 35–6, *37*, 93, 110, 144
bed hangings 55–56, 83, 150, 151, *152*
bedchambers 83–90
Bedford, John of Lancaster, Duke of 30
beds 83–8, *88–91*
Belgium 9
Berkeley, Sir Maurice 148
Berkeley Castle, Gloucestershire 117, 148
Bess of Hardwick *see* Shrewsbury, Elizabeth
    Talbot, Countess of
Bisham Abbey, Berkshire 67–71
Black Book of the Garter 77, *78*
Boleyn, Anne 5, 46, 55, 80, *80*, 87, 88, 90
Bolton, John 30, 128
Bonvisi, Antony 106
Bonvisi family 15, 30
Book of Common Prayer 26
books 102, *103*, 154
Bostocke, Jane, sampler *70*
Bosworth, Battle of (1485) 7, 29, 31
botanical motifs *62–3*, 63, 90, *96*, 154–5, *154–5*
Botry (variously spelled Botre), William 4, 108
Brabant 9, 142
braccio 164
Bramantino 123
brazilwood 26, 164
Brion, Martin de, description of the Holy Land
    103, *149*
Bristowe, Nicholas 109, 113
British Empire 23, 162
British School: *The Family of Henry VIII 4–5*

The Field of Cloth of Gold 1
broadcloth 8, 12, 20, 117, 164
brocading 164
brocatelle 132, *132*, 164
broom 126, 164
Browne, Anthony 50
Bruegel, Pieter the Elder, *Die niederländische
    Sprichwörter* 116
Bruges 9, 13, 18
Brussels 9, 18, 23, 35, 55, 139
Bruyn, Nicolaes de, *Animalium quadrapedum* 67
Bry, Theodor de, *Great and Small Voyages* 22, 23,
    128, *129*
buckthorn 164
Burghley House 110
Burgundy 15, 30–3, 35
Burgundy, dukes of 9, 11
Burton, James 110–12
Burton, John 108

Cabot, Sebastian 21
Caesar, Julius 48
caffa 164
Calais 11, 31, 38, 148
cambric 80, 108, 164
Cambridge University 144
camlet *25*, *66*, 106, *128*, *163*, 164
canopies 76–7
carders *118–19*, 119, 164
carding 164
Carey, George 115
Caron, Antoine, drawing of the Château d'Anet
    114–15
carpets 134–8
    1547 Inventory 93, 138
    acquisition 106
    cleaning 112
    designs 135
    dyes 22–3
    embroidered 138, *138–9*
    production of 134–5

Turkey carpets 134–5, *135, 137*, 138, 161, 162
Carsidoni, Anthony 106
Carter, John: drawing of a Flemish tapestry *84–5*
   sketch of one of the Troy tapestry panels 31, *33*
   sketch of the Painted Chamber in Westminster
    Palace *32*
cartoons, tapestries 31, 54, *140*, 164
Casa de la Contratación de las Indias 11
Cavalcanti, Giovanni 15, 106, 162
Cavalcanti family 15, 132, 154
Cavendish, George 112
Cawarden, Sir Thomas 113
Cecil, Robert 22, 62, 115, 161, 162
Cecil, Sir Thomas 110
Cecil, Sir William, Lord Burghley 17, 20, 21, 59,
   60, 62, 71
celures 76, 77, 83, 87, 164
chalice veils 30, 164
Chandos, Lady Dorothy 67, 71
Charles II, King 138
Charles V, Emperor 17–18, 54–5, 112, 127
Charles VIII, King of France 12, *28*
Charles the Bold, Duke of Burgundy 9, 11, 17, 31
Charles de Florence *1*, 36
chasubles 132, *133*, 164
Château Vert pageant *4–5*
childbirth *84–5*, 87
China 12
Christian prayers and meditations 93, *100*
Christianity 13, 135
Christ's College, Cambridge 35–6, 144
Church of England 55
churchwork 134, 164
Cicero, 'Four Orations' *3*, 113
ciphers 59, 87, 88, 93, 164
Civil War (1642–51) 30
close stools 102, *102*
cloth of arras *see* arras
cloth of gold *1*, *3*, 30, *98*, 128, 132–4, *132–4*, 165
cloth of silver 67, *73*, 132, *132*, 148
cloths of estate 30, 76–7, *79*, *81*, 83, *86*, 93, *134*, 151, 164

cloves 165
cochineal 21, 26, 127, *127*, 165
College of Saint-Omer, Artois 30
Columbus, Christopher 13
commodes 102, *102*
Commonwealth Sale (1649) 30, 48, 56, 128, 138
Compagni, Bartolomeo 17, *17*
Constable, Lady Katheryn 67
Constantinople 12
copes *11*, 30, 35, 59, 108, 165
Corinth 26
Corsi, Antonio 30
Corsi, William 132
Cortes, Hernán 127
Cossa, Francesco del, *The Allegory of March 69*
cotton 126, 165
couching 150, 151, 165
counterfeit arras 15, 43, 110, 142, 165
counterpanes 83, 165
court, travels 113–15
coverlets 106–7, 165
coverpains 80, *81*, 165
Cowdray House, Sussex 50
Cranmer, Thomas 55
cream of tartar 126
Cromwell, Thomas 15, 93, 106, 107, 108
curtains *92*, 93
cushions *64*, 93, 99, *100–1*, 151, *158–9*
cutwork 148, 151, *152*, 165

Dacre, Thomas, Baron 15
damask 12, 35, 80, 93, *96*, *111*, 132, 165
Damula, Marc Antonio 54
David, King 39, 46, 161–2
Day, John 93
Dee, Maurice 15
Denny, Sir Anthony 109
Derby, Thomas Stanley, 1st Earl of 29, 35
Devonshire, Countess of 5
Diderot, Denis, *Encyclopédie 139*
Dido, Queen of Carthage 46, 56, *57*, 93

dining 80, *80–1*
distaff 119, 165
Drake, Sir Francis *21*
Drase, Segar 110–12
Dudley, Mary 63
Dudley, Robert 108
Dürer, Albrecht 154
dyed in the wool 165
dyes 126–8
   alum 2, 9, 12, 126, 164
   Persian carpets 22–3
   recipes 23–6, 126–7
   silk *27*
   trade 21
   wool 120, *120*, 126, *126*

East India Company 22
Edward III, King 30
Edward IV, King 8, *11*, 12, 31, 110, 112
Edward VI, King 17, 48, 49–51, 71, 102
   cloths of estate 77
   coronation 49–50, *50–1*, 127–8
   portraits *4–5*, *52*, *82–3*, 135
Egypt 135
Elizabeth I, Queen 55–71
   acquisition of textiles 108
   bedchambers 90
   birth *84–5*, 90
   coronation 1–2, 49, 80
   emblems and symbols 2, 62, 73, 90
   embroidery 57, 58, *58*, 59, 90, 155
   New Year Gift Roll 67
   Oath of Supremacy 20
   'On Monsieur's Departure' 59–60
   portraits *4–5*, *61*, *64*, *65*, *79*, 93, *94–5*, *100*
   preparation for ceremonies 112–13
   repurposing textiles 108
   Stowe Inventory 71
   table linen 80
   tapestries 18, 49, 55–7
   trading companies 21–2

travels 115
Elizabeth of York 31–3, *86*, 87
ell xiv, 165
ell-sticks 15, 165
Eltham Ordinances 76
emblems 62–3, 73, 90
embroidery 57–9, 63–71, 165
  carpets 138, *138–9*
  gifts 67
  language of 67–71
  patterns 23, 63–7, 90, 151–5, *157*
  recycling 108
  samplers 102
  techniques 147–55
Enghien 110
England's Commercial Policy 8
Essex, Robert Devereux, 2nd Earl of 18, *60*
Eworth, Hans: double portrait of Philip II of
    Spain and Mary I *53*
  Elizabeth I and the Three Goddesses 56
Eyck, Jan van, *The Madonna with Canon van der
    Paele 14*
Eytzinger, Michael *10*

Fabricius, Gervasius, 'Album amicorum' *68*, *146*
The Family of Henry VIII 76
Field of Cloth of Gold (1520) xi, *1*, *1*, 3, 15, 30,
    36–40, *38–9*, 46, 60, 73, 106, 148, 162
Fillastre, Guillaume, *Toison d'Or* 31
Fitzroy, Henry 77, 102
Fitzwilliam, Ann 64
Fitzwilliam, Sir William 64
Flanders 9, 18, 20, 142, 144
flax 122, *123*, 144
Flemish School, *The Meeting of Henry VIII and the
    Emperor Maximilian I 42–3*
Flodden, Battle of (1513) 15
Florence 12, 23, 30, 106, 123, 132
floss 165
Fontainebleau, school of: testers *91*, *152*
Foschi, Pier Francesci de Jacopo, portrait of
    Bartolomeo Compagni *17*
Fox, Richard 31
France 9, 12–13
  embroidery 150–1
  Field of Cloth of Gold 36–40, *38–9*
  tapestries 30–1, 46, 142
Francis I, King of France xi, *1*, 38–40, 46, 90, 113
Frescobaldi, Leonardo 38
Frescobaldi family 15
frieze 39, 165
frizado 165
Frye, Susan 60
fulling 122, *122*, 165
fustian 87, 88, 129, 165

Gage, Sir John 109

Galle, Philip 123
Gallo, Antonio 13
Geminus, Thomas, *Morysse and damashin 148*,
    150, 154
Genoa 11–12, 23, 128, 132
Gentleman's Magazine 31
Gheeraerts, Marcus the younger, 'Rainbow
    Portrait of Elizabeth I' *61*
Ghent 9, 18, 152
Gibson, Richard 4, 5, 106, 108, 112
Giese, Georg 135, *136*
gilt 128, 165
Giustiniani, Mariano 113
Giustiniani, Sebastiano 38, 46, 106
gold 128, *128–9*
  cloth of gold *1*, 3, 30, *98*, 128, 132–4, *132–4*, 165
  embroidery 150
  recycling 108
'Golf Book' *6*
Gómez de Cervantes, Gonzalo 127, *127*
Gormont, Remy de, *Le livre de moresque* 154
Great Fire of London (1666) 105
Great Wardrobe 5, 71, *104*, 105–15, 161
  acquisition of textiles 31, 106–8
  Edward VI's coronation 127–8
  management of stocks 108–12
  preparation and transportation of textiles 112–15
  value of stock 105
Green Cloth 109–10
Greenwich Palace 39, 41–2, 99
Grenier, Jean 31
Grenier, Pasquier 31, 110
Gresham, Sir John 15
Gresham, Sir Richard 15–17, 43, 46, 106, 162
Gresham, Sir Thomas *16*, 17
Grey, Lady Jane 51
grosgrain 166
grotesque 88, *91*, *92*, 150, *152*, 166
ground weave 166
Guild of Silk Weavers, Venice *131*
Guildford, Sir Henry *98*
guilds 7–8, 23, 106

Habsburg dynasty 17–18, 21, 35, 119, 142, 161
Haddon Hall, Derbyshire 33, *34*, 77
Hakluyt, Richard 22–3, 162
  A notable historie 23
  The Principall navigations... 22, 23
Hall, Edward 36, 39
  *The union of the two noble and illustre fameies of
    Lancastre & Yorke* 93, *99*
Hampton Court Palace 41, 73
  1547 Inventory *3*, 87, 88, 90
  bedchambers 87–8
  carpets 93
  cushions 99
  hierarchy of court 4

King's Lodgings 75–6
  Paradise Chamber 77, 108, 138
  preparation for ceremonies 112
  privy chambers 77
  tapestries x, *x*, 17, 43–9, 55–6, 93, 108
  tapestry conservation 142
handkerchiefs 144
Hannibal 35
Hanse 9, 12
Hardwick Hall, Derbyshire 48–9, 59, 64
Harris, Anne 109–10
Harrison, Edmund 138
Hatton, Sir Christopher 18, 60, 142
Hayes, John 57
Helmingham herbal and bestiary *155*
Heneage, Thomas 107
Henry, Duke of Cornwall 102
Henri II, King of France 90, 144
Henry VI, King 12
Henry VII, King 12, 13, 15, 105, 161
  becomes king 7, 8, 29–30
  coronation 112
  death of Elizabeth of York *86*, 87
  ecclesiastical textiles 30
  heraldic textiles 71–3
  tapestries 30–6, 77, 110, 142
  trade embargo 11
Henry VIII, King 42–3
  1547 Inventory *3*, 12, 30, 42, 77, 83, 87, 88, 90, 93,
    102, 132, 134, 138, 142, 150, 151
  acquisition of textiles *1*, 106–8
  becomes king 15
  bedchambers 87–90, *88–9*
  carpets 138, 161
  clothes 117
  cloths of estate 77, 93
  coronation 36
  Field of Cloth of Gold xi, *1*, 30, 36–40, 46, 73, 162
  horse cloths 147–8
  illuminated manuscripts 154
  and King David 39, 46, 161–2
  marriages 55
  pageants 4–5
  portraits 4–5, *76*, 78, *82–3*, 93, 135, 150
  preparation for ceremonies 112
  privy chambers *74*, *75*, 77
  psalter *103*
  table linen 80
  tapestries x, 33, 43–9, 73, 88, 107, 142, 161–2
  tents 40–2
  tournaments 40–1, *40–1*
  travels 113
  heraldry 147
  herbals 154–5, *155*
  Herbert, Henry Somerset, Lord 71
  Hercules 35
  Herwijck, Steven van (attrib.), 'Hampden Portrait'

of Queen Elizabeth I *79*

Hewetson, William 109

Heydon family 15

Heylyn, Peter, *Ecclesia restaurata* 108

Hilliard, Nicholas 60, 62

   Young Man among Roses 60, 62

Hogenberg, Frans *10*

Holbein, Hans the younger *1*, 42, 75, 93, 135, 152

   The Ambassadors 93, 97, 135

   portrait of Georg Giese 135, *136*

   portrait of Sir Henry Guildford *98*

Holbein carpets 135, *135, 137*, 161

Holdenby, Northamptonshire 18

holland (linen fabric) 83, 122, 144, 166

Holland (place) 122, 144

Holtwheler, Harry 128

Holy Roman Empire 12, 17

Homer, *Odyssey* 131

Horenbout, Gerard 152–4

   The Visitation 154

Horenbout, Lucas, *Henry VIII at prayer in his*

   closet 78

Horenbout, Susanna 152–4

horse trappers 36, 40, *40–1*, 108, 128, 147–8, 167

House of Lords 7

Howard, Charles, 2nd Baron Howard of

   Effingham *143*, 144

Hubblethorne, Morgan 22–3

Hundred Years War (1337–1453) 30

Huntly, George Gordon, Earl of 108

Husee, John 110

Huys, Frans 80

Hyckes, Richard 18–19

Ibgrave, William 148

India 9

indigo 26, 166

Intercursus Magnus (1496) 11, 12

Islamic carpets 13, 93, 134–5, *135*

Italy 8

   carpets 13

   cloth of gold 132

   dyes 23–6, 126–7

   embroidery 150

   lace 144

   merchant bankers 11–12

   merchants 15

   silk 12, 106, 123

   velvet 132

James I, King 59, 108, 144, 161

James IV, King of Scotland 15

Jesuit order 30

Joanna of Castile 17

John of Lancaster 90

John de Paris 150–1

Jones, William 108

Katherine of Aragon 18, 36, 40, *40–1*, 102, 161

   divorce 46, 55

   inventory 42–3, 77, 83

   marriage to Prince Arthur 30, *31*

kermes dye 26, 126–7, 166

kersey 8, 15, 166

King Edward VI and the Pope 82 3

King's Book of Payments 15, 36, 107

knot pile 134–5, 166

lac 166

lace 144–7, *145, 146*, 166

lampas 15, 166

lawn 87, 122, 166

Laon 122

Laudonnière, René 23

laundry 109–10

Lavenham 20

Le Moyne de Morgues, Jacques *v*, *22*, 23, 128

   La clef des champs 23, *62–3*, 63–4, 138, 155, *156–7*

   Great Voyages 129

   medlar pear *62*

Leicester, Robert Dudley, Earl of 19–20, 60, 62,

   77, 113

Leicester House, London 20

Leiden 119

Leighton, Lady 67

Levant Company 22

light *2–3*, 110

linen 122–3, *123*, 144, 166

Lisle, Arthur Plantagenet, Viscount 110

Lisle, Lady 110

livery 50, 128, 166

Lock, William 106, 109

Lockey, Rowland, *Lady Margaret Beaufort 37*

Lombards 12

looms *see* weaving

Lotto, Lorenzo 135

Lotto carpets 135, *135*

Lovekyn, George 147, 148

Low Countries *10*, 17–18

   refugees 18, 20

   tapestries 31, 55, 110, 139, 142

   trade 9–11, 13

Lucca 12, 128, 132

Lumley, Lady 67

Luxembourg 9

madder 126, 127, 166

Margaret of York 11

Marlowe, Christopher, *Dido, Queen of Carthage* 56

Mary, Queen of Scots 58–9, *59*, 60, 64, 108

Mary I, Queen 21, 99

   cloths of estate 77

   coronation 71

   embroidery 57–8

   marriage 18, 54

   portraits *4–5, 53, 73, 153*

   reign 51–5

   tapestries 49, 54

Mary II, Queen 77

Mary of Burgundy 17

Mascall, Leonard, *A profitable boke...* 23

Master of the Catholic Kings, *The Marriage at*

   Cana 81, 134

'Master John', portrait of Edward VI *52*

materials 117–28

   cloth of gold 132–4

   dyes 126–8

   gold and silver 128, *128*

   linen 122–3

   silk 123–4

   wool 117–22

Maximilian I (Archduke) 17 (Emperor) 41, *42–3*

Medici, Catherine de' 144

Medici, Giuliano 12

Medici, Lorenzo 12

Medici family 9, 12, 123

Mediterranean 11

Melville, Sir James 60

mercers 12, 109, 166

mercery 166

Merchant Adventurers 21, 166

Merchant Taylors 8, 106

merchants 8, 15–17, 21–3, 26, 106

Meulen, Steven van der (attrib.), 'Hampden

   Portrait' of Queen Elizabeth I *79*

Mexico 21, 26, 127

Middle East 93

Milan 132, 144

millefleurs tapestries *3*, 33, *34*, 93, *94–5*, 113, 166

miniatures 60–2, *60*, 154

'The Miroir or Glasse of the Synnefull Soul' 58, *58*

monasteries 7

   dissolution of 48, 55, 108, 147

Montmorency, Duke of *3*, 113

Mor, Antonis: portrait of Mary I *73, 153*

   portrait of Sir Thomas Gresham *16*

mordants 12, 126, 166

More, Sir Thomas 55, 93

moresque *148*, 150, 154, 166

Mostnick, Jan 110

Muscovy Company 21

nail xiv, 166

nap 119, 166

napery 80, 109, 144

napkins 80, *80*, 109–10, *111, 145*

Nashe, Thomas 56

National Trust 18

Native Americans 23

Nebuchadnezzar, King 35

needlework 166

   see also embroidery

Netherlands 8, 9, 13, 161
New Year Gift Roll (1589) 67
Nonsuch Palace 93
Norfolk, Thomas Howard, Duke of 142
Norris, Henry 76, 106
Norris, John 75, 76–7
North Africa 93
Northumberland, John Dudley, Duke of 50, 51
Norwich 20, 142

Office of the Tents 113
Oliver, Isaac, 'Rainbow Portrait of Elizabeth I' *61*
orphrey 30, *133*, 166
Ottoman Empire 13, 21, 36–8, 54, 135, 161, 162
Oudenaarde 18
Ovid, *Metamorphoses 92*

pageants 4–5
paned 33, 42–3, 132, 148, 166
Pannemaker, Willem de 48, *48*, 54, *54*
Parker, John 106, 154
Parr, Katherine 57, 58, *58*, 154
Parry, Blanche 67, 108
patterns, embroidery 23, 63–7, 90, 151–5, *157*
Peake, Robert the elder (attrib.), 'Procession
    Portrait' of Elizabeth I 64, *65*
Pembroke, Mary Herbert, Countess of 23, 63, 64
Perrenot de Granvelle, Nicolas 55
Persia 12, 22–3, 135
pests 110
Petrarch, Francesco, *I trionfi* 43–6, *44–5*
Philip II, King of Spain 18, 20, 21, *53*, 54
Philip IV, King of Castile (also Philip the Fair,
    Duke of Burgundy) 17, 31
Philip the Bold, Duke of Burgundy 30
piece-goods 166
pillowberes 83, 166
Pine, John *143*
Pintoricchio, *Penelope at her Loom 130*
Platter, Thomas 138
plied threads 166
pomegranate motifs 37, 42, 77, 93, *96*, *98*, 132, 134,
    134
Port Royale, Florida *22*, 23
Portinari, Tommaso ('Thomas Portunary') 12
Portugal 9, 11
pouncing *see* pricking
'Prayers of Queen Katherine Parr' 58, *58*
pricking 63, 166
printing presses 154
privacy 3–4, 75–6
Privy Chamber 105, 109, 154
privy chambers 75–102
    bedchambers 83–90
    cloths of estate 76–7
    dining 80
    small items and ephemera 102

walls and floors 93–9
Privy Council 22
Protestants, in Low Countries 17, 18
Provence 26

quivers 102

Radcliffe, Mrs 115
Raleigh, Sir Walter 23, 63
Raphael 46
    'The Miraculous Draft of Fishes' *140*
Rawson, Avery 106–7
rayne 87, 167
red dyes 127–8
Reformation 2, 23–6, 63, 108
Removing Wardrobes 105
Renaissance 43, 46, 59, 60, 75
repurposing textiles 108
Richard, Duke of York 11
Richard II, King 30
Richard III, King 7, 11, 29
Richmond Palace 30, 31, 67
Robenet (embroiderer) 128
Roman Catholic Church 46
Romulus and Remus 93
Rosetti, Giovanventura, *Plictho de larte de tentori*
    23–6, *27*, 126–7
ruffs 144, 147
rush 77, 167
Russell, Anne 71
Russell, Lady Elizabeth (nee Cooke) 71
Russell, Elizabeth 71
Ruthall, Thomas, Bishop of Durham 108

Sachs, Hans, *Das Ständebuch* 129, *131*, 154
St James's Palace, London 113
St Mary's Church, Cambridge 112–13
samplers *70*, 102
Samson 35
sarcenet 87, 93, 167
satin of Bruges 167
satin weave 167
Saul, King 35
saye 167
scarlet 87, 102, 117, 126–7, 167
Scheldt, river 9
Scudamore, Lady 115
Senesco, George 108
serge 167
sewing kits 102
Seymour, Jane *4–5*, 43
Sforza family 144
shafts, looms 129, 167
shearing sheep *6*, 8, *118–19*
Sheldon, Ralph 18–19
Sheldon, William 18
Sheldon tapestry workshop 18–20, *18–19*

ships, merchant 15
Shrewsbury, Elizabeth Talbot, Countess of (Bess
    of Hardwick) 18, 48–9, 55, 59, 64, *64*, 67, 142
Shrewsbury, George Talbot, 6th Earl of 59
Sidney, Mary *see* Pembroke, Mary Herbert,
    Countess of
Sidney, Sir Philip 60
    Arcadia 63
Sidney family 63
silk: damask *96*
    dyeing 27, 127
    Great Wardrobe 106
    production 123–4, *124–5*
    trade 12–13
    wall hangings 93
    weaving *13*, *131*
silver 108, 128, *128–9*, 132
skein 127, 167
Skelton, John 46
slips 64, *64–5*, 152, 155, *158–9*, 167
Somerset, Duchess of 50
Somerset, Edward Seymour, Duke of 50
Somerset House Conference (1604) 135, *160*, 161–2
Somerset Place 105
Spain 9, 11, 12, 17–18, 21, 161–2
Spanish Armada *143*, 144, 161
Spenser, Edmund 3
    The Faerie Queene 56–7
sperver 167
Spierincx, Francis *143*, 144
spindles *116*, 119, 167
Spinelly, Thomas 15
spinning 119, *120–1*
Stafford, William, *A compendious or briefe exami-
    nation of certayne ordinary complaints...* 26
Stanhope, Sir Michael 50
Staple (town or city) 167
staple (fibres in wool) 167
Staplers' Company 8, 167
starch 147
Stonyhurst vestments 30, 132, *133*
storage of textiles 110
Stow, John, *Annales [...] of England* 147
Stowe Inventory 71
Straet, Jan van der, *Vermis sericus* 123–4, *124–5*
strapwork 58, 88, *91*, 135, 167
Strete, Cornelius van de 110
Stuart dynasty 49, 59
Stubbes, Philip, *The anatomie of abuses* 147
stuff 109, 167
Swanenburg, Isaac Claesz van 119
    Het ploten en kammen 118–19
    *Het spinnan het schere van de ketting en het weven
    120–1*
    Het vollen en verven 122, 126
sweet rush 167
symbols 62–3, 73, 90

Syria 12, 135

tabby weave 128–9, 167
table linen 80, *80–1*, 109–10, *111*, 144
tablecloths 75, 80, *81*, 144
taffeta 17, 71, 88, *89*, 102, 167
tannin 126, 167
tapestries 167
    Abraham tapestries 48–9, *48–9*
    cartoons 31, 54, *140*, 164
    'The Conquest of Tunis' 54–5, *54*
    Dido and Aeneas tapestries 46–8, *47*, 56, *57*, 93
    Elizabethan 55–7
    English tapestry industry 18–20
    at Hampton Court x, *x*, 17, 43–9, 55–6, 93, 108
    Henry VII's collection 30–6, 110
    Henry VIII's collection 33, 43–9, 73, 88, 107, 142, 161–2
    Low Countries 18, 31, 55, 110, 139, 142
    maintenance 110–12
    millefleurs *3*, 33, *34*, 93, *94–5*, 113, 166
    'The Planets' 55
    in privy chambers 93
    'The Triumphs of Petrarch' 43–6, *44–5*
    Troy tapestries *28*, 31, *33*
    weaving 129, 139–44, *139*
    wool 117
    see also wall hanging
The Tapestry Hangings of the House of Lords 143
tapestry weave 167
techniques 128–55
    carpets 134–8
    cloth of gold 132–4
    embroidery 147–55
    lace 144–7
    tapestries 139–44
    weaving 128–32, *130–1*
Teerlinc, Levina (attrib.), *Elizabeth I of England Receiving Dutch Ambassadors 94–5*, 99
tennis rackets 102
tenterhooks 167
tenters 122, 167
tents *38–9*, 39, 40–2, *42–3*, 73, 113–15, *114–15*, 148
Teschemacher, Mr 31
testers 76, 77, 87, 88, *91*, *152*, 167
Thérouanne, siege of (1513) 42
Thomas of Britain 12
threads 117, 167
tick 167
tissue (cloth of tissue) 12, 36, 132, 147, *152*, 167
Tournai 139, 147
Tours 39
towels 80, *81*, 109
Tower of London 33, 35, 43, 71, 93, 99, 105
trade 7–11, 12–13, 20, 21–3, 26
transportation of textiles 113–15
trappers, horse 36, 40, *40–1*, 108, 128, 147–8, 167

Treaty of London (1518) 1, 36–8, 112
tree bark, mordants 126
Troy tapestries *28*, 31, *33*
Tunis 54–5, *54*
Turkey carpets 13, 134–5, *135*, 138, 161, *162*
twill weave 167

underwear 123, 144
Urbino, Federico da Montefeltro, Duke of 31
Uriah the Hittite 46, 161–2

valances 88–90, *89*, *90*, *92*, 148, *150–1*, 168
Valencia 26
Valois dynasty 35
Vaughan, Margery 109
Vaughan, Stephen 17, 109
Vaux Passional *86*, 87
vegetable dyes 126
velvet *72*, 129–30, *132–4*, 168
Venice 9, 21
    carpets 106, 135
    cloth of gold 132
    dyes 23–6, 126
    lace 144
    merchant bankers 11–12
    silks 12, *13*, *131*
venice gold 46, 62, 71, 87, 132, 168
Venus *47*, 56
verdigris 168
verdure 35, 43, *79*, 93, 142, 168
Vermeyen, Jan Cornelisz 54, *54*
Verreyken, Louis 161
Vinciolo, Federico 144
'The Virtues Challenge the Vices' *141*
Vroom, Hendrik Cornelisz *143*, 144

Waldstein, Baron 138
wall hangings 42–3, 93
    see also tapestries
Walle, Pieter van der 93
Walsingham, Lady 67
Walsingham, Sir Francis 22, 62
War of the League of Cambrai (1508–16) 41
Warbeck, Perkin 11
warp 128–9, *131*, 134, 139, *139*, 168
Wars of the Roses (1455–85) 12, 15, 29
Warwick 19–20
Watts, Richard, *The young man's looking-glass* 119
weaving 128–32, *130–1*, 139–44, *139*
weft 128–9, *131*, 134, 139, 168
weld 126, 168
Welshman, Davy 15
Westminster Abbey, London 30, 49–50, *51*, 112
Westminster Palace *see* Whitehall Palace
Westminster Tournament Roll *40–1*, 43
Wewyck, Meynnart, *Lady Margaret Beaufort 37*
White, Nicholas 59

Whitehall Palace, Westminster 4–5, 31, *32*, 71, *84–5*, 102, 105, 144
Whitney, Geoffrey, *A choice of emblemes* 21, 62–3
whorl *116*, 119, 168
William III, King 77, *102*
Windsor, Sir Andrew 108–9
Windsor Castle 30, 90
Wingfield, Anthony 113
woad 20, 126, 168
Wolsey, Cardinal Thomas *1*, 15, 113, 161
    bedding 88, 106–7
    carpets 56, 93, 106
    close stools 102
    cloths of estate 77
    curtains 93
    Eltham Ordinances 76
    tapestries 17, 43–6, 108
    Treaty of London 36–8, 112
wool *6*, 7–11, 15, 17, 20, 117–22, *118–22*, 126, *126*
woolfell 168
'Woolsack' 7
Worcester, Earl of 107
worsted 20, 168
Wraton, Piers 112
Wriothesley, Thomas 17, 57
Wyat, Sir Henry 112

yarn 117, 119, *120–1*, 122, 128, 168
York 142

Picture Credits